So You Want to Sing
A Guide for Professionals

*A Project of the National Association of
Teachers of Singing*

So You Want to Sing: A Guide for Professionals is a series of works devoted to providing a complete survey of what it means to sing within a particular genre. Each contribution functions as a touchstone work for not only professional singers, but students and teachers of singing. Titles in the series offer a common set of topics so readers can navigate easily the various genres addressed in each volume. This series is produced under the direction of the National Association of Teachers of Singing, the leading professional organization devoted to the science and art of singing.

So You Want to Sing Music Theater: A Guide for Professionals, by Karen S. Hall, 2013.

So You Want to Sing Rock 'n' Roll: A Guide for Professionals, by Matthew Edwards, 2014.

So You Want to Sing Rock 'n' Roll

A Guide for Professionals

Matthew Edwards

Allen Henderson
Executive Editor, NATS

A Project of the National Association of
Teachers of Singing

ROWMAN & LITTLEFIELD
Lanham • Boulder • New York • London

Published by Rowman & Littlefield
A wholly owned subsidiary of The Rowman & Littlefield Publishing Group, Inc.
4501 Forbes Boulevard, Suite 200, Lanham, Maryland 20706
www.rowman.com

16 Carlisle Street, London W1D 3BT, United Kingdom

British Library Cataloguing in Publication Information Available

Library of Congress Cataloging-in-Publication Data

Edwards, Matthew, 1979–, author
 So you want to sing Rock 'n' Roll : a guide for professionals / Matthew Edwards.
  pages cm. — (So you want to sing)
 Includes bibliographical references and index.
 ISBN 978-1-4422-3193-1 (pbk. : alk. paper) — ISBN 978-1-4422-3194-8 (ebook)
 1. Singing—Instruction and study. 2. Rock music—Instruction and study. I. Title.
 MT820.E38 2014
 783'.066143—dc23
 2014016172

∞™ The paper used in this publication meets the minimum requirements of American National Standard for Information Sciences—Permanence of Paper for Printed Library Materials, ANSI/NISO Z39.48-1992.

Printed in the United States of America

Unless otherwise noted, illustrations in the book are courtesy of the author.

Note that Somatic Voicework is a trademark of Jeannette LoVetri and the Voice Workshop, New York.

To Jackie and Everett, this is "Your Song."
Thank you for a wonderful life.

CONTENTS

CONTENTS

FOREWORD

So You Want to Sing Rock 'n' Roll: A Guide for Professionals, the second of the So You Want to Sing series, is simply a marvel. Whether you are a skeptical (with good reason) beginning or experienced rock singer, a classical voice teacher, a coach, or something else, I can guarantee you will find yourself clinging to every word in this book. Why? That was my experience as series editor for the project while reading and editing Matt Edward's outstanding work. Whatever your goals or reasons for purchasing this book, you will become enlightened and educated about rock singing in ways you simply couldn't imagine. It's an exciting and fun ride!

I can't think of a better choice than Matt to write this book. His journey started in high school when he began singing in rock bands and participated in theater classes. Matt took a detour during college, where he studied and performed classical music when no other training options were available. During his college years, he came back to his rock roots. While studying classical singing, he continued to teach, as a graduate assistant, mostly music minors who were interested in singing contemporary commercial music (CCM), and there were many rock singers among them. He quickly realized the classical techniques he taught them for juries were not helping them and were not appropriate for the CCM music they wanted and were singing outside of lessons. At this point, he began experimenting with his own rock singing and helping his students learn singing techniques appropriate to contemporary genres. As a coach, he also quickly realized the impact that audio enhancement played in rock singing's final product.

Matt has worked with passion, drive, and dedication on this important project. His knowledge is impressive, and his writing clear and engaging with plenty of humor. While it may be difficult to teach how to sing in a book, Matt comes as close as possible to achieving just that.

I believe that in this important series we will make many important discoveries about how to teach singing in new ways. You will find a treasure trove of information waiting for you in Matt's book. I am extremely proud to have him as part of the project and feel very lucky to work with him. I learned a tremendous amount reading his work, and I predict you will too!

Karen Hall
Series Editor

ACKNOWLEDGMENTS

Our greatest weakness lies in giving up. The most certain way to succeed is always to try just one more time.

—Thomas A. Edison

There are so many people to thank for all of the experiences that have led to the knowledge that informs my life's work. Mom, I cannot thank you enough for all of the music lessons, rides to rehearsals, meals on the go, and countless hours of noise-making that you endured. Dad, when I was twelve you told me that if I wanted to buy more music gear I needed to start mowing yards to pay for it. That was one of the best things you ever did for me. You taught me to work for what I wanted and that success in life does not come easy. To my brothers, Nathan and Steven, thanks for all the jam sessions and memories. To the best in-laws anyone could ask for, John and Noreen Zito, thank you for always being there and for all of your support. I want to thank my teachers Beverley Rinaldi, Kay Griffel, Gary Race, Paul Transue, and Peter Sicilian for sharing their knowledge and love of teaching with me. To Jeanie LoVetri, thank you for teaching me to teach and sharing your knowledge with me. You continue to be a source of inspiration to this day, and I am eternally grateful for all you have taught me. I'd also like to thank the following:

- My voice department colleagues at Shenandoah University: Kathryn Green, David Meyer, Karen Keating, Aimé Sposato,

Michael Forest, Medea Namoradze, Byron Jones, Phillip Sargent, Lucy Hoyt, Edrie Means Weekly, Margaret Brooks, and Amy Call-Murray

- My theater department colleagues: Tom Albert, Carolyn Coulson, Will Ingham, Kirsten Trump, Mac Bozman, and J. J. Ruscella

- My CCM Voice Pedagogy Institute colleagues: Ed Reisert, Tom Arduini, Marcelle Gauvin, and Robert Doyle

- Dean Michael Stepniak for his ongoing support and visionary leadership

- President Tracy Fitzsimmons for all that she does for the students at Shenandoah University and her continued support for our work in the conservatory

- To my students past and present—you have taught me more than you know, and I am honored to have worked with each and every one of you

To all of my friends who supported me and believed in my work when others questioned why we need to teach rock singers as rock singers, thank you. I particularly want to thank Mark Jones, Jan and Shannon DeAngelo, Chuck and Angie Bush, Adam and Airicia Holcomb, Mandy and Jerrad Holloway, Maria Aimionotis, and Christian Maire. Jonathan Flom, thank you for being my partner in crime in the music theater department at SU. If it were not for Jonathan and his vision for the program, my position at Shenandoah University would not exist. There is no one I would rather co-teach with and nowhere else I would rather be.

I am grateful for all of those who gave their time and energy to helping me with this publication along the way: Kathryn Green, Jeannette LoVetri, David Meyer, Warren Freeman, Edrie Means Weekly, and Jonathan Flom. I especially want to thank Christina Howell for her numerous hours of proofreading and editing.

Without the support of the Karen Hall, the series editor, this project would have never been achievable. Her tireless work throughout the process made it possible to bring this book together in six short months. Thank you to her, Allen Henderson, and Bennett Graff for all of their time and effort in bringing this publication to print.

Finally, I want to thank my incredible wife, Jacqlyn, and my son, Everett. Jackie, you have been with me since the very beginning of my career at the Cleveland Institute of Music. You are always there for me no matter what and you never let me give up. I am forever thankful. Everett, you are not even old enough yet to understand any of this. But I want you to know that your little smiles, laughs, and hugs make every day of my life better than the last.

INTRODUCTION

Beginnings are always messy.

—John Galsworthy

In July of 2013 while at the Voice Foundation Annual Symposium: Care of the Professional Voice, Allen Henderson, executive director of the National Association of Teachers of Singing (NATS), asked me if we could have lunch and talk. When he asked me if I would be interested in contributing to an NATS book series, I said sure. Little did I know that I would end up writing an entire book on rock 'n' roll.

The evolution of my career has been unique. When I was in high school I wanted to be a rock star and played in several bands. I also fell in love with acting and was an active part of the theater program at my high school. When it came time to decide my post-graduation plans, I was offered two options by my parents—move out or go to college. I chose the latter and attended the local university, Wright State, for music education, with the hopes of becoming a music teacher and performing in a band on the side. During my second week of school, I was approached by the director of the opera program and was asked to audition. Within a week I was cast as the speaker, second priest, and second man in armor in the *The Magic Flute*. The opera hook was set, and I dove in. I was soon cast in Dayton Opera's chorus and eventually transferred to the Cleveland Institute of Music, which had one of the finest operatic training programs of the time. My mentors there, Beverley Rinaldi and Gary Race, transformed me from a singer into an artist. Rinaldi also offered me my first opportunity to teach in a university setting as her work-study teaching assistant, an opportunity for which I am eternally grateful.

After graduation, I performed with Lyric Opera Cleveland and Cincinnati Opera outreach before attending Louisiana State University on a graduate assistantship, which eventually became a teaching assistantship. It was while I was at LSU that I started teaching rock singers. The singers in my studio were all music minors and mainly interested in singing contemporary commercial music (CCM) repertoire, not classical music. I realized early on that the classical techniques I was teaching them for their juries were not enough to help them sing the musical styles they were performing outside of lessons. I began re-exploring my own rock voice, reading every article and book I could find, while experimenting with my students in their lessons. Soon, I was hired by LA-based Maple Jam Records as a vocal coach for The Terms, a band that was based in Baton Rouge. I started working with their backup singers and eventually joined the band in rehearsals alongside their Grammy Award–winning producer Greg Ladanyi. That experience changed my teaching. It was then that I realized how significantly the recording process influenced live performance demands and how audio enhancement technology played a part in producing the final product. I also began to realize how easily vocal training could take away the special vocal qualities that made each artist unique.

Even though teaching was my passion, I continued to pursue my operatic career while maintaining a private studio and only teaching pop/rock and music theater performers. I eventually moved to Binghamton, New York, to join Tri-Cities Opera (TCO) as a member of their resident artist program. While singing with TCO, I continued to teach private students, worked with regional recording studios and rock singers, and even ran a small semi-professional theater company for two years. When I saw an advertisement for the NATS intern program in 2009, I applied and was accepted to intern with Jeannette LoVetri.

Jeanie tied all of the pieces together for me and taught me how to get results using functional training. That experience along with attending the CCM Institute and earning certification in Levels I–III of Somatic Voicework permanently changed my teaching. A year later I found myself joining the faculty of Shenandoah University as the first tenure-track faculty member in the United States whose sole position was to teach music theater singers to sing pop/rock.

My career path involved so many twists and turns because, at the time I entered the field, there was no formal degree path to prepare me for what I wanted to do. Fortunately, today there are two graduate programs in the United States offering CCM voice pedagogy degrees, but those are hardly enough to train all of the singers who are interested in pursuing a career in CCM voice pedagogy. Allen's conversation with me at the Voice Foundation was an exciting moment because it meant that NATS was taking a significant step toward forwarding the acceptance of CCM styles and CCM voice pedagogy within the profession. I am honored and delighted to contribute to this project. I hope you enjoy reading this book as much as I have enjoyed writing it, and I hope we have a chance to meet in the future. Those of us who are working in these fields are pioneering the way forward, and it is only through our collected efforts that we will be able to continue the progress that has been made thus far.

All the vocal exercises in chapter 4 can also be viewed at http://www .SoYouWanttoSing.org.

STILL LIKE THAT OLD TIME ROCK 'N' ROLL
A History Lesson

If you don't know history, then you don't know anything. You are a leaf that doesn't know it is part of a tree.

—Michael Crichton

The history of rock 'n' roll is complex, with many factors influencing its development. Innovations overlap each other and there are conflicting claims of who did what first. Scholars continue to investigate the history of every type of music, including rock 'n' roll, and attempt to uncover every nuance and detail of artist, song, and genre. Because there are several wonderful books on rock history already in print, this chapter will provide only brief overviews of some of the most important historical events that laid the groundwork for rock 'n' roll as well as highlight artists who made significant contributions to the development of rock.

Before There Was Rock

From Africa to America

The roots of the rock 'n' roll tree dig deeply into African[1] soil. Natives of Africa used percussion instruments daily for communication, ceremonial activities, and entertainment. Early European explorers of the African continent shared stories about the extensive drumming they observed during their travels and compared the communicative abilities of the African drums to the rhythmic tapping of the telegraph. Western tribes primarily used percussive instruments while eastern tribes also used string instruments, including zithers and harps. Perhaps the most relevant detail for our purposes is that all instruments there, including the voice, function primarily as rhythm maker—a stark contrast to European traditions where voices function almost exclusively as melody makers (Bane, 1982).

Another important feature of African musical traditions is the absence of written musical notation. In the Western classical tradition of Europe, one person (the composer) writes the music and other people (the musicians) perform the music. In order for everyone to do what the composer expected, the musicians had to have those musical ideas written down. Even before the invention of the printing press in the fifteenth century, monks kept steady employment and their fingers ink-stained copying music for performers (Grout & Palisca, 1996). In Africa, music transferred from person to person through direct participation in the creative process (Bane, 1982). Audiences for Western classical music in Europe experienced music by attending a church service, court performance, or public performance, and while they may have either talked among themselves or sat quietly, they did not participate in the music making (Weber, 1997). By contrast, music making in Africa was a communal event experienced through direct participation of everyone in attendance as a way to share mutual experiences, reflect on the struggles of everyday life, and worship the gods. Those without drums to play would stamp their feet, use rhythm sticks they made out of bones, use bells, or clap their hands (Bane, 1982; Jones, 2005c).

In the early days of the American colonies, settlers attempted to recreate the musical traditions of their European homelands. Colonial songs contained European conventions and never developed into anything uniquely American beyond the subjects of the texts (Crawford, 2001). However, with the arrival of slaves from Africa, new musical traditions became available to performers, and the combination of these European harmonic traditions and rhythmic elements from Africa led directly to what we know now as rock 'n' roll. Slavery, the Great Awakening, congregational singing, honky-tonks, African American popular music, U.S. population shifts, the GI Bill, the Brits, and Elvis Presley all paved the way for modern rock 'n' roll.

Slavery and Music on the Plantation

Slave owners soon discovered that the drums used in the slaves' music were not solely for music making; they were also being used as communication devices. The rhythmic patterns of the drums had no connection to the

English language, but they did mimic elements of African languages that only the slaves could understand. When the slave owners realized that the drums were being used for communication, they quickly banned them to prevent rebellion (Bane, 1982).

Rhythm making was such an essential feature of African music that, even without the drums, slaves found ways to be rhythmic. Without instruments, they resorted to physical actions to create beats and made vocal choices that added rhythm to the music. An acceptable musical outlet for the slaves, religious songs became subject to this rhythmic treatment. Plantation owners felt an obligation to "save the souls" of their slaves. While at church, slaves participated by singing along with the hymns, and, since their masters insisted they only sing songs in the fields that the masters could understand, they sang hymns from the church and added melodic and rhythmic embellishments derived from their own traditions. Songs performed in that manner became known as spirituals. Spirituals eventually developed into new styles, such as gospel and the secular storytelling form we call the blues (Bane, 1982; Crawford, 2001).

Music in the Church

Many of the original settlers of the United States were Puritans who immigrated, seeking religious freedom. The Puritan religion was part of the Christian faith and had its roots in the Anglican church (Bane, 1982; Jones, 2005d). Early settlers came to believe that Puritan rules regarding daily life had limited relevance to life in America, and they began to question some of their beliefs. When Evangelist George Whitefield came to the United States from England in 1739, he stirred up the populace by preaching a new message of hellfire and brimstone. With a message and style of delivery unfamiliar to most Americans, Whitefield fascinated parishioners accustomed to hearing monotonous Puritan ministers preaching long, boring sermons (Jones, 2005b). In order to accommodate the attendees of these traveling worship services, organizers erected large tents, and the events became known as "tent revivals." Tent revivals frequently turned into spirit-filled spectacles. They provided the perfect venue for whites to take on some of the traditions they had observed in Southern blacks,[2] specifically their song traditions and body movements (Bane, 1982; Crawford, 2001; Jones, 2005b). This movement of evangelical worship led America into what is called the First Great Awakening.

3

During the First Great Awakening, worshipers found a new desire for religious freedom with less control from church hierarchies. Leaders of the movement declared that all church members had both the right and responsibility to participate in worship services and church leadership (Jones, 2005a). Because of parishioners' newfound responsibility, congregational singing became increasingly important. Services featured church songs from Europe, as well as any other type of music to which parishioners could add religious texts. By the late 1700s, publishers were eager to publish the extremely popular and highly lucrative church songbooks. Church leaders, eager to help parishioners learn to sing the new music, developed the shape-note system. These same leaders developed singing schools to help teach the art of singing in four-part harmony (Bane, 1982; Crawford, 2001; Seeger, 1957).

Easily memorized and singable, revival songs provided a release from daily stresses and cares of the common man. However, it wasn't long before leaders in the church began taking steps to remove what they perceived as "primitive music" from the revival churches. From the Civil War forward, music was codified and handed over to church choirs where it could be controlled and contained by those in power (Bane, 1982). When church music making was taken from the masses and handed to the elite, the masses began to seek out other music-making opportunities, which led to the growth of popular music.

The Blues, Hillbilly, and Country Music

The blues grew out of gospel music, which has its roots in the field songs of Southern slaves. To reduce the monotony of fieldwork, slaves sang songs in a call and response pattern where a large group of singers repeated the lyrics and melody sung by the leader (Szatmary, 1996). This call and response pattern formed the basis of the twelve-bar blues. Lyrically, the twelve-bar blues begin with a four-measure phrase that is repeated in the second four measures and then concluded with new lyrics over the final four measures. Harmonically, the first four measures sustain a I chord, measures five and six introduce the IV chord, measures seven and eight return to the I, and measures nine and ten set up the final cadence with a V chord, which resolves to I in measures eleven and twelve (Everett, 2009).[3]

To qualify as a honky-tonk, a whiskey bar in the South had to offer live music and alcohol and cater to a working-class clientele. The owners of the honky-tonks had one goal in mind when offering live music—to keep people dancing and drinking. To make money working in the honky-tonks, a traveling musician had no choice but to play songs those audiences liked. This meant that blues musicians had to learn hillbilly songs and hillbilly singers had to learn the blues. Musicians also had to learn popular songs of the day, often written by European-trained composers, which they then embellished with their own stylizations. Because recordings were not readily available, these songs were transferred in the oral tradition, with each new performer adding new variations. Whites learned from blacks and blacks learned from whites, and when the styles intermingled, they informed each other. Eventually the combination of the two led to new genres, such as rockabilly (Bane, 1982).

While music producers considered rhythm and blues to be the music of low-income black Americans and hillbilly and country western the music for low-income whites (Covach, 2009), the lines between the styles are indistinct. In the simplest terms, hillbilly and blues songs employed only a solo guitar, whereas country music added other melody-making instruments, such as violin, and other chord-producing instruments, such as mandolin and banjo to the mix. Because the styles flourished alongside each other in the South, the boundaries were often difficult to define, but what really separated the styles from each other was race. The United States was deeply segregated in the early twentieth century, and record executives reflected this separation in music marketing. Therefore, even though the styles became more and more similar because of the "cross-pollination" of the performers, sales categories distinguished white artists under the term "country western" and black artists under the term "rhythm and blues" (Garofalo, 2005).

African American Popular Music

Even though music producers marketed the different styles separately, white audiences continued to find black music fascinating. When possible, they watched slaves gathering to sing and dance in "ring shouts" after a long day's work (Crawford, 2001) and attended commercially produced minstrel shows. Segregation made attending some live performances problematic for white audiences, but the publishing of these tunes in the form of sheet music allowed white audiences to enjoy them at home. Ragtime came into popularity in the 1890s when publishers began printing sheet music versions of songs that had gained popularity on the vaudeville circuit. By

1910, nearly every Southern city with a large black population had its own vaudeville theater whose purpose was to entertain the black population with popular songs of the day. These theaters served as the breeding ground for ragtime and, eventually, the "popular blues," a Europeanized version of a rural music style that had been evolving in the South.[4] By 1912, there was an explosion of blues sheet music on the market, fueled in large part by W. C. Handy's music publishing company in Memphis, Tennessee (Abbott & Seroff, 1996; Crawford, 2001).

Perhaps one of the most important developments in the commercialization of the blues occurred on February 14, 1920. The white vaudeville shouter Sophie Tucker had scheduled a recording session that day but had to cancel at the last minute. Perry Bradford, a black songwriter/producer who was eager to record his song "Crazy Blues," convinced record executives at OKeh Records to let him record the song with African American singer Mamie Smith (Garofalo, 2005). This album, pressed and distributed for commercial sale, surprised everyone by selling 75,000 copies within the first month. Record labels suddenly began scurrying to find other blues artists to record in order to take advantage of the public's interest in the music (Ward, Stokes, & Tucker, 1986).

In the 1910s and the 1920s, more than 1.3 million blacks left the South to seek employment in the Northern industrial cities (Higgs, 1976). The great migration brought not only the people but also their musical culture to the North. As Southern blues musicians moved into the cities, they began gigging in local bars and clubs. The artists formed combos and followed in the steps of jazz musicians, adding drums, bass guitar, and the newly invented electric guitar to their music. Electrically amplified instruments increased the overall volume levels of the stage, so singers began to electronically amplify their voices using microphones (Covach, 2009). Recording studios opened in many of the major cities, providing opportunities for musicians to make their music available to larger audiences. Sun Records in Memphis, Chess Records in Chicago, King Records in Cincinnati, and Atlantic Records in New York all became successful by recording blues artists (Covach, 2009). These records, originally called "race" records and pressed primarily for a black audience, soon became reclassified when industry executives discovered that whites were buying the records as well. "Rhythm and blues," a less offensive title than "race" records, had the added benefit of attracting even more white customers (Covach, 2009).

Icons You Need to Know

Robert Johnson was one of the first blues musicians to record his own music. Songs such as "Sweet Home Chicago," "Crossroads," and "Stop Breaking Down" influenced bands, such as Cream, the Rolling Stones, and Buddy Guy. Johnson recorded twenty-nine tracks from 1936 to 1937 before dying at the young age of twenty-seven from strychnine poisoning. Johnson sang in the traditional blues style, accompanied only by guitar. This set his music apart from the commercialized European-blues style heard on the vaudeville stage and printed in sheet music (George-Warren & Romanowski, 2001).

Enter Elvis Presley

Elvis Aaron Presley, born January 8, 1935, in Tupelo, Mississippi, changed rock 'n' roll forever. Presley's mother, a sewing-machine operator, and his father, a truck driver, regularly attended an Assembly of God church where young Presley regularly heard traditional Southern gospel singing. When Presley was three, his father was arrested for passing bad checks and was sentenced to eight months in prison. After he was released, the family fell on hard times and spent the rest of Presley's childhood trying to stay above the poverty line.

Presley received his first guitar around the age of eleven and began teaching himself to play. The family moved to Memphis in 1948 when he was almost thirteen years old, a move that had a major impact on his musical future. It was in Memphis that Presley first heard blues musicians and their records. Not only could young Elvis listen to blues records on WDIA, a black radio station in Memphis, but he could also take trips to downtown Memphis and stroll up and down Beale Street to meet the musicians in person.

Presley graduated from high school in 1953 and immediately went to work in a tool factory before driving trucks like his father. In the summer of 1953, Presley went to the Memphis Recording Service, a subsidiary of Sun Records that allowed anyone to make a recording for a fee, and laid down his first two songs. Sam Phillips, the owner of Sun Records, had noticed the increasing popularity of R&B music among white teenagers but also knew that parents were not fond of their children listening to race records. Phillips and his fellow executives knew they had a problem. How could they make a profit on a musical style that had such negative connotations? Phillips is cited as frequently having said, "If I could find a white man with the Negro sound and the Negro feel, I could make a billion dollars." When Phillips heard Presley recording in his studio, he recognized the chance of a lifetime (Ward et al., 1986).

Phillips put two country musicians in the studio with Presley, playing rhythm guitar and slap bass, to record three songs, including "That's All Right," a blues tune originally recorded by Arthur Crudup. A local DJ named Dewey Phillips started spinning the album two days later, and Presley quickly began to attract national attention. By 1956, RCA Records cut a deal to buy Presley's contract from Sun Records. RCA put their significant resources behind him, and on January 28, 1956, they arranged his national television debut on the Dorsey Brothers' Stage Show. Because television connected the person with the music, producers knew that Elvis's face (being both white and handsome) would bring in record sales. By 1957 Presley was everywhere. He was on TV, on the radio, and in the movies (George-Warren & Romanowski, 2001). He was the first performer to combine music, image, and attitude (Morrow, 2009). Elvis Presley was the world's first rock star.

How Big Business Changed the Future of American Music

Audio Recordings

Thomas Edison invented the cylindrical recorder in 1877 (Jenkins, 2001), and for the first time ever humans could capture sound and replay it in their homes. By the end of the nineteenth century, several entrepreneurs had established businesses dedicated to the burgeoning audio recording industry. By 1925, electronic amplification set the stage for a monumental change in the way that Americans experienced music. Early recordings mainly consisted of instrumental dance music, operatic works, and symphonic works. Two significant recording events in the nineteen-teens changed the face of the audio recording industry. In 1917, the Victor Recording Company recorded the Original Dixie Land Band, and in 1920 OKeh Records recorded the song "Crazy Blues" sung by Mamie Smith. These records sparked an interest in two black music styles that were to have an important impact on rock 'n' roll: jazz and the blues (Crawford, 2001).

Radio

By the end of the 1920s, radio had worked its way into millions of American households. This fascinating invention allowed performers to enter listeners' homes and form an intimate bond with them. Radio also allowed audiences to listen to music without having to purchase it. During the Great Depression, radio became an important marketing tool for performers since most Americans had little to no discretionary income and would only spend money to purchase music by familiar artists. The American Society of Composers, Authors, and Publishers (known as ASCAP) collected royalties from radio stations for its clientele of mainstream popular and classical artists. When the organization was unable to settle a dispute with broadcasters during the 1940s, ASCAP's artists were taken off the air, which meant that broadcasters had to seek out non-ASCAP artists to keep broadcasting music. Keeping their business model alive meant turning to country, folk, and rhythm and blues music (Mooney, 1968; Regal, 2005).

Alan Freed

A discussion about radio and rock 'n' roll would not be complete without mentioning Alan Freed. Freed was a radio disc jockey in Cleveland, Ohio, at a station whose broadcasts covered northeastern Ohio while also reaching north into Ontario and east into western New York and western Pennsylvania (Fong-Torres, 2001). In 1951, Freed heard from a local record store owner that white teenagers had been buying a lot of race records. Freed returned to his radio station and played a few of the best sellers on the air, which were an immediate hit (Garofalo, 2005). His listening audience quickly began to expand, and the popularity of his "Moondog Show" increased. Freed knew that parents would be quite upset if they found out their children were listening to race records over the air, so he decided to start calling the music "rock 'n' roll." Since the term was colorblind; the audience was left to decide if the artists were black or white (Regal, 2005). Rock 'n' roll was poised to take over.

The Portable Radio

Another important technological development occurred around the same time that rock 'n' roll was gaining airplay. In 1954, Texas Instruments introduced the first mass-produced portable transistor radio. In 1957, Sony introduced its own version with a more attractive case, leather carrying strap, and an earphone, all of which made it marketable to a wider demographic. Portable radios made it possible for teenagers to listen to music anywhere they went. It also meant that they could listen to any type of music they wanted to without their parents hearing it (Regal, 2005).

The "Whitening" of Rock 'n' Roll

Rock has always stood in the middle of a struggle between the roots of the music and the corporations interested in taking it over to make a profit. Some of the earliest and best-known record labels, such as Chess and Sun, were independent businesses that catered to local audiences and tastes. But once corporations took over, their desire to "clean up" rock music is readily apparent.

Pat Boone is a prime example of how the music industry used its power in an attempt to limit the integration of blacks into American popular culture. With corporate backing, Boone became famous by reworking songs by black artists for a primarily white middle-class audience. Boone not only rewrote the lyrics to make the songs more "vanilla" (Szatmary, 1996) but also created performances of the music that were musically cleaner and more "square." He became an acceptable alternative to artists, such as Elvis Presley, Jerry Lee Lewis, and Chuck Berry, whom parents perceived as hyper-sexualized. Clearly successful, Boone landed thirty-eight top-forty hits, supplanting the original artists in the spotlight as well as in the record store. Since copyright laws were not the same as they are today, performers such as Boone, who reworked the songs of black artists, were not obligated to share profits with the original songwriters. As a result, many of the original songwriters never achieved the financial success their songs brought to other artists and had to either support themselves with day jobs or tour constantly in order to stay financially above water (Ward et al., 1986).

Television

When it arrived in the 1940s, television supplanted radio as the dominant force in music broadcasting. By 1953, American households owned twenty-seven million television sets (Szatmary, 1996), and programs such as the *Ed Sullivan Show* and Dick Clark's *American Bandstand* broadcast live performances throughout the United States featuring bands performing for screaming throngs of teenage fans (Ward et al., 1986). Image began to matter at least as much as sound when video cameras zoomed in to give viewers an up-close look at the band members. Soon it became clear that while musicians may come to national prominence on the radio, television was how they would rocket to stardom (Fong-Torres, 2001).

The Growth of Consumerism

The economic boost from World War II created another important shift in American culture that contributed to the explosion of rock 'n' roll and other popular music forms. The gross national product of the United States grew from \$91.1 billion in 1939 to \$300 billion in 1950. In the process, the economy created seventeen million new jobs. Americans suddenly found themselves with income above and beyond the threshold needed to sustain daily life. They bought appliances, clothes, cars, and music. Their children earned allowances, and many spent their extra money on entertainment. As more Americans began to purchase music, advertisers who had previously controlled the musical standards through their sponsorship began to lose control of public taste (Girard & Miller, 2008). The recording industry and radio broadcasters found themselves with no choice but to meet consumer demands.

The GI Bill and Population Growth on College Campuses

Over eight million veterans returning from World War II took advantage of the GI Bill and attended college. These young adults were not only learning together but also having fun together sharing cultures, beliefs, and music. The unbridled growth of their demographic established their position as a prominent economic force in the evolution of American culture. College students outside of parental control could listen to whatever music they liked. They could dance, drink, experiment with drugs, and have relations with members of the opposite sex. It was a much different higher-education demographic from what had existed before World War II, when only children of the upper middle class and wealthy elite could afford to attend college (Mann, 2001).

Population Trends

The large shift in population from rural to urban living strongly influenced musical tastes. In 1880, the urban population of the United States was a modest 16 percent of the total population. By 1960, that number had swelled to 70 percent. The overall percentages of whites and blacks in urban settings were nearly equal in 1960 with 70 percent and 73 percent, respectively (Carter et al., 2006). In contrast to rural areas where there were greater distances between dwellings, population density in the nation's urban centers led to a greater likelihood of close contact with members of other races. As whites and blacks walked across town, they heard each other's music wafting from apartments and music clubs. As whites got to know their new neighbors, they began to sympathize with the struggles blacks were facing simply because of the color of their skin and began to rethink social norms (Szatmary, 1996).

The British Invasion

The arrival of the Beatles in 1964 shook up the music business. Because the band hailed from England and was under the control of an English label, they did not have to make any excuses for the fact that their music was based on black influences, and more importantly, they didn't have to cater to the tastes of American parents (Gregg, McDonogh, & Wong, 2013a). The Beatles and other British musicians were a threat to the American establishment because corporate executives had no control over them. The Beatles took profits away from American labels and forced the labels to compete on the Brits' terms.

Rock through the Decades

Indicating the exact date or song that marks the beginning of rock 'n' roll is difficult since there are numerous works that could claim to be the first. For instance, both "Good Rockin' Tonight" (1947) and "Rocket '88" (1951) could easily qualify as early rock songs. Artists such as Charlie Christian, T-Bone Walker, Lionel Hampton, and even Hank Williams could be said to have included elements of rock 'n' roll in their music.

For the purposes of this text, I will highlight what I believe to be some of the most important milestones in the history of rock. The information is sorted by decade, although delineating this music in that manner can make the study of rock history somewhat confusing. In reality, there are no clear delineations of when one style ends and another begins. Each style overlaps the other, both influenced by those that came before it and influencing those that came after it.

Historical events have also had a significant influence on the development of musical styles. Each of the following sections begins with an outline of important world events followed by developments in music and a brief list of icons and artists that you need to know. The "icons" are artists whose impact on music is indisputable. The "artists to know" are performers who made significant contributions and have undoubtedly earned their place in rock history. It is impossible to list all of the artists that you need to know in a single chapter. As you read, be aware that this is only a starting place for your research. In order to truly understand all of the developments in rock 'n' roll and the artists who were part of its evolution, you will need to refer to other sources as well.

The 1950s

1950 The Korean War begins. Senator Joseph McCarthy instigates a communist witch hunt in the United States.

1951 The color TV is introduced, and President Truman signs a peace treaty with Japan officially ending World War II.

1953 DNA is discovered; Joseph Stalin dies.

1954 Segregation is ruled illegal in the United States. The first report warning that cigarette smoking may cause cancer is issued.

1955 Disneyland opens, James Dean dies, and the McDonald's Corporation is founded.

1956 Elvis Presley gyrates his pelvis on the *Ed Sullivan Show*, and the TV remote control and Velcro are invented.

1957 Dr. Seuss publishes *Cat in the Hat*, and the Soviets launch Sputnik into outer space, marking the beginning of the space age.

1958 NASA is founded, Legos are introduced, and the hula-hoop becomes popular.

1959 Fidel Castro becomes dictator of Cuba, and *The Sound of Music* opens on Broadway.

Overview

The 1950s saw the emergence of many new genres. Blues, rhythm and blues, and new styles of pop music were quickly evolving and taking over the music industry as record companies tried to cater to teen audiences (George-Warren & Romanowski, 2001). Doo-wop groups such as the Mills Brothers, the Ravens, the Orioles, the Cadillacs, and the Fleetwoods merged elements of jazz, gospel, pop, and the blues to create something new and exciting (Garofalo, 2005). Ironically, the older generation of record executives actually helped fuel the younger generations' interest in rock 'n' roll. Even though the majority of adults looked upon the music with great disdain, radio and record executives saw an opportunity to make substantial new profits. Slowly, radio stations began spinning more rhythm and blues songs on the radio while record labels began signing more rhythm and blues acts.

Having survived both the Great Depression and World War II and accustomed to living a hard life, parents of the younger generation did not want their children to face the same struggles. They wanted to shelter their children from violence, sex, and what they saw as other forms of indecency. Children, of course, saw their parents as overly conservative and completely out of touch. When these children reached their teenage years, they began to rebel and rock 'n' roll was the perfect platform (Ward et al., 1986).

While parents of the baby boomers enjoyed social dancing in their youth, their children had yet to find their own dancing style until Chubby Checker showed them how to do "the twist." However, the twist was not their parents' idea of an acceptable dance. Cultured parents were accustomed to couples dancing with synchronized steps and limited pelvic gyrations. The twist was raw, uncontrolled, and overtly sexual with no real steps involved. It was glorified street dancing with nothing but twisting and shaking. Lower class, raw, and dirty; parents hated it. Musically speaking, the twist was significant because it was the first rock 'n' roll song where the rhythm itself was more important than the harmonic and melodic material of the song. After the success of the twist, audiences and record producers alike put increasing importance on whether or not a song was danceable (Bane, 1982).

Icons to Know

Little Richard was born Richard Penniman on December 5, 1935, in Macon, Georgia (Larkin, 1995). Richard was a pianist and a vocalist whose flamboyant performance antics helped songs such as "Long Tall Sally," "Rip It Up," "Lucille," "Good Golly Miss Molly," and "Tutti Frutti" land on both the R&B and pop charts. Richard's music gained national attention at a time when blacks were still not widely accepted in popular music spheres. Little Richard's music made people want to move, and it was only a short time before artists like Chubby Checker and Elvis Presley influenced an entire generation to get up and dance (York, 1982).

Chuck Berry was born on January 15, 1926, in San Jose, California, but grew up in St. Louis, Missouri, where his father moved the family when Berry was a young child. Berry began playing the guitar in his teens, playing jazz, swing, and the blues. His first song to hit the charts was "Maybelline," which owed its success in part to Alan Freed, who began spinning it on his New York City radio show. Berry was a rock artist when it was difficult for blacks to gain widespread acclaim. Yet his ability to write hit after hit, such as "Roll Over Beethoven" and "Johnny B. Goode," along with many others, earned him repeated spots on the charts and influenced artists for generations to come (York, 1982).

Antoine Domino, better known as "Fats" Domino, was a pianist and a vocalist from New Orleans. Domino went to work in a factory after leaving school and began playing local clubs on the side, eventually playing alongside legends Amos Milburn and Professor Longhair. In 1949, fellow musicians Lew Chudd and David Bartholomew of Imperial Records heard him play and took him to the studio to record his first top-ten R&B hit, "The Fat Man." He sold over sixty-five million records with hit songs including "Blueberry Hill," "My Blue Heaven," and "I'm in the Mood for Love" (George-Warren & Romanowski, 2001).

Buddy Holly was born Charles Hardin Holly in 1936. Even though his image didn't fit the rebellious and wild persona associated with many other rock artists of the time, he was still able to achieve national success with covers of songs such as "Shake, Rattle, and Roll" (Bill Haley) and "Rip It Up" (Little Richard). His own songs were also successful, with hits such as "That'll Be the Day" and "Oh Boy." Holly died tragically in a plane wreck in Mason City, Iowa, on February 3, 1959, with fellow musicians Richie Valens and the Big Bopper (York, 1982).

Artists to Know

The Everly Brothers, Bill Hayley & The Comets, Ray Charles, The Clovers, The Platters, Bo Diddley, Jerry Lee Lewis, Ricky Nelson, Carl Perkins, Sam Cooke, James Brown, Ritchie Valens, Frankie Lemon & The Teenagers, The Cadillacs, El-Dorados, The Crows, The Checkers

The 1960s

1960   Alfred Hitchcock's *Psycho* is released, lasers are invented, the FDA approves the birth control pill, and the civil rights era picks up momentum with the lunch counter sit-in at Woolworths in Greensboro, North Carolina.

1961   The failed Bay of Pigs invasion is masterminded by the CIA, the Berlin wall is built, JFK gives his "Man on the Moon" speech, the Peace Corps is founded, and the Russians launch the first man into space.

1962   The first James Bond movie is released, the first person is killed attempting to cross the Berlin wall, the first Wal-Mart opens, and Marilyn Monroe dies.

1963   Members of the Ku Klux Klan bomb the 16th St. Baptist church in Birmingham, Alabama, killing four black children. JFK is assassinated in Dallas and Martin Luther King Jr. helps organize the March on Washington, where he gives his "I Have a Dream" speech.

1964   The Beatles become popular in the United States, Muhammad Ali becomes world heavyweight champion, the Civil Rights Act is signed into law, Nelson Mandela is sentenced to life in prison, and the G.I. Joe doll is introduced.

1965   Racial tensions ignite riots in Los Angeles leading to 34 deaths, 1,032 injuries, and $40 million in damage. Malcolm X is assassinated, and the United States sends troops to Vietnam.

1966   The Black Panther party is established, the first Kwanzaa is celebrated, the first mass protests are organized against the Vietnam draft, and the National Organization for Women is founded.

1967   The first heart transplant is performed, the first Super Bowl is held in Los Angeles, and Thurgood Marshall becomes the first African American Supreme Court justice.

1968   Martin Luther King Jr. is assassinated, the Zodiac Killer strikes, and Robert F. Kennedy is assassinated.

1969   Charles Manson orders his followers to go on a killing spree at the home of film director Roman Polanski; Woodstock is held in White Lake, New York; Neil Armstrong becomes the first man on the moon; and *Sesame Street* premiers.

Overview

The 1960s saw the emergence of several new genres: Motown, funk, disco, folk rock, progressive rock, psychedelic rock, hard rock, heavy metal, fusion, singer/songwriter, and country rock. In the 1960s, the baby boomers began to display the economic power that came with the sheer size of their demographic (George-Warren & Romanowski, 2001). The commercialization of rock music and the growing power of the major record labels slowly erased regional differences. By 1963, there were fifty million car stereos, which allowed teens to listen to any type of music they wanted as they drove around town. Especially in larger cities, radio listeners heard music by both black and white artists (Szatmary, 1996). Rock music became a medium for sharing cultural differences throughout the United States. Racial barriers also began to erode, thanks to factors including the 1964 Civil Rights Act, the Voting Rights Act, and the Economic Opportunity Act (Szatmary, 1996).

Social Change

As racial barriers were falling, social unrest fueled by other injustices gave birth to new causes for the people. A number of assassinations occurred during the 1960s including John F. Kennedy, Martin Luther King Jr., and Malcolm X. These murders fueled numerous conspiracy theories and, in the case of Martin Luther King Jr., inspired huge protests that occasionally turned violent. Another important catalyst for the militant protest movement can be found in the Vietnam War. The first American troops arrived in Vietnam in 1961. The Gulf of Tonkin Resolution of 1964 sent more troops to Vietnam, and by 1968 the American presence had grown to over a half-million troops. This generation had relative economic stability; they could afford to turn their attention to the world around them and do something about it. Students on college campuses in the United States realized that their futures and livelihoods were in danger and took their concerns to the streets. They rebelled by burning draft cards, drastically changing their clothing, hair, and behavior, and in some cases fleeing to Canada (Ward et al., 1986). Their rebellious and militant attitudes fueled a whole new era of music that was full of anger. It was the perfect breeding ground for artists such as Jimi Hendrix, Janis Joplin, and Creedence Clearwater Revival (Szatmary, 1996).

The Emergence of the Drug Culture

Teens in the 1960s were disillusioned with the societal norms that emerged during their parents' generation. The social uprisings and controversies surrounding the Vietnam War led to teenage suspicions of the institutions central to American life, such as schools, big business, government, the military, and the police. Teens and young adults wanted to explore new ways of thinking outside of parental norms and began experimenting with marijuana and LSD after the book *The Psychedelic Experience* was published in 1964, offering readers information on how to expand their minds with drugs. The Byrds' drug-influenced song "8 Miles High," landing on the

U.S. charts in 1966, clearly demonstrates drugs becoming widely accepted by the youth culture (Ward et al., 1986).

Motown

Barry Gordy had a strong desire to help black artists from the blues, gospel, and R&B genres move into the mainstream. Gordy formed Motown Records as an avenue for launching these artists' careers. He taught his artists how to walk, dress, talk, sing, and dance in a manner that he thought would more closely align with the societal norms of the day, and it worked. Hit songs such as "The One Who Really Loves You," "Shop Around," "Please Mr. Postman," and "Stop! In the Name of Love" all came out of Motown and found their place on the charts (Covach, 2009).

The British Invasion

At the same time that rock 'n' roll was becoming mainstream in the United States, it was also taking the United Kingdom by storm. American records were hot sellers to the British youth. The Brits started imitating the sounds they heard on those records and began writing their own music and gigging. Liverpool alone had over three hundred live music clubs (Simonelli, 2012).

The BBC and Radio Luxembourg controlled the British radio waves. The BBC was the government channel and only dedicated twelve hours per week to rock 'n' roll. Radio Luxembourg played rock 'n' roll more regularly, but the major record labels funded it, so its content was controlled by the music industry. British teenagers were attracted to rock 'n' roll as well as the image that it portrayed of teenage lives in the United States. From the 1950s to the early 1960s, the American and UK charts mirrored each other, with Americans dominating both (Covach, 2009).

After seeing the Beatles perform at the Cavern Club in their hometown of Liverpool in 1961, Brian Epstein became the band's manager and began pursuing a recording contract for the band. By the end of 1962, the Beatles achieved the distinction of being the first Liverpool band to land a record on the UK charts. In 1963, Epstein convinced Capitol Records, the American branch of EMI Records, to release the single "I Want to Hold Your Hand." He then began booking gigs in the United States, and in February 1964, the Beatles landed in New York marking the beginning of what many call "The British Invasion" (Covach, 2009).

Woodstock

The epic festival known as Woodstock took place from August 15 to 17, 1969, on a six-hundred-acre dairy farm outside of Bethel, New York, owned by Max Yasgur (Larkin 1995d). In the festival, American youth found a place to unite and share their anger against American culture and the Vietnam War (Szatmary, 1996). Fans began showing up a week before the festival to set up camp. The roster of artists included The Who, Joe Cocker, Janis Joplin, Joan Baez, Arlo Guthrie, Creedence Clearwater Revival, the Grateful Dead, Santana, Ravi Shankar, and many others. With over 300,000 people in attendance, the festival demonstrated music's influence and hold on the younger generation (Larkin, 1995d). Woodstock made it clear that rock music had evolved from its early days into something new and exciting. Bands were pushing the envelope of musical creativity; the fans loved it, and it was clear that rock was here to stay (Gregg et al., 1986).

Icons to Know

Movies in the 1960s were increasingly filmed in California and regularly showcased the beach, with films like *Beach Party* and *Blue Hawaii*. The Beach Boys capitalized on the popularity of beach life and helped invent "surf music" with songs like "Surfin' Safari" and "Surfin' U.S.A." As the band matured and became more enmeshed in the drug culture, they began moving toward the psychedelic realm. They relocated to Holland to record their 1973 album "Holland," which reached number thirty-six on the U.S. charts and number twenty on the UK charts. Although they did land a few songs on the charts later in their careers, they failed to land any smash hits in the United States that paralleled their earlier successes (Stambler, 1989a).

The seed of the Beatles came in 1957 when Paul McCartney joined the Quarrymen as a guitarist, where John Lennon was already a member. Within a year, McCartney and Lennon sought two additional band members to form their own group that they initially called "Johnny and the Moondogs" but eventually renamed the "Silver Beatles" before dropping "silver" and becoming "The Beatles" (Larkin, 1995a). In 1962, the band recorded their first hit, "Love Me Do," which reached number one on the UK charts in just four weeks. The band pushed the musical limits of rock 'n' roll and influenced countless bands in the UK and the United States. Unfortunately, struggles among band members led to irresolvable grievances, and the Beatles dissolved in 1970 (Stambler, 1989b).

The Byrds originally consisted of band members Jim McGuinn, Chris Hillman, David Crosby, Gene Clark, and Mike Clarke. McGuinn had played extensively in the folk music scene in Greenwich Village. David Crosby had been playing folk clubs around the United States, and Gene Clark had been playing with Randy Spark's New Christy Minstrels. Chris Hillman had worked as an actual cowboy, bringing country influences to the group, and Mike Clarke brought jazz influences into the mix. Record producer Jim Dickinson had worked as an A&R (artists and repertoire) man for folk and jazz music and thought there was an opportunity to create a new sound following the Beatles success. Dickinson brought the eclectic group of musicians together to form The Byrds and pushed them into the national spotlight in 1965. Their chart-topping cover of Bob Dylan's "Mr. Tambourine Man" fused elements of rock 'n' roll and folk music and is widely recognized as the first folk rock recording (York, 1982c). More successful in the recording studio than on the live stage, The Byrds scored a number of hits with songs written by other writers, including Bob Dylan. Even though the group went through several personnel changes, they managed to stay together through the early 1970s (Stambler, 1989c).

Like the Beatles, the Rolling Stones drew influences from American blues and created something new and exciting. However, whereas the early Beatles gave rock a cleaned-up image with wholesome lyrics and slick outfits, the Stones played rock from an earthy, grungy, and destructive point of view (York, 1982i). They wore their hair long and exchanged smiling faces for scowls. Song titles like "Their Satanic Majesty's Request" left no doubt that the Stones did not "want to hold your hand." Many of their early concerts turned into riots, and their disruption of the *Ed Sullivan Show* caused the host to temporarily ban rock bands. Through the years their style changed, at times becoming smoother and more melodic. But they were always known as the bad boys of the British Invasion (Larkin, 1995c).

The Doors, led by Jim Morrison, recorded their debut album in 1967. Originally calling themselves the "Psychedelic Rangers," the drug-infused style they exemplified clearly places them at the forefront of psychedelic rock. Unfortunately, Morrison died in a Paris apartment of unknown causes in 1971, and although the band attempted to continue without him, the sparks of creativity that Morrison brought to the band were gone (York, 1982g).

The Grateful Dead was one of several bands that found fame during the Haight Ashbury movement in San Francisco. Originally called the Warlocks, the group began as a conventional rock band. Around 1965, they started playing at La Honda, a known center for LSD use in the Haight Ashbury district. They began playing under the influence of narcotics and allowed the influence of the drugs to guide their musical choices (Stambler, 1989d). The Dead, as they were commonly known, infused rock influences with styling from other genres, such as jazz and country music. In concert, it was not unusual for single songs to develop into extended improvisations that barely resembled the group's recordings (Covach, 2009). The Dead played Woodstock and continued to tour off and on in different incarnations over the next few decades.

The Yardbirds originally called themselves the "Metropolis Blues Quartet" but changed their name in 1962 when guitarist Eric Clapton joined the group (Hardy & Laing, 1987d). The band began by playing covers of American blues artists and achieved initial success when chosen to take over for the Rolling Stones as the house band at the Crawdaddy Club in Richmond, Surrey, England. Their first U.S. album in 1965, *For Your Love*, produced only one hit, the title track. Their second U.S. album, *Having a Rave Up*, produced several hits but inspired Clapton's departure because he felt the band was becoming too commercial (George-Warren & Romanowski, 2001). The Yardbirds never quite realized their commercial potential, being overshadowed by groups such as Herman's Hermits, The Dave Clark Five, and the Beatles, but they did score a few hits, such as "Shapes of Things," "Heart Full of Soul," and "Over, Under, Sideways, Down." Most importantly, the band signifies a return to rock's blues origins that influenced countless other bands in the 1960s and 1970s (York, 1982j).

Jimmy Page who was originally a guitarist with the Yardbirds, joined up with Robert Plant in 1969 to form Led Zeppelin. Hard rock was a relatively new genre at the time, yet the group was still able to land airplay with their song "Communication Breakdown." The radio play helped them build their fan base for their first full album "Whole Lotta Love" in 1969. The band changed the face of rock album art, continued to push the aural borders of rock 'n' roll with their songwriting, and soon built a superstar reputation with their lively stage performances. "Stairway to Heaven," released in 1971, cemented their legendary status and continues to be a common staple in aspiring rock guitarists' repertory (York, 1982h).

Janis Joplin was one of the most exceptional female vocalists of the late 1960s. Born in 1943 in Port Arthur, Texas, Joplin drew her influences from the blues artists of the South. When she moved to San Francisco to join the counterculture revolution, she began playing as a soloist in folk clubs before joining Big Brother and the Holding Company. The band played a lively combination of rock and the blues and was the perfect setting for Joplin to showcase her vocals with hits such as "Piece of My Heart" and "Ball and Chain." In late 1968, Joplin left Big Brother and the Holding Company to pursue other options, eventually singing with both Squeeze and Full Tilt. Her attempts after leaving Big Brother and the Holding Company never quite lived up to the standard she had set for herself on their album *Cheap Thrills*. The pressure proved to be too much for Joplin to handle and she turned to heroine, eventually overdosing on October 4, 1970 (Hardy & Laing, 1987b).

Jimi Hendrix was born in Seattle, Washington, in 1942 and rose from his poor upbringings to become a rock 'n' roll superstar. Hendrix taught himself to play guitar by listening to the old blues players. In 1961, he joined the military as a paratrooper and started his musical career playing in military clubs. After leaving the military, he worked as a backup guitarist for many of the legends of the blues and rock including B. B. King, Sam Cooke, Ike and Tina Turner, Little Richard, and others. Chas Chandler, who had played bass for the Animals, recognized Hendrix's talent and took him to England in 1966 to form the Jimi Hendrix Experience. Hendrix's career quickly skyrocketed, gaining him attention from artists, including Eric Clapton and Pete Townshend. By the end of 1967, he had toured throughout Europe and released "Hey Joe," "Purple Haze," and "Are You Experienced?" When John Phillips of the Mamas and the Papas asked Paul McCartney if the Beatles could play the Monterey Pop Festival, McCartney declined and suggested Hendrix. Upon McCartney's insistence that they give the unknown Hendrix a chance, Phillips booked him. When Hendrix finished his set at the festival with a rendition of "Wild Thing," lit his guitar on fire, and smashed it into pieces on the stage, he instantly became a star.

Even though Hendrix was the first black artist to have a mainly white fan base, it came with a price. Hendrix felt enormous pressure to bridge the racial divide, which was not why he had become a musician. In 1968, he tried giving up his wild onstage antics and let the music speak for itself, but the shift was not received well by the paying public. In 1969, Hendrix reached the highlight of his career by playing at Woodstock, but he struggled to find himself and his path after the famous festival and began a downward spiral of drugs and alcohol that ended in his death on September 18, 1970 (Covach, 2009; George-Warren & Romanowski, 2001).

Artists to Know

Roy Orbinson, Cream, Jefferson Airplane, The Monkees, Van Morrison, The Turtles, The Hollies, Frank Zappa & The Mothers of Invention, The Moody Blues, Iron Butterfly, Bo Diddley, The Spencer Davis Group, Blood Sweat and Tears, James Brown, Herman's Hermits, Steppenwolf, The Mamas & The Papas, The Kinks, The Dave Clark Five, The Animals, The Drifters, The Four Tops, Simon & Garfunkel, The Velvet Underground

The 1970s

1970 The Beatles break up, American college students are massacred by the National Guard at Kent State University in Ohio, a Palestinian terrorist group hijacks five airplanes, and the floppy disk drive is introduced.

1971 VCRs are introduced.

1972 *M*A*S*H* premiers on TV, pocket calculators are introduced, and the world is shocked by a terrorist attack at the Olympics in Munich, where two members of the Israeli Olympic team, along with nine hostages, are murdered.

1973 The United States pulls out of Vietnam, *Roe v. Wade* makes abortion legal, and the Sears Tower is built in Chicago.

1974 Richard Nixon resigns after the Watergate scandal.

1975 Microsoft is founded by Bill Gates and Paul Allen.

1977 Elvis dies, *Roots* the miniseries appears on TV, and *Star Wars* is released.

1978 The first test tube baby is born, and 909 followers of prophet Jim Jones commit suicide in Jonestown, Guyana.

1979 Sony introduces the Walkman, a portable cassette player.

Overview

The 1970s saw the anger of the 1960s slowly fade away. Politically charged songs such as Creedence Clearwater Revival's "Fortunate Son" were replaced by peaceful ballads liked "Lean on Me." The decade saw the rise of soft rock with new and old artists, including Elvis, taking the stage to show their softer side. Singer/songwriter Carole King released her successful *Tapestry* album, selling ten million copies and charting hits such as "It's Too Late," "I Feel the Earth Move," and "Will You Love Me Tomorrow?"

The baby boomers were now having babies of their own and were moving away from the angry days of their youth toward a more peaceful existence (Morrow, 2009).

The seventies also saw a split in radio format. AM radio had been the primary source for music until the early 1970s. As rock developed and the music grew more complex, FM and its ability to transmit higher quality recordings became attractive to radio stations. Top-forty stations were initially slow to adopt FM format, and thus it became the platform for non-top-forty musicians. FM radio embraced harder rock styles and its DJs became fascinated with extended rock songs and album-oriented rock (AOR). FM offered an opportunity for songs like Iron Butterfly's seventeen-minute long "In-A-Gadda-Da-Vida" to get airplay at a time when the typical length of a song was around three minutes (Garofalo, 2005; Regal, 2005).

The 1970s also saw the rise of the one-hit wonder. One-hit wonders could be extremely profitable, and record labels began taking chances on unknown artists hoping to strike it rich with just one good song. Artists such as Focus, who landed a spot on the charts with "Hocus-pocus," do not jump into one's mind when thinking about the 1970s, but their songs are often recognized (George-Warren & Romanowski, 2001). For other artists such as Pink Floyd, Deep Purple, and Led Zeppelin, a hit song could get them labeled as sellouts. Those artists focused on selling out concerts instead of being one-hit wonders and used albums as an artistic outlet. This not only had an impact on the artists' business model but also their vocal demands. If you recorded a song in the studio with extreme vocals, you had better be prepared to sing the song the same way night after night on tour.

The Kent State University massacre of May 4, 1970, had a profound effect on music. On April 30, 1970, President Nixon announced an escalation of the Vietnam War—the United States was sending troops into Cambodia. Students began protesting the president's actions in the middle of the campus on what was known as "The Commons." The situation quickly grew out of hand. Students stormed the ROTC building on campus and burned it to the ground, and they threw bottles at police officers who were trying to contain the protests. On Saturday, May 2, Ohio governor Jim Rhodes declared a state of emergency and sent the National Guard to the campus. On May 4, two thousand students gathered on The Commons and the National Guard attempted to disperse the crowd. When students began throwing rocks and tear gas at the soldiers, the Guard turned their guns on the unarmed students. Over sixty-seven shots were fired in thirteen seconds, and when the smoke cleared, four students were dead and nine were injured (Eagles, 2001). University students throughout the United States were shocked. Their protests and calls for social change had resulted in the United States government turning its guns on its own people. The antiestablishment temperament of the youth gave way to a more introspective and distanced view on life and the music changed as well (Szatmary, 1996).

Icons to Know

Yes was formed in 1968 in London, England, and became one of the most successful progressive rock bands ever. Yes combined virtuosic playing with constantly evolving melodies and three-part vocal harmonies that critics disliked but audiences loved (George-Warren & Romanowski, 2001). They released a series of albums from 1971 to 1974 including *The Yes Album*, *Fragile*, *Close to the Edge*, *Tales from Topographic Oceans*, and *Relayer*. *Fragile* produced one hit single, "Roundabout," but the most critics saw the rest of their work as self-indulgent and pretentious (Covach, 2013).

Deep Purple was known as one of the loudest hard-rock bands around at the height of their career (York, 1982f). The band did not begin as a heavy-metal group. When they formed in 1968 in Hertford, England, they were a more traditional rock band performing songs with piano chops that were classically influenced. They released their first U.S. hit single in 1968, "Hush," followed by a cover of Neil Diamond's "Kentucky Woman." By 1974, the band had sold fifteen million albums and had gained a following in the UK, United States, Australia, and Japan. The band underwent numerous personnel changes but played together with various incarnations into the 1990s (George-Warren & Romanowski, 2001).

Black Sabbath formed in Birmingham, England, and followed in the footsteps of the Rolling Stones, becoming known as one of the darker, Satanic inspired rock bands. Fronted by singer Ozzy Osbourne, the band was hated by music critics and radio DJs, and yet the band still managed to sell eight million records by 1979. Instead of relying on corporate marketing support to build its fan base, the group cemented its reputation through nonstop touring. They erected giant crosses on the stage for shock value and wrote songs that mainly dealt with death, destruction, and the apocalypse. When they began to slowly back away from their dark image in the mid-seventies, their fan base began to fade. When Osbourne left the band, the group tried to stay together with a new lead singer, Ronnie James Dio. However, they were never able to regain the fans or audience base they had with Osbourne at the mic (George-Warren & Romanowski, 2001).

The Ramones formed in 1974 after its four members graduated from high school in Forest Hills, Queens. The band started playing twenty-minute gigs at the underground club CBGB in Manhattan and was quickly signed to their first record deal. The band's music was simple: a few repetitive chords, no solos, fast and furious rhythms, with minimalistic vocal melodies and lyrics. Their 1976 album was less than thirty minutes long and contained notable songs such as "Blitzkrieg Bop," "Beat on the Brat," and "Now I Wanna Sniff Some Glue." The band remained active until 1996, yet major commercial success always seemed to elude them. Their title track for Stephen King's *Pet Cemetery* was perhaps their greatest national exposure. Even though they never achieved top-ten successes like some of their peers, their influence can be seen in numerous artists of the generations that follow (George-Warren & Romanowski, 2001).

Born in 1949, Bruce Springsteen is one of the most popular rock singer-songwriters to come out of the 1970s. Springsteen's first band, Steel Mill, gained popularity on the Atlantic coast and in San Francisco after a series of tour dates in 1969. The group was offered a record contract from Fillimore, but turned it down. Steel Mill broke up in 1971, after taking on bassist Steve Van Zandt. At that point, Springsteen realized he would be better off as a solo artist. However, his ties to his original band mates would remain throughout his career, with many of them performing as members of Springsteen's E Street Band. Springsteen's biggest success, "Born To Run," was advertised with posters declaring that Springsteen was the future of rock. His nearly constant touring and high energy on stage earned him a reputation as one of the best live performers of his generation. Springsteen produced hit after hit for the next three decades and continues to perform today (Hardy & Laing, 1987).

KISS formed in 1972 with band members Gene Simmons, Paul Stanley, Peter Criss, and Ace Frehley. The band members covered their faces with grease paint to create a spectacle and started playing around New York City. KISS developed a grandiose stage show, complete with special effects, that drew criticism from mainstream audiences and positive attention from heavy-metal fans. They released their first album in 1974 and hit the U.S. charts in 1976 with their album *Alive*. The band eventually earned eighteen gold and twelve platinum albums.

Artists to Know

Elton John, Black Sabbath, The Who, Queen, The Eagles, Chicago, The Clash, Lynyrd Skynyrd, Alice Cooper, Aerosmith, Rush, Steve Miller Band, James Taylor, Jethro Tull, Bachman-Turner Overdrive, Electric Light Orchestra, Heart, Emerson, Lake & Palmer, AC/DC, Three Dog Night, Deep Purple, Fleetwood Mac, Iggy Pop, Average White Band, Cat Stevens, Peter Frampton, ZZ Top, KISS, Neil Young, Moody Blues, Kansas, Styx, Linda Ronstadt, Jim Croce, AC/DC, Jackson Brown, Three Dog Night, Boston, The Who, David Bowie

The 1980s

1980 John Lennon is assassinated, the first Pacman video game is released, the Rubik's cube becomes popular, and MTV is introduced on three hundred cable networks.

1981 AIDS is identified, the first woman is appointed to the Supreme Court, Ronald Reagan is almost assassinated by John Hinckley Jr., and IBM introduces personal computers.

1982 Michael Jackson's *Thriller* and the Steven Spielberg movie *E.T.* are both released.

1983 Cabbage Patch Kids are introduced, and MTV expands its reach with contracts for two thousand cable networks.

1985 The hole in the ozone layer is discovered.

1986 Space shuttle Challenger explodes, and a nuclear reactor in Chernobyl, USSR, explodes resulting in the worst nuclear power plant disaster in history.

1988 Pan Am flight 103 is bombed over Lockerbie, Scotland, a terrorist attack that the Libyan government eventually claims responsibility for.

1989 The Berlin wall falls, the Exxon Valdez oil spill creates an environmental disaster in Alaska, and student protestors are massacred in China's Tiananmen Square.

Overview

The 1980s saw the continued expansion of rock subgenres. Terms such as new wave, gothic rock, hardcore punk, electroclash, glam metal, and soft rock can all be used to define the various movements that developed in this decade (Covach, 2009). Technological advances, home cassette recorders, car cassette decks, "Walkmans" that played cassettes on the go, and the debut of MTV also significantly influence the music of this decade.

Rise of the Music Video

MTV was launched on August 1, 1981, as the nation's first twenty-four-hour music video channel. Record companies were skeptical at first, but when viewership expanded from 2.5 million in 1981 to 17 million in 1983, they took notice. By 1983, featuring a song on MTV was predicted to boost record sales by 15 to 20 percent. The visual aspect of music videos gave youths a chance to escape from daily life, and a band's looks began to matter as much, if not more, than its music (Szatmary, 1996). Record companies saw the potential benefits, and soon MTV was signing exclusive deals with record labels and rewriting the expectations for rock performers. No longer was it good enough to have a great song; you needed to also have a great video to go with it. There was one caveat in the early years: if you were a minority, there was little to no chance your video would ever play on air.

In 1983, there were over eight hundred acts with videos in rotation on MTV; only sixteen of those acts were black performers. That slowly began to change when Michael Jackson released his album *Thriller*. Earning twelve Grammy nominations, landing seven songs in the top ten, and holding the number-one spot for an album thirty-seven weeks in a row, the album ensured that MTV could not ignore Jackson. His first two videos "Beat It" and "Billie Jean" did not receive immediate acceptance from MTV executives, but eventually public pressure forced them to give in, and Jackson's stardom opened the gates for other black artists (Garofalo, 2005).

Heavy metal continued to expand in the eighties with thrash metal bands such as Metallica, Anthrax, Megadeath, and Slayer. Death metal bands such as Death, Cannibal Corpse, Morbid Angel, and Deicide also had followings. Alternative rock grew on college campuses across the United States as a reaction to the commercialism that had taken over much of rock. Campus bands produced their own albums and self-distributed them at their live shows and local record stores.

Bands from previous decades began making comebacks in the eighties. The Beach Boys recorded "Kokomo," the Steve Miller Band recorded "Abracadabra," and The Kinks recorded "Come Dancing." There was also a movement toward recapturing the musical spirit of the 1960s. Perhaps the best known of these artists was Bruce Springsteen, whose bad-boy singer/songwriter image helped him land hit after hit on the Billboard charts.

Icons to Know

Billy Joel was born in 1949 and first pursued professional boxing before forming his first band, the Hassles. The Hassles were signed to United Artists and recorded two albums before breaking up. Joel tried several other partnerships before moving to California where he began earning a living as a piano bar player. In 1974, he recorded his first album for Columbia, *Piano Man*, and saw its title track rocket to the top forty. Numerous albums followed, including *Street Life Serenade*, *Turnstiles*, and *The Stranger*, that established Joel as a major force in rock 'n' roll (George-Warren & Romanowski, 2001).

Patricia Andrzejewski was born in New York in 1953 and grew up on Long Island. At the age of seventeen, she began training as an opera singer at New York's prestigious Juilliard School. She quickly grew frustrated with the disciplined approach at Juilliard and left the school. Soon she married her high school sweetheart Dennis Benatar and changed her name to Pat Benatar. Dennis and Pat moved to Virginia where she worked as a singing waitress before returning to New York City in 1975. Once she returned to the city, she tried to start a career as a cabaret artist, but struggled to gain an audience. She changed her act and started singing rock 'n' roll, eventually getting signed by Chrysalis in 1978. In 1979, she released *Heat of the Night* and landed the single "Heartbreaker" on the top 30, earning her platinum record status (Hardy & Laing, 1987c). Her 1980 album *Crimes of Passion*, produced two hit singles, "Hit Me with Your Best Shot" and "Treat Me Right," eventually selling four million copies. *Precious Time* charted "Promises in the Dark" and "Fire and Ice" in 1981, reaching multiplatinum status. After a string of hits, Benatar took a brief hiatus in 1984 to give birth to her first daughter. She returned in 1985 with three hit singles and then attempted to record a blues album called *True Love* that failed to produce any hits. Her next album, *Gravity's Rainbow*, also failed to achieve success. After her label was bought out by EMI in 1995, she stepped out of the spotlight (George-Warren & Romanowski, 2001).

Artists to Know

Foreigner, Journey, Motley Crue, Dire Straits, U2, Def Leppard, Guns N' Roses, R.E.M., Bon Jovi, Duran Duran, John Mellencamp, Genesis,

Rush, Van Halen, Fleetwood Mac, Judas Priest, Heart, Bob Seeger, Tears for Fears, Chicago, Pete Townshend, Motley Crue, Talking Heads, The Cure, Iron Maiden, Judas Priest, Def Leppard, Elton John, Rod Stewart, Bob Seeger, Don Henley, Yes, Scorpions, Whitesnake, Kenny Loggins, Men at Work, Chicago, Tracy Chapman

The 1990s

1990   The Hubble telescope is launched into space and Nelson Mandela is freed from prison.

1991   Operation Desert Storm is set into motion by President George H. W. Bush in response to Iraq's invasion of Kuwait, and the Soviet Union dissolves, creating twelve independent states.

1992   The Cold War ends after the fall of the Soviet Union, and the brutal beating of Rodney King by Los Angeles police officers leads to six days of riots, leaving fifty-three people dead.

1993   ATF and FBI agents raid the Waco, Texas, compound of the Branch Davidian cult resulting in a fifty-one-day standoff. Seventy-six men, women, and children die as a result of a fire started by their leader. Lorena Bobbitt forever changes the repercussions of marital infidelity, and the World Trade Center is bombed for the first time.

1994   O.J. Simpson is arrested for murder.

1995   Home-grown terrorists blow up the Oklahoma City federal building, killing 168 people. Israeli prime minister Yitzach Rabin is assassinated.

1996   Mad cow disease is identified in Britain, and "The Unabomber," Ted Kaczynski, is arrested for sending multiple package bombs through the mail from 1978 to 1995.

1997   Princess Diana is killed in a car crash after being chased by paparazzi.

1998   President Clinton is impeached for perjury related to the Paul Jones and Monica Lewinsky scandals. *Titanic* is released with critical acclaim becoming the most successful movie ever.

1999   High school seniors Eric Harris and Dylan Klebold go on a killing spree at Columbine High School leaving twelve students and one teacher dead. Northeastern University computer science student Shawn Fanning launches his Internet file-sharing service Napster.

Overview

The economic situation in the 1990s was depressing. In 1992, the average worker was only earning $391 a week, a 5 percent decline from income levels in 1979, when adjusted for inflation. The unemployment rate was 7 percent, or a whopping 13 percent if it included underemployed workers and those who had given up looking for work. There were also changes to the American family structure that influenced Generation X. In the 1970s, only 10 percent of households were headed by a single parent. By 1992, that number had increased to 26 percent. Generation X not only had little hope for economic success but also was discouraged about the possibility of their personal lives not working out, either (Szatmary, 1996).

In the 1990s, alternative bands that had originally formed as a reaction against commercialism began to find commercial success. Fueled by the success of Nirvana, record labels began signing bands such as Goo Goo Dolls, Bush, Green Day, Live, and Pearl Jam. With the record labels' help, alternative artists started landing songs on the Billboard charts. Artists were eager to explore new musical possibilities and began combining elements of everything from country to hip-hop in their writing. A whole new set of subgenres emerged as well, including alternative metal, grunge, ska, pop punk, and nu metal, which were outlets for the anger and frustration felt by Generation X (Szatmary, 1996). The growth of these subgenres was fueled by Internet chat rooms and websites that allowed fans to socialize and share the music of new artists specific to their tastes (Selverne, 2004).

The 1990s gave birth to the modern American music festival. Lollapalooza was based on the successful multicity music festivals found in Europe and debuted in 1991 with a twenty-one-city tour. The headlining bands in 1991 included: Jane's Addiction, Nine Inch Nails, Henry Rollins, Ice-T and Body Count, Living Colour, Butthole Surfers, and Siouxsie and the Banchees. The tour was a huge success, and in 1992 it expanded to include thirty-five stops and a second stage to showcase emerging talents (Lollapalooza, 2013). The festival became a strong political force as well. Booths were set up for organizations such as the College Democrats, Rock the Vote, PETA, the Coalition for the Homeless, and the Cannabis Action Network. As the artists playing the festival became mainstream, Lollapalooza grew in popularity and soon became one of the major summer destinations in the United States.

The release and subsequent success of Alanis Morrisette's *Jagged Little Pill* was an important turning point for women. As in other fields of society,

31

women in rock music have often been underrepresented. That began to change around 1996 with numerous acts gaining widespread popularity. Performers such as Natalie Merchant, Tori Amos, Ani DiFranco, Gwen Stefani (No Doubt), Delores O'Riordan (Cranberries), and Shawn Colvin all found success. By 1999, they were dominating the Grammy Awards, winning for Best Dance Recording, Best Pop Album, and Best Rock Song.

Perhaps the most important development of the 1990s was Internet file sharing. When Shawn Fanning launched Napster on June 1, 1999, the music industry was forever changed. Consumers no longer had to copy CDs or record radio broadcasts to get their favorite songs for free, they could simply go online and share with millions of people throughout the world. Record companies not only lost control over distribution, they lost millions if not billions of dollars in profits (Selverne, 2004).

Icons to Know

Nirvana was formed in 1987 by Kurt Cobain, Dave Grohl, and Chris Novoselic and conveyed the vast array of emotions that Generation X'ers were feeling, especially the sense that they would never have a better life than their parents. The band merged punk-rock musicality with memorable lyrics and catchy melodies. Their single "Smells Like Teen Spirit" led their 1991 album to sell ten million copies, bringing the band, and alternative music, into the mainstream (Walser, n.d.).

Pearl Jam was a Seattle alternative-rock band that found success with its 1991 debut album, *Ten*. The self-produced album landed two hit songs on the charts, "Alive" and "Jeremy." The band reinvented itself several times over the next fifteen years, experimenting with new sounds and new band members. Many of the band members also worked on other side projects between Pearl Jam records. One of the band's most interesting successes was charting five albums in one week. They accomplished this feat by commercially releasing twenty-five recordings of live concerts in one week in September 2000. The band was trying to outsmart online bootleggers who were sharing lower quality files online, and the plan worked. Six months later, they released another set of live recordings and landed seven on the album charts at the same time (Walser, n.d.).

No Doubt was a popular grunge band in the 1990s fronted by female lead singer Gwen Stefani. The band signed with Interscope Records in 1991 and released its first album, *No Doubt*, with disappointing results. They released their second album, *The Beacon Street Collection*, in 1995 followed by *Tragic Kingdom* that same year. After repeated airplay, their single "I'm Just a Girl" reached the top thirty on the charts, and album sales began to climb. In 1996, the band landed another single, "Don't Speak," before slowly fading away from mainstream popularity. The band reemerged with albums in 2000 and 2001, but Stefani's desire to pursue solo work led to the bands demise ("No Doubt," 2006).

Alanis Morrisette was born in June 1974 in Ottawa, Ontario, Canada. She gained attention in Canada first, before capturing international attention in the mid-1990s. Morrisette began writing songs at the age of nine and released her first single at the age of ten, "Fate Stay with Me," which gained her local attention. She signed her first publishing deal at age fourteen, releasing two albums before signing with Maverick Records in 1994 and relocating to Los Angeles. Her 1995 album, *Jagged Little Pill*, included numerous hits including "You Oughta Know," "All I Really Want," and "Ironic." By 1998, the album had sold sixteen million copies in the United States and twenty-eight million internationally. Subsequent albums were released in 1998, 2002, 2004, and 2008, but none of them enjoyed the same success as *Jagged Little Pill* ("Alanis Morissette," 2006).

Artists to Know

Green Day, Bush, Red Hot Chili Peppers, Savage Garden, Third Eye Blind, Hootie & The Blowfish, Lisa Loeb, Nine Inch Nails, Weezer, Tool, Garbage, Screaming Trees, Primus, Creed, Blind Melon, Korn, Sheryl Crow, The Offspring, Sublime, Stone Temple Pilots, Sonic Youth, Dave Matthews Band, Beck, Rage Against the Machine, Alice in Chains, Oasis, Radiohead, The Smashing Pumpkins, U2, Phish

The 2000s

2000   The decade begins with concerns about whether or not computers will interpret the year "00" as 1900 or 2000, instigating the Y2K crisis. The Supreme Court decides the presidential election in favor of Republican George W. Bush, against the popular vote, due to ballot counting discrepancies in Florida.

2001   The terrorist attacks of September 11 devastate the American people and make Al Qaeda and Osama bin Laden household names. The Enron scandal leads to the largest bankruptcy in American history.

2002   Queen Elizabeth, the Queen Mother of England, dies in her sleep; the Beltway sniper attacks kill ten random victims around Washington, D.C.; and the United States Department of Homeland Security is established.

2003   The United States, led by George W. Bush, invades Iraq under false claims that the country has weapons of mass destruction.

2004   Television personality Martha Stewart is arrested for insider trading, and German Armin Meiwes recruits a willing victim online to be murdered and cannibalized, earning him eight years in prison.

2005   Pope John Paul II dies at the age of eighty-four; Joseph Ratinger, a German with former ties to the Nazi party, is elected Pope; and Michael Jackson is found not guilty on ten charges of child abuse.

2006   Vice President Dick Cheney accidentally shoots one of his colleagues while on a duck hunting trip in Texas, wildlife expert Steve Irwin dies from a stingray attack, and musician Malachi Ritscher sets himself on fire to protest the Iraq War. President George W. Bush signs the Military Commissions Act of 2006, allowing expedited military trials for enemy combatants, denying habeas corpus for those combatants, and giving the president the authority to define torture.

2007   Gunman Seung-Hui Cho kills thirty-two people at Virginia Tech University.

2008   Somali pirates hijack seven ships off the coast of Somalia, and American investor Bernie Madoff is arrested for orchestrating the largest Ponzi scheme in history, having stolen $64.8 billion from investors.

2009   President Obama is awarded the Nobel Peace Prize for his diplomatic efforts.

Overview

The subgenre expansion of the 1990s continued into the 2000s. Metalcore, technical-death metal, folk metal, rap-rock, emo, and screamo all found an audience in the 2000s. Record companies continued to struggle with how to earn revenue and reduce online pirating. At the same time, websites such as Pandora, Spotify, and Rhapsody offered independent labels and bands unprecedented opportunities to have their songs heard nationwide. The 2000s became the decade of the independent musician; in some ways returning the industry to the earliest days of rock 'n' roll when independent labels were the dominant force.

The 2000s also marked the return of political music and the singer/songwriter. The September 11, 2001, attack on the World Trade Center threw the United States into the world spotlight and set the stage for the ongoing "War on Terror." There was a great deal of skepticism before the war, but with the so-called evidence of weapons of mass destruction, public opinion shifted in favor of invading Iraq. Once the public learned that that they had been lied to and there were no weapons of mass destruction, their opinions of the war began to change. But there was something different this time around. Whereas in the past radio stations were mainly independent and could play whatever they wanted, in the 2000s an ongoing series of mergers had consolidated most of the radio stations in the country under the umbrella of a few corporate empires. Wealthy corporations and their executives now had control over what was played on air nationwide. The CEOs of those corporations were not antigovernment and were not in favor of playing protest music on their stations (Garofalo, 2005). Artists such as The Dixie Chicks found themselves thrust into the national spotlight and bombarded with negativity for taking a stand against a government they believed was corrupt. Radio stations across the country turned against the group, removing their music from the air, and organizing CD-crushing parties for ex-fans (Reuters, 2003).

The return of the singer/songwriter was perhaps one of the more exciting musical movements of this decade. Artists such as John Mayer and Jason Mraz wrote with a simpler approach to music and were still able to achieve commercial success (Garofalo, 2005). Thanks to a plethora of Internet music platforms, up-and-coming singer/songwriters were able to get their music heard nationwide while building their regional reputations. A new wave of independent artists began to find success one song at a time, success often driven by appearances on television commercials, television shows, and movie soundtracks.

YouTube, an Internet video-sharing site founded in 2005 (Rowell, 2011), had a significant impact on the worldwide music industry during this decade. Because YouTube allowed anyone to upload a video for free, major record labels and independent artists were finally on a level playing field. Independent artists around the world began recording and uploading cover songs and originals, competing for views and a chance at national stardom. Artists such as Justin Bieber, Rebecca Black, and Karmin all gained national attention on YouTube and turned that exposure into mainstream success.

Artists to Know

Sara Bareilles, Jazon Mraz, Regina Spektor, The White Stripes, The Shins, Boys Like Girls, Linkin Park, Muse, Foo Fighters, 30 Seconds to Mars, Avenged Sevenfold, Barenaked Ladies, Disturbed, Staind, Maroon 5, Fountains of Wayne, Fuel, Godsmack, Paramore, Incubus, Nickleback, My Chemical Romance, John Mayer, Fall Out Boy, Queens of the Stone Age, Bullet for My Valentine, The Fray, Adam Lambert, Muse

Notes

1. While most history books use "Africa" to identify the roots of rock, "Sub-Saharan Africa" is more accurate. However, in keeping in line with the existing texts, I will use "Africa" throughout this book.

2. Racial segregation, slavery, and other race-related issues play a significant role in rock history. While some texts use the terms "African Americans" and "Caucasians," most sources use "black" and "white." It is impossible to make a choice that does not cause some controversy. Since firsthand sources from the time period being discussed predominantly use the terms "black" and "white," those will be used throughout the text.

3. If you are unfamiliar with musical notation and chord structure, I suggest you consult Amy Appleby's *You Can Read Music*.

4. Musicians who often had little to no formal training wrote the traditional blues. When their compositions were published in sheet music form, professional composers, many of whom studied in or came from Europe, arranged them. These European-trained composers added structure to the rhythm, harmony, and melody, making them more accessible to trained performers. However, the result was often disconnected from the authentic feel of the original composition.

Bibliography

Abbott, L., & Seroff, D. (1996). "They cert'ly sound good to me": Sheet music, southern vaudeville, and the commercial ascendancy of the blues. *American Music*, *14*(4), 402–54. Retrieved from http://www.jstor.org/stable/3052302.

Alanis Morissette. (2006). "Morissette, Alanis." In *Encyclopedia of popular music*, 4th ed. New York: Oxford University Press. Retrieved October 17, 2013, from http://www.oxfordmusiconline.com/subscriber/article/epm/62744

Bane, M. (1982). *White boy singin' the blues*. New York: Da Capo Press.

Carter, S. B., Gartner, S. S., Haines, M. R., Olmstead, A. L., Sutch, R., Wright, G. (Eds.). (2006). "Urban and rural territory—population, by size of place:

1790–1990." In *Historical statistics of the United States: Earliest times to the present: Millennial edition.* (Vol. 1, pp. 103–8). New York: Cambridge University Press.

Covach, J. (2009). *What's That Sound? An Introduction to rock and its history.* New York: W. W. Norton.

Covach, J. (2013). Yes. In Grove music online. New York: Oxford University Press. Accessed October 28, 2013, http://www.oxfordmusiconline.com/subscriber/article/grove/music/46092.

Crawford, R. (2001). *An introduction to America's music.* New York: W. W. Norton & Company.

Eagles, C. (2001). Kent State and Jackson State. In *The Oxford companion to United States history.* New York: Oxford University Press. Retrieved October 26, 2013, from http://www.oxfordreference.com/view/10.1093/acref/9780195082098.001.0001/acref-9780195082098-e-0850.

Everett, W. (2009). *The foundations of rock: From Blue Suede Shoes to Suite: Judy Blue Eyes.* New York: Oxford University Press.

Fong-Torres, B. (2001). *The hits just keep on coming: The history of top 40 radio.* San Francisco: Backbeat Books.

Garofalo, R. (2005). *Rockin' out: Popular music in the U.S.A.* Upper Saddle River: Pearson Education.

George-Warren, H., & Romanowski, P. (Eds.). (2001). *The Rolling Stone encyclopedia of rock and roll.* New York: Simon & Schuster.

Girard, P. J., & Miller, R. (Eds.). (2008). *The Greenwood encyclopedia of daily life in America* (Vol. 2, p. 760). Westport, CT: Greenwood Press.

Gregg, R., McDonogh, G. W., & Wong, C. H. (Eds.). (2013a). The Beatles. In *Encyclopedia of contemporary American culture* (p. 74). New York: Routledge.

Gregg, R., McDonogh, G. W., & Wong, C. H. (Eds.). (2013b). Rock 'n' roll. In *Encyclopedia of contemporary American culture* (pp. 624–25). New York: Routledge.

Gregg, R., McDonogh, G. W., & Wong, C. H. (Eds.). (2013c). Woodstock. In *Encyclopedia of contemporary American culture* (p. 787). New York: Routledge.

Grout, D. J. A., & Palisca, C. V. A. (1996). *A history of western music.* New York: W. W. Norton & Company.

Hardy, P., & Laing, D. (Eds.) (1987a). Bruce Springsteen. In *Encyclopedia of rock.* New York: Schirmer Books.

Hardy, P., & Laing, D. (Eds.) (1987b). Janis Joplin. In *Encyclopedia of rock.* New York: Schirmer Books.

Hardy, P., & Laing, D. (Eds.) (1987c). Pat Benatar. In *Encyclopedia of rock.* New York: Schirmer Books.

Hardy, P., & Laing, D. (Eds.) (1987d). The Yardbirds. In *Encyclopedia of rock.* New York: Schirmer Books.

Higgs, R. (1976). The boll weevil, the cotton economy, and black migration 1910–1930. *Agricultural History, 50*(2). Retrieved from http://www.jstor.org/stable/3741334.

Jenkins, C. (2008). A question of containment: Duke Ellington and early radio. *American Music, 26*(4), 415–41. Retrieved from http://www.jstor.org/stable/40071718.

Jenkins, R. (2001). Thomas Edison. In *The Oxford companion to United States history*. New York: Oxford University Press. Retrieved from http://www.oxfordreference.com/view/10.1093/acref/9780195082098.001.0001/acref-9780195082098-e-0458.

Jones, L. (2005a). Christianity: Christianity in North America. In *Encyclopedia of religion*. (Vol. 3, pp. 1708–17). Farmington Hills: Macmillan Reference USA.

Jones, L. (2005b). George Whitefield. In *Encyclopedia of religion*. (Vol. 14, pp. 9726–28). Farmington Hills: Macmillan Reference USA.

Jones, L. (2005c). Music: Music and religion in Sub-Saharan Africa. In *Encyclopedia of religion*. (Vol. 9, pp. 6256–60). Farmington Hills: Macmillan Reference USA.

Jones, L. (2005d). Puritanism. In *Encyclopedia of religion*. (Vol. 11, pp. 7518–21). Farmington Hills: Macmillan Reference USA.

Larkin, C. (Ed.) (1995a). Beatles. In *The Guinness encyclopedia of popular music* (Vol. 1, pp. 323–28). New York: Stockton Press.

Larkin, C. (Ed.) (1995b). Little Richard. In *The Guinness encyclopedia of popular music* (Vol. 4, pp. 2517–18). New York: Stockton Press.

Larkin, C. (Ed.) (1995c). Rolling Stones. In *The Guinness encyclopedia of popular music* (Vol. 5, pp. 3564–70). New York: Stockton Press.

Larkin, C. (Ed.) (1995d). Woodstock Festival. In *The Guinness encyclopedia of popular music* (Vol. 6, pp. 4552–53). New York: Stockton Press.

Lollapalooza. (2013). From http://www.lollapalooza.com [retrieved October 20, 2013].

Mann, C. (2001). GI Bill. In *The Oxford companion to military history*. New York: Oxford University Press. http://www.oxfordreference.com/view/10.1093/acref/9780198606963.001.0001/acref-9780198606963-e-486 [retrieved October 25, 2013].

Mooney, H. F. (1968). Popular music since the 1920s: The significance of shifting taste. *American Quarterly, 20*(1), 67–85. Retrieved from http://www.jstor.org/stable/2710991

Morrow, C. B. (2009). *Rock and roll*. Watertown: Imagine!

No Doubt. (2006). In *Encyclopedia of popular music*, 4th ed. New York: Oxford University Press. Retrieved October 17, 2013, from http://www.oxfordmusiconline.com/subscriber/article/epm/65236.

Regal, B. (2005). *Radio: The life story of a technology*. Westport, CT: Greenwood Publishing Group.

Reuters. (2003). Dixie Chicks pulled from air after bashing Bush (March 14, 2003). CNN. Retrieved from http://www.cnn.com/2003/SHOWBIZ/Music/03/14/dixie.chicks.reut/.

Rowell, R. (2011). YouTube: *The company and its founders*. North Mankato: ABDO Publishing Company. Retrieved from http://books.google.com/books?id=WaUfjvXY1K0C&pgis=1.

Seeger, C. (1957). Music and class structure in the United States. *American Quarterly, 9*(3), 281–94.

Selverne, M. (2004). Music Industry. In *Baker's biographical dictionary of popular musicians since 1990*. (pp. 777–83). New York: Schirmer Reference.

Simonelli, D. (2012). Working class heroes: Rock music and British society in the 1960s and 1970s. Plymouth: Rowman & Littlefield. Retrieved from http://books.google.com/books?id=mnrwy7P3KvQC&pgis=1.

Stambler, I. (1989a). "Beach Boys." In *The encyclopedia of pop, rock, and soul*. (pp. 42–44). New York: St. Martin's Press.

Stambler, I. (1989b). Beatles. In *The encyclopedia of pop, rock, and soul*. (pp. 44–47). New York: St. Martin's Press.

Stambler, I. (1989c). Byrds. In *The encyclopedia of pop, rock, and soul*. (pp. 86–89). New York: St. Martin's Press.

Stambler, I. (1989d). The Grateful Dead. In *The encyclopedia of pop, rock, and soul*. (pp. 221–23). New York: St. Martin's Press.

Szatmary, D. P. (1996). A time to rock: A social history of rock and roll. New York: Schirmer Books.

Walser, R. (n.d.) Nirvana. In *Oxford music online*. New York: Oxford University Press, accessed October 17, 2013, http://www.oxfordmusiconline.com/subscriber/article/grove/music/49152.

Walser, R. (n.d.) Pearl Jam. In *The encyclopedia of popular music*, 4th ed. New York: Oxford University Press, accessed October 17, 2013, http://www.oxfordmusiconline.com/subscriber/article/epm/39255.

Ward, E., Stokes, G., & Tucker, K. (1986). *Rock of ages: The Rolling Stone history of rock & roll*. New York: Rolling Stone Press.

Weber, W. (1997). Did people listen in the 18th century? *Early Music, 25*(4). Retrieved from http://www.jstor.org/stable/3128412.

York, W. (1982a). (Ed.) Little Richard. In *Who's who in rock music*. (p. 216). New York: Charles Scribner's Sons.

York, W. (1982b). Yes. In *Who's who in rock music*. New York: Charles Scribner's Sons.

York, W. (Ed.) (1982c). Byrds. In *Who's who in rock music*. (p. 50). New York: Charles Scribner's Sons.

York, W. (Ed.) (1982d). Charles Hardin "Buddy" Holly. In *Who's who in rock music*. (p. 165). New York: Charles Scribner's Sons.

York, W. (Ed.) (1982e). Chuck Berry. In *Who's who in rock music*. (p. 27). New York: Charles Scribner's Sons.

York, W. (Ed.) (1982f). Deep Purple. In *Who's who in rock music*. (p. 88). New York: Charles Scribner's Sons.

York, W. (Ed.) (1982g). Doors. In *Who's who in rock music*. (p. 96). New York: Scribner.

York, W. (Ed.) (1982h). Led Zeppelin. In *Who's who in rock music*. (p. 209). New York: Charles Scribner's Sons.

York, W. (Ed.) (1982i). Rolling Stones. In *Who's who in rock music*. (pp. 304–5). New York: Charles Scribner's Sons.

York, W. (Ed.) (1982j). Yardbirds. In *Who's who in rock music*. (p. 400). New York: Charles Scribner's Sons.

CHAPTER TWO

SINGING MUSIC THEATER
AND VOICE SCIENCE

Scott McCoy

This chapter presents a concise overview of how the voice functions as a biomechanical, acoustic instrument. We will be dealing with elements of anatomy, physiology, acoustics, and resonance. But don't panic: The things you need to know are easily accessible, even if it has been many years since you last set foot in a science or math class!

All musical instruments, including the human voice, have at least four things in common: a *power source*, *sound source* (vibrator), *resonator*, and a system for *articulation*. In most cases, the person who plays the instrument provides power by pressing a key, plucking a string, or blowing into a horn. This power is used to set the sound source in motion, which creates vibrations in the air that we perceive as sound. Musical vibrators come in many forms, including strings, reeds, and human lips. The sound produced by the vibrator, however, needs a lot of help before it becomes beautiful music—we might think of it as raw material, like a lump of clay that a potter turns into a vase. Musical instruments use resonance to enhance and strengthen the sound of the vibrator, transforming it into sounds we identify as a piano, trumpet, or guitar. Finally, instruments must have a means of articulation to create the nuanced sounds of music. Let's see how these four elements are used to create the sounds of singing.

Pulmonary System: The Power Source of Your Voice

The human voice has a lot in common with a trumpet: Both use flaps of tissue as a sound source, both use hollow tubes as resonators, and both rely on the respiratory (pulmonary) system for power. If you stop to think about it, you quickly realize why breathing is so important for singing. First and foremost, it keeps us alive through the exchange of blood gasses—oxygen in, carbon dioxide out. But it also serves as the storage depot for the air we use to produce sound. Most singers rarely encounter situations in which these two functions are in conflict, but if you are required to sustain an extremely long phrase, you could find yourself in need of fresh oxygen before your lungs are totally empty.

Misconceptions about breathing for singing are rampant. Fortunately, most are easily dispelled. We must start with a brief foray into the world of physics in the realm of Boyle's law. Some of you no doubt remember this principle: The pressure of a gas within a container changes inversely with changes of volume. If the quantity of a gas is constant and its container is made smaller, pressure rises. But if we make the container bigger, pressure goes down. Boyle's law explains everything that happens when we breathe, especially when we combine it with another physical law: *Nature abhors a vacuum.* If one location has reduced pressure, air flows from an area of higher pressure to equalize the two, and vice versa. So if we can create a zone of reduced air pressure by expanding our lungs, air automatically flows in to restore balance. When air pressure in the lungs is increased, it has no choice but to flow outward.

As we all know, the air we breathe goes in and out of our lungs. Each lung contains millions and millions of tiny air sacs called *alveoli*, where gasses are exchanged. The alveoli also function like ultra-miniature versions of the bladder for a bag pipe, storing the air that will be used to set the vocal folds into vibration. To get the air in and out of them, all we need to do is make the lungs larger for inhalation and smaller for exhalation. Always remember this relationship between cause and effect during breathing: We inhale because we make ourselves larger; we exhale because we make ourselves smaller. Unfortunately, the lungs are organs, not muscles, and have no ability on their own to accomplish this feat. For this reason, your bodies came from the factory with special muscles designed to enlarge and compress your entire thorax (ribcage), while simultaneously moving your lungs. We can classify these muscles in two main categories: Any muscle that has the ability to increase the volume capacity of the thorax serves an *inspiratory* function; any muscle that has the ability to decrease the volume capacity of the thorax serves an *expiratory* function.

Your largest muscle of inspiration is called the *diaphragm* (figure 2.1). This dome-shaped muscle originates at the bottom of your sternum (breast-

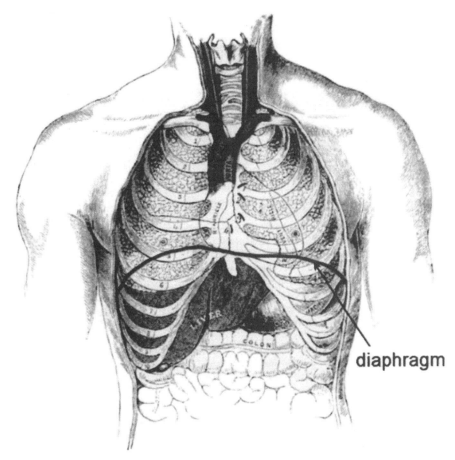

Figure 2.1. Location of diaphram. Dr. Scott McCoy.

bone) and completely fills the area from that point around your ribs to your spine. It's the second largest muscle in your body, but you probably have no conscious awareness of it or ability to directly control it. When we take a deep breath, the diaphragm contracts and the central portion flattens out and drops downward a couple inches into your abdomen, pressing against all of your internal organs. If you release tension from your abdominal muscles as you inhale, you will feel a gentle bulge in your upper or lower belly, or perhaps in your back, resulting from the displacement of your innards by the diaphragm. This is a good thing and can be used to let you know you have taken a good inhalation.

The diaphragm is important, but we must remember that it cannot function in isolation. After you inhale, it relaxes and gently returns to its resting position through an action called *elastic recoil*. This movement, however, is entirely passive and makes no significant contribution to generating the pressure required to sustain phonation. Therefore, it makes no sense at all to try to "sing from your diaphragm"—unless you intend to sing while you inhale, not exhale!

Eleven pairs of muscles assist the diaphragm in its inhalatory efforts, which are called the *external intercostal* muscles (figure 2.2). These muscles start from ribs one through eleven and connect at a slight angle downward to ribs two through twelve. When they contract, the entire thorax moves

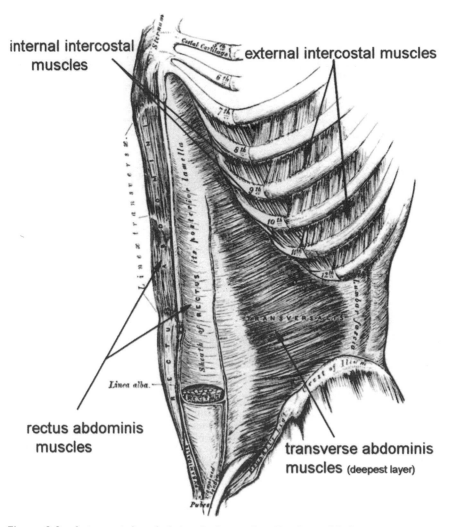

Figure 2.2. Intercostal and abdominal muscles. Dr. Scott McCoy.

up and out, somewhat as a bucket handle moves. With the diaphragm and intercostals working together, you are able to increase the capacity of your lungs by about three to six liters, depending on your gender and overall physical stature; thus, we have quite a lot of air available to power our voices.

Eleven additional pairs of muscles are located directly under the external intercostals, which, not surprisingly, are called the *internal intercostals* (figure 2.2). These muscles start from ribs two through twelve and connect upward to ribs one through eleven. When they contract, they induce the opposite action of their external partners: The thorax is made smaller, inducing exhalation. Four additional pairs of expiratory muscles are located in the abdomen, beginning with the *rectus* (figure 2.2). The two *rectus abdominis* muscles run from your pubic bone to your sternum and are divided into four separate portions, called *bellies* of the muscle (lots of muscles have multiple bellies; it is coincidental that the bellies of the rectus are found in the location we colloquially refer to as our belly). Definition of these bellies results in the so-called ripped abdomen or six-pack of body builders and others who are especially fit.

The largest muscles of the abdomen are called the *external obliques* (figure 2.3), which run at a downward angle from the sides of the rectus, covering the lower portion of the thorax, and extend all the way to the spine. The *internal obliques* lie immediately below, oriented at an angle that crisscrosses the external muscles. They are slightly smaller, beginning at the bottom of the thorax, rather than extending over it. The deepest muscle layer is the *transverse abdominis* (figure 2.2), which is oriented with fibers that run horizontally. These four muscle pairs completely encase the abdominal region, holding your organs and digestive system in place while simultaneously helping you breathe.

Your expiratory muscles are quite large and can produce a great deal of pulmonary, or air, pressure. In fact, they can easily overpower the larynx. Healthy adults generally can generate more than twice the pressure that is required to produce even the loudest sounds; therefore, singers must develop a system for moderating and controlling airflow and breath pressure. This practice goes by many names, including "breath support," "breath control," and "breath management," all of which rely on the principle of *muscular antagonism*. Muscles are said to have an antagonistic relationship when they work in opposing directions, usually pulling on a common point of attachment, for the sake of increasing stability or motor control. You can see a clear example of muscular antagonism in the relationship between your biceps

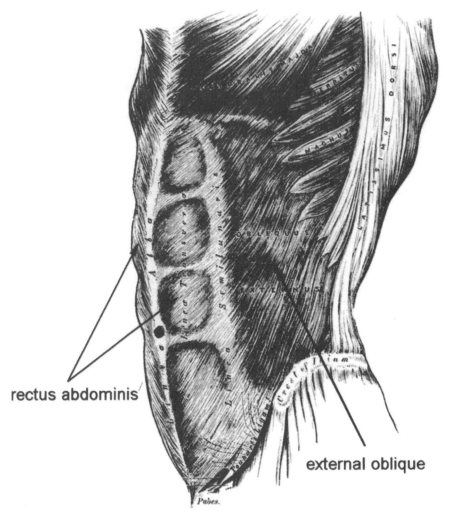

rectus abdominis

external oblique

Figure 2.3. External oblique and rectus abdominus muscles. Dr. Scott McCoy.

(flexors) and triceps (extensors) when you hold out your arm. In breathing for singing, we activate inspiratory muscles (e.g., diaphragm and external intercostals) during exhalation to help control respiratory pressure and the rate at which air is expelled from the lungs.

One of the things you will notice when watching a variety of singers is that they tend to breathe in many different ways. You might think that voice teachers and scientists, who have been teaching and studying singing for hundreds, if not thousands, of years, would have come to agreement on the best possible breathing technique. But for many reasons, this is not the case. For one, different musical and vocal styles place varying demands on breathing. For another, humans have a huge variety of body types, sizes, and morphologies. A breathing strategy that is successful for a tall, slender woman might be completely ineffective in a short, robust man. Our bodies actually contain a large number of muscles beyond those we've already discussed that are capable of assisting with respiration. For an example, consider your *latissimi dorsi* muscles. These large muscles of the arm enable us to do pull-ups (or pull-downs, depending on which exercise you perform) at the fitness center. But because they wrap around a large portion of the thorax, they also exert an expiratory force. We have at least two dozen such muscles that have secondary respiratory functions, some for exhalation and some for inhalation. When we consider all these possibilities, it is no surprise at all that there are many ways to breathe that can produce beautiful singing. Just remember to practice some muscular antagonism—maintaining a degree of inhalation posture during exhalation—and you should do well.

Larynx: The Vibrator of Your Voice

The larynx, sometimes known as the voice box or Adam's apple, is a complex physiologic structure made of cartilage, muscle, and tissue. Biologically, it serves as a sphincter valve, closing off the airway to prevent foreign objects from entering the lungs. When firmly closed, it is also used to increase abdominal pressure to assist with lifting heavy objects, childbirth, and defecation. But if we gently close this valve while we exhale, tissue in the larynx begins to vibrate and produce the sounds that become speech and singing.

The human larynx is a remarkably small instrument, typically ranging from the size of a pecan to a walnut for women and men, respectively. Sound is produced at a location called the *glottis*, which is formed by two flaps of tissue called the *vocal folds* (a.k.a. vocal cords). In women, the glottis is about the size of a dime; in men, it can approach the diameter of a quarter. The two folds are always attached together at their front point but open in the shape of the letter *V* during normal breathing, an action called *abduction*. To phonate, we must close the V while we exhale, an action called *adduction* (just like the machines you use at the fitness center to exercise your thigh and chest muscles).

Phonation only is possible because of the unique multilayer structure of the vocal folds (figure 2.4). The core of each fold is formed by muscle, which is surrounded by a layer of gelatinous material called the *lamina propria*. The *vocal ligament* also runs through the lamina propria, which helps to prevent

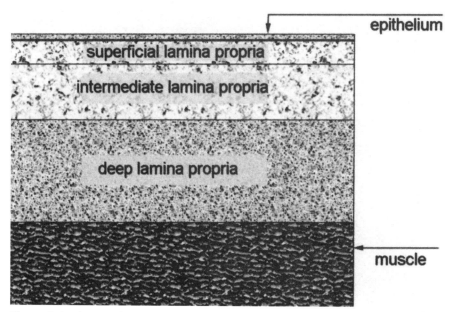

Figure 2.4. Layered structure of the vocal fold. Dr. Scott McCoy.

injury by limiting how far the folds can be stretched for high pitches. A thin, hairless epithelial layer that is constantly kept moist with mucus secreted by the throat, larynx, and trachea surrounds all of this. During phonation, the outer layer of the fold glides independently over the inner layer in a wavelike motion, without which phonation is impossible.

We can use a simple demonstration to better understand the independence of the inner and outer portions of the folds. Explore the palm of your hand with your other index finger. Note that the skin is attached quite firmly to the flesh beneath it. If you poke at your palm, that flesh acts as padding, protecting the underlying bone. Now explore the back of your hand. You will observe that the skin is attached quite loosely—you can easily move it around with your finger. And if you poke at the back of your hand, it is likely to hurt; there is very little padding between the skin and your bones. Your vocal folds combine the best attributes of both sides of your hand. They provide sufficient padding to help reduce impact stress, while permitting the outer layer to slip like the skin on the back of your hand, enabling phonation to occur. When you are sick with laryngitis and lose your voice (a condition called *aphonia*), inflammation in the vocal folds couples the layers of the folds tightly together. The outer layer can no longer move independently over the inner, and phonation becomes difficult or impossible.

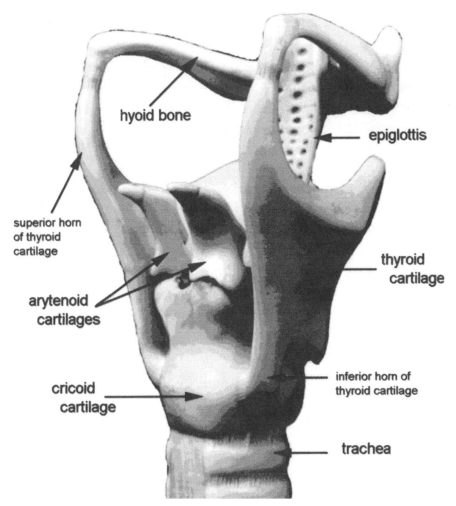

Figure 2.5. Cartilages of the larynx, viewed at an angle from the back. Dr. Scott McCoy.

The vocal folds are located within the five cartilaginous structures of the larynx (figure 2.5). The largest is called the *thyroid cartilage*, which is shaped like a small shield. The thyroid connects to the *cricoid* cartilage below it, which is shaped like a signet ring—broad in the back and narrow in the front. Two cartilages that are shaped like squashed pyramids sit atop the cricoid, called the *arytenoids*. Each vocal fold runs from the thyroid cartilage in front to one of the arytenoids at the back. Finally, the *epiglottis* is located at the top of the larynx, flipping backward each time we swallow to prevent food and liquid from entering our lungs. Muscles connect between the

49

various cartilages to open and close the glottis and to lengthen and shorten the vocal folds for ascending and descending pitch, respectively. Because they are sometimes used to identify vocal function, it is a good idea to know the names of the muscles that control the length of the folds. We've already mentioned that a muscle forms the core of each fold. Because it runs between the thyroid cartilage and an arytenoid, it is named the *thyroarytenoid* muscle (formerly known as the *vocalis* muscle). When the thyroarytenoid, or TA muscle, contracts, the fold is shortened and pitch goes down. The folds are elongated through the action of the *cricothyroid,* or CT muscles, which run from the thyroid to cricoid cartilage.

Vocal color (timbre) is created by the combined effects of the sound produced by the vocal folds and the resonance provided by the vocal tract. While these elements can never be completely separated, it is useful to consider the two primary modes of vocal fold vibration and their resulting sound qualities. The main differences are related to the relative thickness of the folds and their cross-sectional shape (figure 2.6). The first option depends on short, thick folds that come together with nearly square-shaped edges. Vibration in this configuration is given a variety of names, including *Mode 1, Thyroarytenoid* (TA) *dominant, chest mode,* or *modal voice.* The alternate configuration uses longer, thinner folds that only make contact at their upper margins. Common names include *Mode 2, Cricothyroid* (CT) *dominant, falsetto mode,* or *loft voice.* Singers vary the vibrational mode of the folds according to the quality of sound they wish to produce.

Before we move on to a discussion of resonance, we must consider the quality of the sound that is produced by the larynx. At the level of the glottis, we create a sound not unlike the annoying buzz of a duck call. That buzz, however, contains all the raw material we need to create speech and singing.

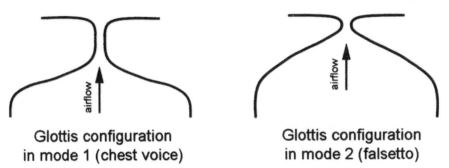

Glottis configuration in mode 1 (chest voice)

Glottis configuration in mode 2 (falsetto)

Figure 2.6. Primary modes of vocal fold vibration. Dr. Scott McCoy.

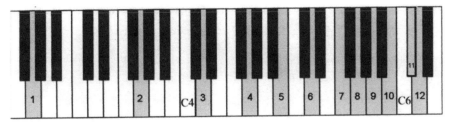

Figure 2.7. Natural harmonic series, beginning at G$_2$. Dr. Scott McCoy.

Vocal or glottal sound is considered to be *complex*, meaning it consists of many simultaneously sounding frequencies (pitches). The lowest frequency within any tone is called the *fundamental*, which corresponds to its named pitch in the musical scale. Orchestras tune to a pitch called *A-440*, which means it has a frequency of 440 vibrations per second, or 440 *Hertz* (abbreviated Hz). Additional frequencies are included above the fundamental, which are called *overtones*. Overtones in the glottal sound are quieter than the fundamental. In voices, the overtones are usually whole number multiples of the fundamental, creating a pattern called the *harmonic series* (e.g., 100 Hz, 200 Hz, 300 Hz, 400 Hz, 500 Hz, etc., or G$_2$, G$_3$, C$_4$, G$_4$, B$_4$), as shown in figure 2.7).[1]

Singers who choose to make coarse or rough sounds, as might be appropriate for rock or blues, often add overtones that are *inharmonic* or not part of the standard numerical sequence. Inharmonic overtones are also common in singers with damaged or pathological voices.

Under most circumstances, we are completely unaware of the presence of overtones—they simply contribute to the overall timbre of a voice. In some vocal styles, however, harmonics become a dominant feature. This is especially true in *throat singing* or *overtone singing*, as is found in places like Tuva. Throat singers tune their vocal tracts so precisely that single harmonics are highlighted within the harmonic spectrum as a separate, whistle-like tone. These singers sustain a low-pitched drone and then create a melody by moving from tone to tone within the natural harmonic series. You can learn to do this, too. Sustain a comfortable pitch in your range and slowly morph between the vowels /ee/ and /oo/. If you listen carefully, you will hear individual harmonics pop out of your sound.

The mode of vocal fold vibration has a strong impact on the overtones that are produced. In mode 1, high frequency harmonics are relatively strong; in mode 2, they are much weaker. As a result, mode 1 tends to yield a much brighter, brassier sound.

Vocal Tract: Your Source of Resonance

Resonance is typically defined as the amplification and enhancement (or en-richment) of musical sound through *supplemental vibration*. What does this really mean? In laymen's terms, we could say that resonance makes instruments louder and more beautiful by reinforcing the original vibrations of the sound source. This enhancement occurs in two primary ways, which are known as forced and free resonance.[2] Any object that is physically connected to a vibrator can serve as a forced resonator. For a piano, the resonator is the soundboard (on the underside of a grand or on the back of an upright); the vibrations of the strings are transmitted directly to the soundboard through a structure known as the bridge, which is also found on violins and guitars. Forced resonance also plays a role in voice production. Place your hand on your chest and say "ah" at a low pitch. You almost certainly felt the vibrations of forced resonance. In singing, this might best be considered your *private* resonance; you can feel it and it might impact your self-perception of sound, but nobody else can hear it. To understand why this is true, imagine what a violin would sound like if it were encased in a thick layer of foam rubber. The vibrations of the string would be damped out, muting the instrument. Your skin, muscles, and other tissues do the same thing to the vibrations of your vocal folds.

By contrast, free resonance occurs when sound travels through a hollow space, such as the inside of a trumpet, an organ pipe, or your vocal tract, which consists of the pharynx (throat), oral cavity (mouth), and nasal cavity. As sound travels through these regions, a complex pattern of echoes is cre-ated; every time sound encounters a change in the shape of the vocal tract, some of its energy is reflected backward, much like an echo in a canyon. If these echoes arrive back at the glottis at the precise moment a new pulse of sound is created, the two elements synchronize, resulting in a significant increase in intensity. All of this happens very quickly—remember that sound is traveling through your vocal tract at over 700 miles per hour.

Whenever this synchronization of the vocal tract and sound source occurs, we say that the system is *in resonance*. The phenomenon occurs at specific frequencies (pitches), which can be varied by changing the position of the tongue, lips, jaw, palate, and larynx. These resonant frequencies, or areas in which strong amplification occurs, are called *formants*. Formants provide the specific amplification that changes the raw, buzzing sound pro-duced by your vocal folds into speech and singing. The vocal tract is capable of producing many formants, which are labeled sequentially by ascending pitch. The first two, F_1 and F_2, are used to create vowels; higher formants contribute to the overall timbre and individual characteristics of a voice. In some singers, especially those who train to sing in opera, formants 3 through 5 are clustered to form a super formant, eponymously called the *singer's formant*, which creates a ringing sound and enables a voice to be heard in a large theater without electronic amplification.

Formants are vitally important in singing, but they can be a bit intimidating to understand. An analogy that works really well for me is to think of formants as being like the wind. You cannot see the wind, but you know it is present when you see leaves rustling in a tree or feel a breeze on your face. Formants work in the same manner. They are completely invisible and directly inaudible. But just as we see the rustling leaf, we can hear and, perhaps, even feel the action of formants by how they change our sound. Try a little experiment. Sing an ascending scale beginning at B-flat$_3$, sustaining the vowel /ee/. As you approach the D-natural or E-flat of the scale, you likely will feel (and hear) that your sound becomes a bit stronger and easier to produce. This occurs because the scale tone and formant are on the same pitch, providing additional amplification. If you change to an /oo/ vowel, you will feel the same thing at about the same place in the scale. If you sing to an /oh/ or /eh/ and continue up the scale, you'll feel a bloom in the sound somewhere around C$_5$ (an octave above middle C); /ah/ is likely to come into its best focus at about G$_5$.

To remember the approximate pitches of the first formants for the main vowels, ee-eh-ah-oh-oo, just think of a C-Major triad in first inversion, open position, starting at E$_4$: ee = E$_4$, eh = C$_5$, ah = G$_5$, oh = C$_5$, and oo = E$_4$ (figure 2.8). If your music theory isn't strong, you could use the mnemonic "**e**very **c**hild **g**ets **c**andy **e**agerly." These pitches might vary by as much as a

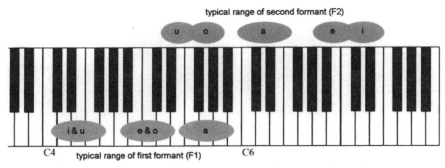

Figure 2.8. Typical range of first and second formants for primary vowels. Dr. Scott McCoy.

minor third higher and lower, but no farther: Once a formant changes by more than that interval, the vowel that is produced *must* change.

Formants have absolutely no preference for what they amplify—they are indiscriminate lovers, just as happy to bond with the first harmonic as the fifth. When men or women sing low pitches, there will almost always be at least one harmonic that comes close enough to a formant to produce a clear vowel sound. The same is not true for women with high voices, especially sopranos, who must routinely sing pitches that have a fundamental frequency *higher* than the first formant of many vowels. Imagine what happens if she must sing the phrase "and I'll leave you forever," with the word "leave" set on a very high, climactic note. The audience won't be able to tell if she is singing *leave* or *love* forever; the two will sound identical. This happens because the formant that is required to identify the vowel /ee/ is too far below the pitch being sung. Even if she tries to sing *leave*, the sound that comes out of her mouth will be heard as some variation of /ah/.

Fortunately, this kind of mismatch between formants and musical pitches rarely causes problems for anyone but opera singers, choir sopranos, and perhaps ingénues in classic music-theater shows. Almost everyone else generally sings low enough in their respective voice ranges to produce easily identifiable vowels.

Second formants can also be important, but more so for opera singers than everyone else. They are much higher in pitch, tracking the pattern oo = E_5, oh = G_5, ah = D_6, eh = B_6, ee = D_7 (you can use the mnemonic "**e**very **g**ood **d**ad **b**uys **d**iapers" to remember these pitches) (figure 2.8). Because they can extend so high, into the top octave of the piano keyboard for /ee/, they interact primarily with higher tones in the natural harmonic series. Unless you are striving to produce the loudest unamplified sound possible, you probably never need to worry about the second formant; it will steadfastly do its job of helping to produce vowel sounds without any conscious thought or manipulation on your part.

If you are interested in discovering more about resonance and how it impacts your voice, you might want to install a spectrum analyzer on your computer. Free (or inexpensive) programs are readily available for download over the Internet that will work with either a PC or Mac computer. You don't need any specialized hardware—if you can use Skype or Facetime, you already have everything you need. Once you've installed something, simply start playing with it. Experiment with your voice to see exactly how the analysis signal changes when you change the way your voice sounds. You'll be able to see how harmonics change in intensity as they interact with your formants. If you sing with vibrato, you'll see how consistently you produce your variations in pitch and amplitude. You'll even be able to see if your tone is excessively nasal for the kind of singing you want to do. Other programs are available that will help you improve your intonation (how well you sing in tune) or to enhance your basic musicianship skills. Technology truly has advanced sufficiently to help us sing more beautifully.

Mouth, Lips, and Tongue: Your Articulators

The articulatory life of a singer is not easy, especially when compared to the demands placed on other musicians. Like a pianist or brass player, we must be able to produce the entire spectrum of musical articulation, including dynamic levels from hushed pianissimos to thunderous fortes, short notes, long notes, accents, crescendos, diminuendos, etc. We produce most of these articulations the same way instrumentalists do, which is by varying our power supply. But singers have another layer of articulation that makes everything much more complicated; we must produce these musical gestures while simultaneously singing words.

As we learned in our brief examination of formants, altering the resonance characteristics of the vocal tract creates the vowel sounds of language. We do this by changing the position of our tongue, jaw, lips, and sometimes palate. Slowly say the vowel pattern /ee-eh-ah-oh-oo/. Can you feel how your tongue moves in your mouth? For /ee/, it is high in the front and low in the back, but it takes the opposite position for /oo/. Now slowly say the word *Tuesday*, noting all the places your tongue comes into contact with your teeth and palate and how it changes shape as you produce the vowels and diphthongs. There is a lot going on in there—no wonder it takes so long for babies to learn to speak!

Our articulatory anatomy is extraordinarily complex, in large part because our bodies use the same passageway for food, water, air, and sound. As a result, our tongue, larynx, throat, jaw, and palate are all interconnected with common physical and neurologic points of attachment. Our anatomical *Union Station* in this regard is a small structure called the *hyoid bone*. The hyoid is one of only three bones in your entire body that does not connect to other bones via a joint (the other two are your *patellae*, or kneecaps). This little bone is suspended below your jaw, freely floating up and down every time your swallow. It is a busy place, serving as the upper suspension point for the larynx, the connection for the root of the tongue, and the primary location of the muscles that open your mouth by dropping your jaw.

Good singing—in any genre—requires a high degree of independence in all these articulatory structures. Unfortunately, nature conspires against us to make this difficult to accomplish. From the time we were born, our bodies have relied on a reflex reaction to elevate the palate and raise the larynx each time we swallow. This action becomes habitual: palate goes up, larynx also lifts. But depending on the style of music we are singing, we might need to keep the larynx down while the palate goes up (opera and classical), or palate down with the larynx up (country and bluegrass). As we all know, habits can be very hard to change, which is one of the reasons that it can take a lot of study and practice to become an excellent singer. Understanding your body's natural reflexive habits can make some of this work a bit easier.

There is one more significant pitfall to the close proximity of all these articulators: Tension in one area is easily passed along to another. If your jaw muscles are too tight while you sing, that hyperactivity will likely be transferred to the larynx and tongue—remember, they are all interconnected through the hyoid bone. It can be tricky to determine the primary offender in this kind of chain reaction of tension. A tight tongue could just as easily be making your jaw stiff, or an elevated, rigid larynx could make both tongue and jaw suffer.

Neurology complicates matters even further. You have sixteen muscles in your tongue, fourteen in your larynx, twenty-two in your throat and palate, and another sixteen that control your jaw. Many of these are very small and lie directly adjacent to each other, and you are often required to contract one quite strongly while its next-door neighbor must remain totally relaxed. Our brains need to develop laser-like control, sending signals at the right moment with the right intensity to the precise spot where they are needed. When we first start singing, these brain signals come more like a blast from a shotgun, spreading the neurologic impulse over a broad area to multiple muscles, not all of which are the intended target. Again, with practice and training we learn to refine our control, enabling us to use only those muscles that will help, while disengaging those that would get in the way of our best singing.

Conclusion

This brief chapter has only scratched the surface of the huge field of voice science. To learn more, you might visit the websites of the National Association of Teachers of Singing, The Voice Foundation, or The National Center for Voice and Speech. You can easily locate the appropriate addresses through any Internet search engine. Remember: knowledge is power. Occasionally, people are afraid that if they know more about the science of how they sing, they will become so analytical that all spontaneity is lost or that they will become paralyzed by too much information and thought. In my forty-plus years as a singer and teacher, I've never encountered somebody who actually suffered this fate. To the contrary, the more we know, the easier—and more joyful—singing becomes.

Notes

1. Pitches are named by the international system in which the lowest C of the piano keyboard is C_1. Middle C therefore becomes C_4, the fourth C of the keyboard.

2. There is nothing pejorative in these terms: Free resonance is not superior to forced resonance.

VOCAL HEALTH AND THE ROCK SINGER

Wendy DeLeo LeBorgne

General Physical Well-Being

The idea of vocal health, vocal wellness, and an overall generally healthy lifestyle may not be the first things that come to mind when thinking about rock performers. Rock stars often have the reputation of staying up late, partying hard, and engaging in less than ideal healthy situations. Sadly, the rock world has lost many great artists due to choices that have led to their demise. From Jimi Hendrix and Janis Joplin to Mike Starr and Amy Winehouse, the rock world has been significantly affected by the influences of popular culture (Oksanen, 2013; Shaw, Whitehead, & Giles, 2010). It may seem that the performers who live and work in this genre do not consider vocal health and physical health as priorities in their performing careers.

However, rock singers, especially, should consider themselves as "vocal athletes" due to the demands placed upon them. The physical, emotional, and performance demands required for optimal output requires that the artist consider training and maintaining their instrument the same way an athlete considers training for an event. With increased vocal and performance demands, it is unlikely that a vocal athlete will have an entire performing career completely injury free. This may not be the fault of the singer, as many injuries occur due to circumstances beyond the singer's control, such as singing through an illness or being on a new medication seemingly unrelated to the voice.

Vocal injury has often been considered taboo to talk about in the performing world, as it has been considered to be the result of faulty technique or poor vocal habits. In actuality, the majority of vocal injuries presenting in the elite performing population tends to be overuse and/or acute injury. In the rock world, a slightly rough or abnormal vocal quality may be quite marketable for the performer. From a clinical perspective over the last seventeen years, younger, less experienced singers with fewer years of training (who tend to be quite talented) generally are the ones who present with issues related to technique or phonotrauma (nodules, edema, contact ulcers), while more mature singers with professional performing careers tend to present with acute injuries (hemorrhage), overuse and misuse injuries (muscle tension dysphonia, edema, gastroesophageal reflux [GERD]), or injuries following an illness. There are no current studies documenting use and training in correlation to laryngeal pathologies. However, there are studies that document that somewhere between 35 percent and 100 percent of professional vocal athletes have abnormal vocal fold findings on stroboscopic evaluation (Korovin & LeBorgne, 2009; Phyland, Oates, & Greenwood, 1999; Hoffman Ruddy, Lehman, Crandell, Ingram, & Sapienza, 2001; Evans, Evans, Carvajal, & Perry, 1996; Koufman, Radomski, Joharji, Russell, & Pillsbury, 1996; Heman-Ackah, Dean, & Sataloff, 2002; Lundy, Casiano, Sullivan, Roy, Xue, & Evans, 1999; Tepe, Deutsch, Sampson, Lawless, Reilly, & Sataloff, 2002). Many times these "abnormalities" are in singers who have no vocal complaints or symptoms of vocal problems. From a performance perspective, uniqueness in vocal quality often gets hired, and perhaps a slight aberration in the way a given larynx functions may become quite marketable. Regardless of what the vocal folds may look like, the most integral part of performance is that the singer must maintain agility, flexibility, stamina, power, and inherent quality (genre appropriate) for their current level of performance, taking into account physical, vocal, and emotional demands.

Unlike sports medicine and the exercise physiology literature where much is known about the types and nature of any given sports injury, there is no common parallel for the vocal athlete model (Yang, Tibbetts, Covassin, Cheng, Nayar, & Heiden, 2012). However, because the vocal athlete utilizes the body systems of alignment, respiration, phonation, and resonance with some similarities to physical athletes, a parallel protocol for vocal wellness may be implemented/considered for vocal athletes to maximize injury-prevention knowledge for both the singer and teacher. This chapter aims to provide information on vocal wellness and injury prevention for the vocal athlete.

Considerations for Whole Body Wellness

Nutrition

You have no doubt heard the saying "You are what you eat." Eating is a social and psychological event. For many people, food associations and eating have an emotional basis resulting in either overeating or malnourishment. Eating disorders and body image issues in performers may have major implications and consequences for the performer on both ends of the spectrum (obesity and anorexia). Singers should be encouraged to reprogram the brain and body to consider food as fuel. You want to use high octane gas in your engine, just as pouring water in your car's gas tank won't get you very far. Eating a poor diet or a diet that lacks appropriate nutritional value will have negative physical and vocal effects on the singer. Poor dietary choices for the vocal athlete may result in physical and vocal effects ranging from fatigue to life-threatening disease over the course of a lifetime. Encouraging and engaging in healthy eating habits from a young age will potentially prevent long-term negative effects from poor nutritional choices. It is beyond the scope of this chapter to provide a complete overview of dietary guidelines for children, adolescents, adults, and the mature adult; however, a listing of additional references to help guide your food and beverage choices for making good nutritional choices can be found online at:

Dietary Guidelines for Americans: http://www.health.gov/dietary
  guidelines
Nutrition.gov Guidelines for Tweens & Teens: http://www.nutrition
  .gov/life-stages/adolescents/tweens-and-teens
Fruits and Veggies Matter: http://www.fruitsandveggiesmorematters
  .org/myplate-and-what-is-a-serving-of-fruits-and-vegetables

For the rock singer on tour, eating well can be a huge challenge. Late nights on a tour bus or in a hotel room result in limited options for well-balanced meals. Therefore, meal planning and stocking the bus with healthy food options becomes necessary to avoid poor food choices. Additionally, performers are generally famished after a two-to-three-hour intensive performance and will need to eat before going to sleep, but bar food is not typically the best option for a light meal and the temptation of alcohol is huge.

Hydration

"Sing Wet, Pee Pale." This phrase was echoed in the studio of Dr. Van Lawrence regarding how his students would know if they were hydrated well enough. Generally, this rule of pale urine during your waking hours is a good indicator that you are well hydrated. Medications, vitamins, and certain foods may alter urine color despite adequate hydration. Due to the varying levels of physical and vocal activity of many performers, in order to maintain adequate oral hydration, the use of a hydration calculator based on activity level may be a better choice than observation of urine color. These hydration calculators are easily accessible online and take into account the amount and level of activity the performer engages in on a daily basis. For rock singers, the use of hazes, fogs, and pyrotechnics may significantly contribute to laryngeal dryness. Rock singers are dynamic onstage performers, with jumping and dancing and in generally engaging their audience when conveying their music; they lose a significant amount of fluid due to perspiration and the act of singing itself.

Laryngeal and pharyngeal dryness as well as "thick, sticky mucus" are often complaints of singers. Combating these concerns and maintaining an adequate viscosity of mucus for performance has resulted in some research. As a reminder of laryngeal and swallowing anatomy, nothing that is swallowed (or gargled) goes over or touches the vocal folds directly (or one would choke). Therefore, nothing that a singer eats or drinks ever touches the vocal folds, and in order to adequately hydrate the mucus membranes of the vocal folds, one must consume enough fluids for the body to produce a thin mucus. Therefore, any "vocal" effects from swallowed products are limited to potential pharyngeal and oral changes, not the vocal folds themselves.

The effects of systemic hydration are well documented in the literature. There is evidence to suggest that adequate hydration will provide some protection of the laryngeal mucosal membranes when they are placed under increased collision forces and will reduce the amount of effort (phonation threshold pressure) to produce voice (Leydon, Sivasanka, Falciglia, Atkins, & Fisher, 2009; Leydon, Wroblewski, Eichorn, & Sivasankar, 2010; Sivasankar & Leydon, 2010; Yiu & Chan, 2003). This is important for the singer because it means that, with adequate hydration and consistency of mucus, the effort needed to produce voice is lessened and your vocal folds are better protected from injury. Imagine the friction and heat produced when you rub your dry hands together and then what happens if you put lotion on your hands. The mechanisms in the larynx to provide appropriate mucus production are not fully understood, but there is enough evidence at this time to support oral hydration as a vital component of every singer's vocal health regime to maintain appropriate mucosal viscosity.

Although very rare, overhydration (hyperhidrosis) can result in dehydration and even illness or death. An overindulgence of fluids essentially makes the kidneys work "overtime" and flushes too much water out of the body. This excessive fluid loss in a rapid manner can be detrimental to the body.

In addition to drinking water to systemically maintain hydration, there are many nonregulated products on the market for performers that claim to improve the laryngeal environment (e.g., Entertainer's Secret, Throat Coat Tea, Greathers Pastilles, Slippery Elm, etc.). Although there may be little detriment in using these products, quantitative research documenting change in laryngeal mucosa is sparse (Brinckmann, Sigwart, van Houten, & Taylor, 2003; Roy, Tanner, Gray, Blomgren, & Fisher, 2003). One study suggests that the use of Throat Coat when compared to a placebo treatment for pharyngitis did show a significant difference in decreasing the perception of sore throat. Another study compared the use of Entertainer's Secret to two other nebulized agents and its effect on phonation threshold pressure (PTP). There was no positive benefit in decreasing PTP with Entertainer's Secret (Roy et al., 2003).

Many singers use personal steam inhalers and/or room humidification to supplement oral hydration and aid in combating laryngeal dryness. There are several considerations for singers who choose to use external means of adding moisture to the air they breathe. Personal steam inhalers are portable and can often be used backstage or in the hotel room for the traveling performer. Typically, water is placed in the steamer and the face is placed over the steam for inhalation. Because the mucus membranes of the larynx are composed of a saltwater solution, one study looked at the use of nebulized saline in comparison to plain water and its potential effects on effort or ease to sound production in classically trained sopranos (Tanner, Roy, Merrill, Muntz, Houtz, Sauder, Elstad, Wright-Costa, 2010). Data suggested that perceived effort to produce voice was less in the saline group than the plain-water group. This indicated that the singers who used the saltwater solution reported less effort to sing after breathing in the saltwater than singers who used plain water. It was hypothesized by the researchers that because the body's mucus is not plain water (rather it is saltwater—think about your tears), when you use plain water for steam inhalation, it may actually draw the salt from your own saliva, resulting in a dehydrating effect.

In addition to personal steamers, other options for air humidification come in varying sizes of humidifiers from room size to whole-house humidifiers. When choosing between a warm-mist or cool-mist humidifier, considerations include both personal preference and needs. One of the primary reasons warm-mist humidifiers are not recommended for young children is the risk of burns from the heating element. Both the warm-mist and cool-mist humidifiers act similarly in adding moisture to the environmental air. External air humidification may be beneficial and provide a level of comfort for many singers. Regular cleaning of the humidifier is vital to prevent bacteria and mold buildup. Also, depending on the hardness of the water, it is important to avoid mineral buildup on the device, and distilled water may be recommended for some humidifiers.

For traveling performers who often stay in hotels, fly on airplanes, or are generally exposed to other dry-air environments, there are products on the market designed to help minimize drying effects. One such device is called "Humidfly," a facemask (http://www.humidiflyer.com/) designed with a filter to recycle the moisture from a person's own breath and replenish moisture on each breath cycle.

For dry nasal passages or to clear sinuses, many singers use neti pots. Many singers use this homeopathic flushing of the nasal passages regularly. When utilized properly, research supports the use of a neti pot as a part of allergy relief and chronic rhinosinusitis control, sometimes in combination with medical management (Brown & Grahm, 2004; Dunn, Dion, & McMains, 2013). Conversely, long-term use of nasal irrigation (without taking intermittent breaks from daily use) may result in washing out the "good" mucus of the nasal passages, which naturally helps to rid the nose of infections. A study presented at the American College of Allergy, Asthma & Immunology (ACAAI) 2009 Annual Scientific Meeting reported that when a group of individuals who were using twice-daily nasal irrigation for one year discontinued using it, they had an increase in acute rhinosinusitits (Nsouli, 2009).

Tea, Honey, and Gargle to Keep the Throat Healthy

Regarding the use of general teas (which many singers combine with honey or lemon), there is likely no harm in the use of decaffeinated tea (caffeine may cause systemic dryness). The warmth of the tea may provide a soothing sensation to the pharynx and the act of swallowing can be relaxing for the muscles of the throat. Honey has been shown to be promising as an effective cough suppressant in the pediatric population (Shadkam, Mozaffari-Khosravi, & Mozayan 2010). The dose of honey given to the children in the study was two teaspoons. Gargling with salt or apple-cider vinegar and water are also popular home remedies for many singers, with the uses being from soothing the throat to curing reflux. Gargling plain water has been shown to be efficacious in reducing the risk of contracting upper-respiratory infections (Satomura, Kitamura, Kawamura, Shimbo, Watanabe, Kamei, Takana, & Tamakoshi, 2005). This author suggests that, when gargling, the singer only "bubble" the water with air and avoid engaging the vocal folds in sound production. Saltwater as a gargle has long been touted as a sore-throat remedy and can be traced back to 2700 BC in China for treating gum disease (http://health.howstuffworks.com/wellness/oral-care/products/saltwater-as-mouthwash.htm). The scientific basis behind a saltwater rinse for everything from oral hygiene to sore throats is that salt (sodium chloride) may act as a natural analgesic (pain killer) and may also kill bacteria. Similar to the effects that not enough salt in the water may have on drawing the salt out of the tissue in steam inhalation, if you oversaturate the water solution with salt and gargle it, it may act to draw water out of the oral mucosa, thus reducing inflammation.

Another popular home remedy reported by singers is the use of apple cider vinegar to help with everything from acid reflux to sore throats. Apple cider vinegar has been reported as a medicinal remedy dating back to 3300 BC, and it became popular in the 1970s as a weight-loss diet cocktail. Popular media reports apple cider vinegar can improve conditions from acne and arthritis to nosebleeds and varicose veins (http://www.healthline.com/natstandardcontent/apple-cider-vinegar). Specific efficacy data regarding the beneficial nature of apple cider vinegar for the purpose of sore throat, pharyngeal inflammation, and reflux has not been reported in the literature at this time. Of the peer-reviewed studies found in the literature, one discussed possible esophageal erosion and inconsistency of the actual product in tablet form (Hill, Woodruff, Foote, & Barreto-Alcoba, 2005). Therefore, at this time, strong evidence supporting the use of apple cider vinegar has not been published.

Medications and the Voice

Medications (over-the-counter, prescription, and herbal) may result in drying effects on the body and often on the laryngeal mucosa. General classes of drugs with potential drying effects include: antidepressants, anti-hypertensives, diuretics, ADD/ADHD medications, some oral acne medications, hormones, allergy drugs, and vitamin C in high doses. The National Center for Voice and Speech (NCVS) provides a listing of some common medications with potential voice side effects including laryngeal dryness. This listing does not take into account all medications so singers should always ask their pharmacist of the potential side effects of a given medication. Due to the significant number of drugs on the market, it is safe to say that most pharmacists will not be acutely aware of "vocal side effects," but if dryness is listed as a potential side effect of the drug, you may assume that all body systems could be affected. Under no circumstances should you stop taking a prescribed medication without consulting your physician first. Because every person has a different body chemistry and reaction to medication, just because a medication lists dryness as a potential side effect does not necessarily mean you will experience that side effect. Conversely, if you begin a new medication and notice physical or vocal changes that are unexpected, you should consult your physician. Ultimately, the goal of medical management for any condition is to achieve the most benefits with the fewest side effects. Some resources for the singer regarding prescription drugs and herbs are:

- http://www.fda.gov/OHRMS/DOCKETS/98FR/06D-0480-GLD0001.PDF

- http://nccam.nih.gov/health/herbsataglance.htm

- http://www.nlm.nih.gov/medlineplus/druginfo/herb_All.html

- http://www.ncvs.org

In contrast to medications that tend to dry, there are medications formulated to increase saliva production or alter the viscosity of mucus. Medically, these drugs are often used to treat patients who have had a loss of saliva production due to surgery or radiation. Mucalitic agents are used to thin secretions as needed. As a singer, if you feel that you need to use a mucalitic agent on a consistent basis, it may be worth getting to the root of the laryngeal dryness by seeking a professional option from an otolaryngologist.

Reflux and the Voice

Gastroesophageal reflux (GERD) and/or laryngopharyngeal reflux (LPR) can have a devastating impact on the singer if not recognized and treated appropriately. Although GERD and LPR are related, they are considered to be slightly different conditions. GERD is the reflux (Latin root meaning "flowing back") of digestive enzymes, acids, and other stomach contents into the esophagus (food pipe). If this backflow is propelled through the upper esophagus and into the throat (larynx and pharynx), it is referred to as LPR. It is not uncommon to have both GERD and LPR, but they can occur independently.

More frequently, people with GERD have decreased esophageal clearing. Esophagitis, or inflammation of the esophagus, is also associated with GERD. People with GERD often feel heartburn. LPR symptoms are often "silent" and do not include heartburn. Specific symptoms of LPR may include some or all of the following: lump in the throat sensation, feeling of constant need to clear the throat/post-nasal drip, longer vocal warm-up time, quicker vocal fatigue, loss of high frequency range, worse voice in the morning, sore throat, bitter/raw/brackish taste in the mouth. If you experience these symptoms on a regular basis, it is advised that you consider a medical consultation for your symptoms. Prolonged, untreated GERD or LPR can lead to permanent changes in the esophagus and/or larynx. Untreated LPR also provides a laryngeal environment that is conducive to vocal fold lesions, as it inhibits normal healing mechanisms.

Treatment of LPR and GERD generally include both dietary and lifestyle modifications in addition to medical management. Some of the dietary recommendations include: eliminating caffeinated and carbonated beverages; smoking cessation; eliminating alcohol; limiting tomatoes, acidic foods, and drinks and limiting raw onions or peppers. Also, avoiding high-fat foods is recommended. From a lifestyle perspective, make changes such as not eating within three hours of lying down, eating small meals frequently (instead of large meals), elevating the head of your bed, avoiding tight clothing around the belly, and bending over or exercising too soon after you eat.

Reflux medications fall into three general categories: antacids, H2 blockers (histamine blockers), and proton pump inhibitors (PPI). There are now combination drugs that include both an H2 blocker and proton pump inhibitor. Every medication has both associated risks and benefits and singers should be aware of the possible benefits and side effects of the medications they take. In general terms, antacids (e.g., Tums, Mylanta, Gaviscon) neutralize stomach acid. H2 blockers such as Axid (nizatidine), Tagamet (cimetidine), Pepcid (famotidine), and Zantac (ranitidine), work to decrease acid production in the stomach by preventing histamine from triggering the H2 receptors to produce more acid. Then there are the PPIs: Nexium (esomeprazole), Prevacid (lansoprazole), Protonix (pantoprazole), AcipHex (rabeprazole), Prilosec (omeprazole), Dexilant (dexlansoprazole). PPIs act as a last line of defense to decrease acid production by blocking the last step in gastric-juice secretion. Some of the most recent drugs to combat GERD/LPR are combination drugs (e.g., Zegrid (sodium bicarbonate + omeprazole) that provide a short-acting response (sodium bicarbonate) and a long release (omeprazole). Because some singers prefer a holistic approach to reflux management, strict dietary and lifestyle compliance is recommended, and consultation with both your primary care physician and naturopath are warranted in that situation. Efficacy data on nonregulated herbs, vitamins, and supplements is limited, but some data do exist.

Substance Abuse and Smoking

Due to the culture that often surrounds the rock singer, the use of uncontrolled substances, tobacco, and marijuana requires a discussion of the potential detriment to the laryngeal mechanism. The "invincible" belief of most late-teens to twenty-somethings has been shown to result in risky behavior, especially in males. Within the section on injury prevention below, there is specific information to arm the teacher/singer with relevant facts so that the performers themselves can make choices based in that knowledge.

Physical Exercise

Vocal athletes, like physical athletes, should consider how and what they do to maintain both cardiovascular fitness and muscular strength. In today's performance culture, it is rare that a performer stands still and sings, especially the rock performer. The range of physical activity can vary from light movement to high-intensity choreography with acrobatics and pyrotechnics. As performers are being required to increase their onstage physical activity level, overall physical fitness is imperative to avoid compromise in the vocal system. Breathlessness will result in compensation by the larynx, which attempts to regulate the air. Compensatory vocal behaviors over time may result in a change in vocal performance. The health benefits of both cardiovascular training and strength training are well documented in the literature for physical athletes but relatively rarely for vocal performers.

Mental Wellness

Vocal performers must maintain a mental focus during performance and a mental toughness during auditioning and training. This important aspect of performance is addressed rarely during training programs in vocal performance, and it is often left to the individual performer to develop their own strategy or coping mechanism. Yet many performers are on anti-anxiety or antidepressant drugs (which may be the direct result of performance-related issues). If the sports world is again used as a parallel for mental toughness, there are no elite-level athletes (and many junior-level athletes) who don't utilize the services of a performance/sports psychologist to maximize focus and performance. It is the recommendation of this author that performers consider the potential benefits of a performance psychologist to help maximize vocal performance. Several references that may be of interest to the singer include: Joanna Cazden's *Visualization for Singers*, and Shirlee Emmons and Alma Thomas's *Power Performance for Singers: Transcending the Barriers*.

Unlike instrumentalists, whose performance is dependent on accurate playing of an external musical instrument, the singer's instrument is uniquely intact and subject to the emotional confines of the brain and body in which it is housed. Musical performance anxiety (MPA) can be career threatening for all musicians, but perhaps the vocal athlete is more severely impacted (Spahn, Echternach, Zander, Voltmer, & Richter, 2010). The majority of literature on MPA is dedicated to instrumentalists, but the basis of definition, performance effects, and treatment options can be considered for vocal athletes (Anderson, 2011; Brantigan, Brantigan, & Joseph, 1982; Brugués, 2011a; Brugués, 2011b; Chanel, 1992; Drinkwater & Klopper, 2010; Fredrikson & Gunnarsson, 1992; Gates, Saegert, Wilson, Johnson, Shepherd, & Hearne, 1985; Kenny, Davis, & Oates, 2004; Lazarus & Abramovitz, 2004; Nagel, 2010; Powell, 2004; Spahn et al., 2010; Studer, Gomez, Hildebrandt, Arial, & Danuser, 2011).

Fear is a natural reaction to a stressful situation, and there is a fine line between emotional excitation and perceived threat (real or imagined). The job of a performer is to convey to an audience through vocal production, physical gestures, and facial expression a most heightened state of emotion. Why would audience members pay top dollar to sit for two or three hours for a mundane experience? There is not only the emotional conveyance of the performance but also the internal turmoil often experienced by the singers themselves in preparation for elite performance. It is well documented in the literature that even the most elite performers have experienced debilitating performance anxiety. MPA is defined on a continuum with anxiety levels ranging from low to high and has been reported to comprise four distinct components: affect, cognition, behavior, and physiology (Spahn et al., 2010). Affect comprises feelings (e.g., doom, panic, anxiety), effected cognition will result in altered levels of concentration, while the behavior component results in postural shifts, quivering, and trembling, and finally physiologically the body's ANS (autonomic nervous system) will activate, resulting in the "fight or flight" response. In recent years, researchers have been able to define two distinct neurological pathways for MPA. The first pathway happens quickly and without conscious input (ANS) resulting in the same fear stimulus as if a person were put into an emergency, life-threatening situation. In those situations, the brain releases adrenaline, resulting in the physical changes of: increased heart rate, increased respiration, shaking, pale skin, dilated pupils, slowed digestion, bladder relaxation, dry mouth, and dry eyes, all of which severely affect vocal performance. The second pathway that has been identified results in a conscious identification of the fear/threat and a much slower physiologic response. With the second neuromotor response, the performer has a chance to recognize the fear, process how to deal with the fear, and respond accordingly.

Treatment modalities to address MPA include psycho-behavioral therapy (including biofeedback) and drug therapies. Elite physical performance athletes have been shown to benefit from visualization techniques and psychological readiness training, yet within the performing arts community, stage fright may be considered a weakness or character flaw precluding readiness for professional performance. On the contrary, vocal athletes, like physical athletes should mentally prepare themselves for optimal competition (auditions) and performance. Learning to convey emotion without eliciting an internal emotional response by the vocal athlete may take the skill of an experienced psychologist to help change ingrained neural pathways. Ultimately, control and understanding of MPA will enhance performance and prepare the vocal athlete for the most intense performance demands without vocal compromise.

Although speculative, rock performers have been observed to have very high highs and then crash to very low lows. It is not surprising that this up-and-down emotional rollercoaster may result in performers self-medicating to ramp up when needed and come down so that they can sleep. Unfortunately, this vicious cycle often results in choosing drugs that alter the typical pathways and brain functions that give the performer a false sense of their actual emotional state.

Vocal Wellness: Injury Prevention

In order to prevent vocal injury and understand vocal wellness in the singer, general knowledge of common causes of voice disorders is imperative. One common cause of voice disorders is vocally abusive behaviors or misuse of the voice to include phonotraumatic behaviors such as yelling, screaming, loud talking, talking over noise, throat clearing, coughing, harsh sneezing, and boisterous laughing. Chronic or less-than-optimal vocal properties, such as poor breathing techniques, inappropriate phonatory habits during conversational speech (glottal fry, hard glottal attacks), inapt pitch, loudness, rate of speech, and/or hyperfunctional laryngeal-area muscle tone may also negatively impact vocal function. Medically related etiologies, which also have the potential to impact vocal function, range from untreated chronic allergies and sinusitis to endocrine dysfunction and hormonal imbalance. Direct trauma, such as a blow to the neck or vocal fold damage during intubation, can impact optimal performance in vocal athletes depending on the nature and extent of the trauma. Finally, external irritants ranging from cigarette smoke to reflux directly impact the laryngeal mucosa and ultimately can lead to laryngeal pathology.

The vocal demands of the rock singer are inherently dangerous due to the intensity, length, and genre-specific vocal ornaments (growling, screaming, etc.) that are essential for rock singers at the amateur and elite level. Because of the vocal demands that cannot be altered, vocal health and hygiene off-stage is crucial for these performers. Vocal hygiene education and compliance may be one of the primary critical components for maintaining the voice throughout a career (Behrman, Rutledge, Hembree, & Sheridan, 2008). This section will provide the singer with information on preventing vocal injury. However, just like a professional sports athlete, it is unlikely that a professional vocal athlete will go through an entire career without some compromise in vocal function. It may be a common upper-respiratory infection that creates vocal fold swelling for a short time or it may be a "vocal accident" that is career threatening. For the rock singer, performing two-to-three-hour shows several nights in a row is akin to engaging in a sporting event at an intense level night after night. The knowledge of how to take care of your voice is essential for any vocal athlete.

71

Train Like an Athlete for Vocal Longevity

Performers seek instant gratification in performance, sometimes at the cost of gradual vocal building for a lifetime of healthy singing. Historically, vocal pedagogues required their students to perform vocalises exclusively for up to two years before beginning any song literature. Singers gradually built their voices by ingraining appropriate muscle memory and neuromotor patterns through development of aesthetically pleasing tones, onsets, breath management, and support. There was an intensive master-apprentice relationship and rigorous vocal guidelines to maintain a place within a given studio. Time off was taken if a vocal injury ensued or careers were ended, and students were asked to leave a given singing studio if their voice was unable to withstand the rigors of training. Training vocal athletes today has evolved and appears driven to create a "product" quickly, perhaps at the expense of the longevity of the singer. Pop stars emerging well before puberty are doing international concert tours, yet many young artist programs in the classical arena do not consider singers for their programs until they are in their mid-twenties to late twenties. Today's rock stars are mainly young (under age thirty-five), perhaps because of the physical aspect of what the popular culture demands or perhaps because of the vocal rigors (and recovery) needed by these voices.

Each vocal genre presents with different standards and vocal demands. Therefore, the amount and degree of vocal training is varied. Some would argue that performing extensively without adequate vocal training and development is ill-advised, yet singers today are thrust onto the stage at very young ages. Dancers, instrumentalists, and physical athletes all spend many hours per day developing muscle strength, memory, and proper technique for their craft. The more advanced the artist or athlete, generally the more specific the training protocol becomes. Consideration of training vocal athletes in this same fashion is recommended. One would generally not begin a young, inexperienced singer without previous vocal training on a Wagner aria. Similarly, in nonclassical vocal music, there are easy, moderate, and difficult pieces to consider, pending the level of vocal development and training.

Basic pedagogical training in alignment, breathing, voice production, and resonance are essential building blocks for development of good voice production. Muscle memory and development of appropriate muscle patterns happens slowly over time, with appropriate repetitive practice. Doing too much too soon for any athlete (physical or vocal) will result in an increased risk for injury. When singers are asked to do "vocal gymnastics," they must be sure to have a solid basis of strength and stamina in the appropriate muscle groups to perform consistently with minimal risk of injury.

Many rock singers who have come into my office do not want to sound "trained." I am in complete agreement with them. These singers have an innate emotional connection to their music, and my job (as a voice pathologist and singing-voice specialist) is to help them become efficient in their performance. Nowhere in the standard vocal pedagogical literature are there exercises to train vocal growling or screaming. However, these are multimillion-dollar artists who are required to perform at vocal extremes consistently and must do so in the healthiest possible manner. Therefore, providing these vocal athletes with healthy alternatives and/or understanding (physiological) of the variety of ways in which you can scream (some healthy, some not), you work to create a vocally healthy rock singer. It is also my strong opinion, that rock stars should "cross train" within the voice studio, just to keep the voice agile and healthy.

Vocal Fitness Program

One generally does not get out of bed first thing in the morning and try to do a split. Yet many singers go directly into a practice session or audition without a proper warm-up. Think of your larynx like your knee, made up of cartilages, ligaments, and muscles. Vocal health is dependent upon appropriate warm-ups (to get things moving), drills for technique, and then cool-downs (at the end of your day). Consider vocal warm-ups a "gentle stretch." Depending on the needs of the singer, warm-ups should include physical stretching; postural alignment self-checks; breathing exercises to promote rib cage, abdominal, and back expansion; vocal stretches (glides up to stretch the vocal folds and glides down to contract the vocal folds); articulatory stretches (yawning, facial stretches); and mental warm-ups (to provide focus for the task at hand). Vocalises, in the opinion of this author, are designed as exercises to go beyond warm-ups and prepare the body and voice for the technical and vocal challenges of the music. They are varied and address the technical level and genre of the singer to maximize performance and vocal growth. Cool-downs are a part of most athletes' workouts. However, singers often do not use cool-downs (physical, mental, and vocal) at the end of a performance. A recent study looked specifically at the benefits of vocal cool-downs in singers and found that singers who used a vocal cool-down needed less effort to produce voice the next day (Gottliebson, 2011).

Systemic hydration as a means to keep the vocal folds adequately lubricated for the amount of impact and friction that they will undergo has been previously discussed in this chapter. Compliance with adequate oral hydration recommendations is important as is the minimization of agents that could potentially dry the membranes (e.g., caffeine, medications, dry air). The body produces approximately two quarts of mucus per day. If not adequately hydrated, the mucus tends to be thick and sticky. Poor hydration is similar to not putting enough oil in the car engine. Frankly, if the gears do not work as well, there is increased friction and heat, and the engine is not efficient.

Speak Well, Sing Well

Optimize the speaking voice, utilizing ideal frequency range, breath, intensity, rate, and resonance. This is especially true for rock singers. The audience needs to understand the words they say, but the singing style is often reflective of popular speech patterns (e.g., glottal fry, hard glottal attacks). Singers generally are vocally enthusiastic individuals who talk a lot and often talk loudly. During typical conversation, the average fundamental speaking frequency (times per second the vocal folds are impacting) for a male varies from 100–150 Hz and 180–230 Hz for women. Because of the delicate structure of the vocal folds and the importance of the layered microstructure's vibrating efficiently and effectively to produce voice, vocal behaviors or outside factors that compromise the integrity of the vibration patterns of the vocal folds may be considered phonotrauma.

Phonotraumatic behaviors can include yelling, screaming, loud talking, harsh sneezing, and harsh laughing. Elimination of phonotraumatic behaviors is essential for good vocal health. The louder one speaks, the further apart the vocal folds move from midline, the harder they impact, and they stay closed longer. A tangible example would be to take your hands, move them only six inches apart and clap as hard and as loudly as you can for ten seconds. Now, move your hands two feet apart and clap as hard, loudly, and quickly as possible for ten seconds. The further apart your hands are, the more air you move, the louder the clap; the skin on the hands becomes red and ultimately swollen (if you do it long enough and hard enough). This is what happens to the vocal folds with repeated impact at increased vocal intensities. The vocal folds are approximately 17 mm in length and vibrate at 220 times per second on A3, 440 on A4, 880 on A5, and over 1,000 per second when singing a high C. That is a lot of impact for little muscles. Consider this fact when singing loudly or in a high tessitura for prolonged periods of time. It becomes easy to see why women are more prone than men to laryngeal impact injuries due to the frequency range of the voice alone.

In addition to the number of cycles per second the vocal folds are impacting, singers need to be aware of their vocal intensity (volume). Check the volume of the speaking and singing voice and, for conversation, consider using a distance of three to five feet as a gauge for how loud you need to be in general conversation (about an arms-length distance). Speaking on cell phones or a Bluetooth device in a car generally results in louder than normal conversational vocal intensity, and singers are advised to minimize unnecessary use of these devices.

Singers should be encouraged to take "vocal naps" during their day. A vocal nap would be a short period of time (five minutes to an hour) of complete silence. Although the vocal folds are rarely completely still (because they move when you swallow and breathe), a vocal nap minimizes impact and vibration for a short window of time. A physical nap can also be mentally and physically refreshing for the singer.

In the popular music world, everything that we hear is amplified, compressed, sometimes distorted, and mixed. Readers are asked to fully understand chapter 7 by Matt Edwards on acoustics and amplification. The biggest vocal health issues that come into my clinic from amateur rock singers are often the result of singers attempting to imitate the intensity and distortion of rock sounds that they hear (unaided by amplification or acoustic morphing), which results in overdriving the vocal mechanism, leading to injury.

Avoid Environmental Irritants: Alcohol, Smoking, Drugs

Arming singers with information on the actual effects of environmental irritants so that they can make informed choices on engaging in exposure to these potential toxins is essential. The glamour that continues to be associated with smoking, drinking, and drugs can be tempered by the deaths of popular stars who engaged in life-ending choices. There is extensive documentation about the long-term effects of toxic and carcinogenic substances, and there are a few key facts to consider when choosing whether to partake.

Alcohol, although it does not go over the vocal folds directly, does have a systemic drying effect. Due to the acidity in alcohol, it may increase the likelihood of reflux, resulting in hoarseness and other laryngeal pathologies. Consuming alcohol generally decreases one's inhibitions and therefore, under the influence of alcohol, you are more likely to sing and do things that you would not typically do.

Beyond the carcinogens in nicotine and tobacco, the heat at which a cigarette burns is well above the boiling temperature of water (water boils at 212° F; a cigarette burns at over 1,400° F). No one would consider pouring a pot of boiling water on their hand, and yet the temperature of a burning cigarette results in significant heat over the oral mucosa and vocal folds. The heat alone can create deterioration in the lining, resulting in polypoid degeneration. Obviously, cigarette smoking has been well documented as a cause for laryngeal cancer.

Marijuana and other street drugs are not only addictive but can also cause permanent mucosal lining changes, depending on the drug used and the method of delivery. If one of your singer colleagues is experiencing a drug or alcohol problem, provide them with information and support on getting appropriate counseling and help. Here are two drug- and alcohol-recovery websites: http://www.recovery.org/topics/addiction-recovery-helplines/ and http://www.samhsa.gov/recovery/.

Smart Practice Strategies for Skill Development and Voice Conservation

Daily practice and drills for skill acquisition is an important part of any singer's training. However, overpracticing or inefficient practicing may be detrimental to the voice. Consider practice sessions of athletes: They may practice four to eight hours per day, broken into one- to two-hour training sessions with a period of rest and recovery between sessions. Although we cannot compare the sports model, without adequate evidence, to the vocal athlete model, the premise of short, intense, focused practice sessions is logical for the singer. As with physical exercise, it is suggested that practice sessions do not have to be all "singing." Rather, structuring sessions so that one-third of a session is spent on warm-up; one-third on vocalise, text work, rhythms, character development, etc.; and one-third on repertoire will allow the singer to function in a more efficient vocal manner. Building the amount of time per practice session to sixty to ninety minutes by increasing the duration by five minutes per week may be effective (e.g., week one–twenty minutes three times per day; week two–twenty-five minutes three times per day, etc.). Extensive recording session (six-plus hours) and band rehearsals that last for over three hours may result in a less-than-optimal environment for the rock singer. It is strongly recommended that all rehearsal sessions be done with microphones, a soundboard, and appropriate amplification.

Vary the "vocal workout" during your week. For example, if you do the same physical exercise in the same way day after day with the same intensity and pattern, you will likely experience repetitive strain injuries. However, cross training or varying the type and level of exercise aids in injury prevention. So, when planning your practice sessions for a given week (or rehearsal process for a given role), consider varying your vocal intensity, tessitura, and exercises to maximize your training sessions, thus building stamina, muscle memory, and skill acquisition. For example, one day you may spend more time on learning rhythms and translation, and the next day you spend thirty minutes performing coloratura exercises to prepare for a specific role. Take one day a week off from vocal training and give your voice a break. This does not mean complete vocal rest (although some singers find this beneficial), but rather a day without singing and limited talking.

Practice Your Mental Focus

Mental wellness and stress management are as important as vocal training for vocal athletes. Addressing any mental health issues is paramount to developing the vocal artist. This may include anything from daily mental exercises/meditation/focusing to overcoming performance anxiety or more serious mental-health issues/illness. Every person can benefit from improved focus and mental acuity.

Specific Vocal Wellness Concerns for the Rock Singer

Of all of the singing genres (classical, music theater, jazz), rock and popular singing is likely the highest revenue generating with many of the artists having substantially less formal vocal training than their classical-music counterparts. The 2012 Billboard Top 40 moneymaking artists brought in $373 million, after all management and expenses were paid out. The top four artists were pop/rock singers (Madonna, Bruce Springsteen, Roger Walters, and Van Halen). Over 90 percent of the revenue generated by these artists came from concerts (www.billboard.com). The cancelation or postponement of a concert or concert tour due to illness or vocal injury would have had a significant impact on revenue. Therefore, keeping these artists vocally healthy is imperative for this multimillion dollar industry.

Physical Fitness

Rock performances are physically, vocally, and often visually spectacular. Due to the physical demands on rock performers, cardiovascular fitness and general physical health guidelines should hold true for rock singers to meet their performance demands. From crowd surfing to riding a bucking bronco on stage, rock shows are physically demanding. Perhaps more than any other music genre, the physical toll of performance on a rock star's body is extreme. The more physically demanding the performance, the more vital it is to schedule shows with a day of rest in between to allow adequate physical recovery. Physical therapy, personal trainers, stunt coordinators, and dance captains are all warranted for rock singers' optimal performances.

Healthy Singing

Rock singing is vocally and emotionally intense, designed to connect with the audience in a different manner from classical singing. Emotionally edgy, the vocalisms heard in rock music are both laryngeal and sound engineered. The singer must learn to minimize the vocal risk and maximize the vocal output. Learning to perform a rock scream in a healthy, amplified manner with distortion is essential. Vocal scooping, creaking, and fry are also stylistic choices that are not only warranted but necessary for the rock artist. Those who sing rock and train rock performers must address how and when to incorporate these ornaments into song. Vocalises that target these tasks should be developed by the teacher and practiced by the singer.

When planning the set lists for live performance, singers and teachers should work together so that the sets begin and end with less vocally intense songs (not low energy/entertaining) to allow for a natural warm-up and cool-down between sets. The most vocally and physically intense songs should be performed in the middle of a set. The physical fitness and staging demands should be considered in this planning. For example, if the singer comes out onto the stage in a cloud of haze, hanging from a set piece, or dancing intensely, he or she may need a vocally easy song to follow, allowing for adequate recovery.

Aside from the tips listed above regarding smoking, alcohol, and substance use, here are two additional considerations for performers in smoky or hazy environments. First, if the singer takes a spray bottle (such as an empty, washed-out window cleaner bottle) and fills it with water, he or she can spritz the air on the stage prior to performance and between sets to settle the dust (the water particles will weigh down the dust and pull it to the floor and out of the artist's face. Second, the use of a small fan that blows the air toward the audience will draw smoky air from the stage and away from the singer (back toward the audience). Depending on your stage set-up, this fan can be placed either at the singer's feet or on speakers. Multiple fans are fine. Water should be kept in various locations on the stage for the rock performer throughout the performance.

Appropriate microphones, amplification, and mixing are essential for vocal survival of the rock singer. Understanding both the utility and limits of a given microphone and sound system are essential for the rock performer, for both live and studio performances. Chapter 7 provides readers an in-depth exploration of this topic.

Not everything a rock singer does is "vocally healthy," sometimes because the emotional expression may be so intense it results in vocal collision forces that are extreme. Even if the rock singer does not have formal vocal training, cross training the instrument (which can mean singing in both high and low registers with varying intensities and resonance options) before and after practice sessions and performance are a vital component to minimizing vocal injury. Taking care of the physical instrument through daily physical exercise, adequate nutrition and hydration, and maintaining focused attention on performance will provide the necessary basis for vocal health during performance. Small doses of high-intensity singing (or speaking) will limit impact stress on the vocal folds. Finally, attention to the mind, body, and voice will provide the singer with an awareness when something is wrong. This awareness and knowledge of when to rest or seek help will promote vocal well-being for singers throughout their careers.

Bibliography

Anderson, L. (2011). Myself or someone like me: A review of the literature on the psychological well-being of child actors. *Medical Problems of Performing Artists*, *36*(3), 146–49.

Behrman, A., Rutledge, J., Hembree, A., & Sheridan, S. (2008). Vocal hygiene education, voice production therapy, and the role of patient adherence: A treatment effectiveness study in women with phonotrauma. *Journal of Speech, Language, and Hearing Research*, *51*, 350–66.

Brantigan, C., Brantigan, T., & Joseph, N. (1982). Effect of beta blockade and beta stimulation on stage fright. *American Journal of Medicine*, *72*(1), 88–94.

Brinckmann, J., Sigwart, H., van Houten, & Taylor, L. (2003). Safety and efficacy of a traditional herbal medicine (Throat Coat) in symptomatic temporary relief of pain in patients with acute pharyngitis: A multicenter, prospective, randomized, double-blinded, placebo-controlled study. *Journal of Alternative and Complementary Medicine*, *9*(2), 285–98. http://www.ncbi.nlm.nih.gov/pubmed/?term=Throat+coat+tea.

Brown, C., & Grahm, S. (2004). Nasal irrigations: Good or bad? *Current Opinion in Otolaryngology, Head and Neck Surgery*, *12*(1), 9–13.

Brugués, A. (2011a). Music performance anxiety—Part 1. A review of treatment options. *Medical Problems of Performing Artists*, *26*(2), 102–5.

Brugués, A. (2011b). Music performance anxiety—Part 2. A review of treatment options. *Medical Problems of Performing Artists*, *26*(3), 164–71.

Cazden, J. (2009). Visualization for Singers (MP3). http://www.amazon.com/Visualizations-Singers-Joanna-Cazden/dp/B002ZYYTEW.

Chanel, P. (1992). Performance anxiety. *American Journal of Psychiatry*, *149*(2), 278–79.

Donahue, E., LeBorgne, W., Brehm, S., & Weinrich, B. (2013). Reported vocal habits of first-year undergraduate musical theater majors in a preprofessional training program: A 10-year retrospective study. *Journal of Voice*, (In Press).

Drinkwater, E., & Klopper, C. (2010). Quantifying the physical demands of a musical performance and their effects on performance quality. *Medical Problems of Performing Artists*, *25*(2), 66–71.

Dunn, J., Dion, G., & McMains, K. (2013). Efficacy of nasal symptom relief. *Current Opinion in Otolaryngology, Head and Neck Surgery*, *21*(3), 248–51.

Elias, M. E., Sataloff, R. T., Rosen, D. C., Heuer, R. J., & Spiegel, J. R. (1997). Normal strobovideolaryngoscopy: Variability in healthy singers. *Journal of Voice*, *11*(1), 104–7.

Emmons, S., & Thomas, A. (1998). *Power Performance for Singers: Transcending the Barriers*. New York: Oxford University Press.

Evans, R. W., Evans, R. I., & Carvajal, S. (1998). Survey of injuries among West End performers. *Occupational and Environmental Medicine*, *55*, 585–93.

Evans R. W., Evans R. I., Carvajal S., & Perry S. (1996). A survey of injuries among Broadway performers. *American Journal of Public Health*, *86*, 77.

Fredrikson, M., & Gunnarsson, R. (1992). Psychobiology of stage fright: The effect of public performance on neuroendocrine, cardiovascular and subjective reactions. *Biology Psychology*, *33*(1), 51–61.

Gates, G., Saegert, J., Wilson, N., Johnson, L., Shepherd, A., & Hearne, E. (1985). Effect of beta blockade on singing performance. *Annals of Otology, Rhinology, and Laryngology, 94*(6), 570–74.

Gottliebson, R. O. (2011). The efficacy of cool-down exercises in the practice regimen of elite singers. Dissertation, University of Cincinnati.

Heman-Ackah, Y., Dean, C., & Sataloff, R. T. (2002). Strobovideolaryngoscopic findings in singing teachers. *Journal of Voice, 16*(1), 81–86.

Hill, L., Woodruff, L., Foote, J., & Barreto-Alcoba, M. (2005). Esophageal injury by apple cider vinegar tablets and subsequent evaluation of products. *Journal of the American Dietetics Association, 105*(7), 1141–44.

Hoffman-Ruddy, B., Lehman, J., Crandell, C., Ingram, D., & Sapienza, C. (2001). Laryngostroboscopic, acoustic, and environmental characteristics of high-risk vocal performers. *Journal of Voice, 15*(4), 543–52.

Kenny, D., Davis, P., & Oates, J. (2004). Music performance anxiety and occupational stress amongst opera chorus artists and their relationship with state and trait anxiety and perfectionism. *Journal of Anxiety Disorders, 18*(6), 757–77. (Pt. 1), 570–74.

Korovin, G, & LeBorgne, W. (2009). A longitudinal examination of potential vocal injury in musical theater performers. The Voice Foundation's 36th Annual Symposium: Care of the Professional Voice; June 3–7, 2009; Philadelphia, PA.

Koufman, J. A., Radomski, T. A., Joharji, G. M., Russell, G. B., & Pillsbury, D. C. (1996). Laryngeal biomechanics of the singing voice. *Otolaryngology Head and Neck Surgery*, 115, 527–37.

Lazarus, A., & Abramovitz, A. (2004). A multimodal behavioral approach to performance anxiety. *Journal of Clinical Psychology, 60*(8), 831–40.

Leydon, C., Sivasankar, M., Falciglia, D., Atkins, C., & Fisher, K. (2009). Vocal fold surface hydration: A review. *Journal of Voice, 23*(6), 658–65.

Leydon, C., Wroblewski, M., Eichorn, N., & Sivasankar, M. (2010). A meta-analysis of outcomes of hydration intervention on phonation threshold pressure. *Journal of Voice, 24*(6), 637–43.

Lundy, D., Casiano, R., Sullivan, P., Roy, S., Xue, J., & Evans, J. (1999). Incidence of abnormal laryngeal findings in asymptomatic singing students. *Otolaryngology, Head and Neck Surgery*, 121, 69–77.

Nagel, J. (2010). Treatment of music performance anxiety via psychological approaches: A review of selected CBT and psychodynamic literature. *Medical Problems of Performing Artists, 25*(4), 141–48.

Nsouli, T. (2009). Long-term use of nasal saline irrigation: Harmful or helpful? American College of Allergy, Asthma & Immunology (ACAAI) 2009 Annual Scientific Meeting: Abstract 32. Presented November 8, 2009.

Oksanen, A. (2013). Female rock stars and addiction in autobiographies. *Nordic Studies on Alcohol and Drugs*, 30, 123–40.

Phyland, D. J., Oates, J., & Greenwood, K. (1999). Self-reported voice problems among three groups of professional singers. *Journal of Voice*, 13, 602–11.

Powell, D. (2004). Treating individuals with debilitating performance anxiety: An introduction. *Journal of Clinical Psychology, 60*(8), 801–8.

Roy, N., Tanner, K., Gray, S., Blomgren, M., & Fisher, K. (2003). An evaluation of the effects of three laryngeal lubricants on phonation threshold pressure (PTP). *Journal of Voice, 17*(3), 331–42. http://www.ncbi.nlm.nih.gov/pubmed/?term= Entertainer%E2%80%99s+Secret

Satomura, K., Kitamura, T., Kawamura, T., Shimbo, T., Watanabe, M., Kamei, M., Takana, Y., & Tamakoshi, A. (2005). Prevention of upper respiratory tract infections by gargling: a randomized trial. *American Journal of Preventative Medicine, 29*(4), 302–7.

Shadkam, M., Mozaffari-Khosravi, H., & Mozayan, M. (2010). A comparison of the effect of honey, dextromethorphan, and diphenhydramine on nightly cough and sleep quality in children and their parents. *Journal of Alternative and Complementary Medicine*, July; *16*(7), 787–93.

Shaw, R. L., Whitehead, C., & Giles, D. C. (2010). Crack down on the celebrity junkies: Does media coverage of celebrity drug use pose a risk to young people. *Health, Risk & Society, 12*(6), 575–89.

Sivasankar, M. & Leydon, C. (2010). The role of hydration in vocal fold physiology. *Current Opinion in Otolaryngology, Head & Neck Surgery, 18*(3), 171–75.

Spahn, C., Echternach, M., Zander, M., Voltmer, E., & Richter, B. (2010). Music performance anxiety in opera singers. *Logopedica Phoniatrica Vocolology, 35*(4), 175–82.

Studer, R., Gomez, P., Hildebrandt, H., Arial, M., & Danuser, B. (2011). Stage fright: Its experience as a problem and coping with it. *International Archives of Occupational Environmental Health, 84*(7), 761–71.

Tanner, K., Roy, N., Merrill, R., Muntz, F., Houtz, D., Sauder, C., Elstad, M., & Wright-Costa, J. (2010). Nebulized isotonic saline versus water following a laryngeal desiccation challenge in classically trained sopranos. *Journal of Speech Language and Hearing Research, 53*(6), 1555–66.

Tepe, E. S., Deutsch, E. S., Sampson, Q., Lawless, S., Reilly, J. S., & Sataloff, R. T. (2002). A pilot survey of vocal health in young singers. *Journal of Voice*, 16, 244–47.

Yang, J., Tibbetts, A., Covassin, T., Cheng, G., Nayar, S. & Heiden, E. (2012). Epidemiology of overuse and acute injuries among competitive collegiate athletes. *Journal of Athletic Training, 47*(2), 198–204.

Yiu, E., & Chan, R. (2003). Effect of hydration and vocal rest on the vocal fatigue in amateur karaoke singers. *Journal of Voice*, 17, 216–27.

LET ME HEAR YOU SCREAM! (ROCK VOCAL PEDAGOGY)

The more technique you have, the less you have to worry about it.

—Pablo Picasso

Introduction

The most common approaches to vocal training that most singers will encounter are a classical or *bel canto* approach and a functional approach. *Bel canto* is a term that literally means "beautiful singing" and is a technique that is strongly associated with Italian operatic tradition. "Functional training is any technique that allows a vocalist to gradually develop mechanical control over any sung sound without sacrificing freedom or authenticity. It conditions the muscles of the vocal mechanism, over time, indirectly, through exercises, to respond automatically" (LoVetri, 2013, p. 80).

While it would be helpful to declare that there is a clear divide between classical and functional training, it is unfortunately not that simple. Defining exactly what qualifies as bel canto training presents several problems. Famed bel canto teacher Giovanni Battista Lamperti asserted, "no definitive system of bel canto has descended to us, except advice by word-of-mouth, from singer to singer" (Brown, 1957, p. i). Voice pedagogy legend Richard Miller said, "No modern teacher can honestly profess to teach some clearly delineated method that is universally recognized as 'the bel canto method'" (Miller, 1996). (See appendix A for more information.) Some classical voice teachers profess to teach a "classical technique," while others say that their method is strictly bel canto. Some bel canto teachers approach vocal training with a solid understanding of how the voice works. However, a great majority primarily use imagery based techniques such as "sing through your dolphin nose," "spin the tone on the breath," and "feel the sound escaping through the top of your head" (Stark, 1999). Confusion can quickly set in.

Functional training is also somewhat difficult to define, but there is at least a common thread that ties all functional teachers together—they train singers with an approach that is firmly rooted in voice science. Instead of relying solely on imagery, the functional teacher uses exercises that target specific elements of the mechanism. The teacher trains the student to have the ability to control registration, respiration, resonance, and vowel quality to produce any type of sound they desire. When each individual element works optimally, the entire mechanism begins to respond automatically to neurological commands (LoVetri, 2013). When this occurs, the voice is able to respond to the emotional instincts of the singer, eliminating the need for imagery, and allowing the artistic soul to lead the way. There are some very good classical and bel canto teachers out there who are actually teaching functionally. But, if they only identify their training method as classical or bel canto, it is impossible to separate them from the more traditional imagery based practitioners.

In 2013, I presented the research "Pop/Rock Singers' Attitudes Towards Professional Training" at the Voice Foundation Annual Symposium: Care of the Professional Voice. I found that singers with no prior training were not familiar with bel canto technique, and the majority saw little to no benefit in learning to sing with Italian vowels or in a foreign language (Edwards, 2013). This data supports anecdotal evidence that suggests rock singers avoid professional training because of its historical roots in the operatic tradition. In 2008, the American Academy of Teachers of Singing published a statement declaring that contemporary commercial music (CCM) singers require a separate and unique approach to singing their chosen repertoire (AATS, 2008). Therefore, it would seem that rock singers' concerns are warranted.

Functional training has recently taken a stronger foothold in the voice-teacher community, thanks to the work of scientists and pedagogues who have dedicated their lives to sharing their knowledge of vocal function with the voice-teaching community. Unfortunately, many singers are unaware that functional teachers exist and they continue to avoid voice lessons. This is problematic. Every professional athlete has a trainer whom they consult on a regular basis to ensure they are in the best shape. Rock singers are vocal athletes, and they need the same type of attention as traditional athletes. Functional training provides that support while allowing the singer to maintain his or her unique vocal qualities. By focusing on improving vocal function and leaving foreign language and operatic repertoire out of the process, rock singers feel safer exploring the possibilities of their own voice. They become less afraid of being turned into an opera singer.

The foundational principles of my own pedagogical approach to functional train come from the work of Jeannette LoVetri and her Somatic Voicework method. Some exercises in this chapter come directly from LoVetri's work and are cited as such. However, since the goal of this text is not to advocate one pedagogy but rather to bring together concepts from multiple sources to inform your singing and/or teaching, I also include exercises from other authors as well as those from my own research and background. Nevertheless, vocal function lies at the heart of all of the exercises in this chapter, and all will help you explore the workings of your own vocal mechanism with a safe and methodical approach.

"Playing Ball"

The vocal mechanism is a complicated system, which is why voice professionals who specialize in the habilitation of the singing voice spend years studying the science behind vocal production. When athletes play a game, they forget what they are working on in their personal training sessions and focus all of their attention on playing ball. As a teacher, I seek an equal end result for my singers. When my students step onto the stage or into the recording studio, I do not want them to think about all of the technical details we work on in lessons. Instead, I want them to focus on telling a story and let the voice respond to their emotions. I believe this is one of the most important benefits of functional training.

How to Use This Chapter

Learning to sing from a book is never easy. The exercises in this chapter may or may not make sense to you or work for you. If you were my private student, we would not necessarily proceed in the order that I present in this chapter. Before we even began a course of action, I would first listen to you sing, discuss your musical style, and talk with you about your performance habits, your goals, and your vocal concerns. After considering all of those elements, I would begin with the exercises that would serve you best as an individual and cultivate your unique sound while protecting your vocal health. During the course of your training, we may or may not work on all of the exercises. I encourage you to first read the whole chapter, take notes, and highlight concepts that stand out to you. After reading the entire chapter, think about the technical difficulties you would like to resolve or goals that you want to achieve and begin working on the exercises that seem best suited to your needs.

If you read a section of this chapter and decide that you are already happy with the way you handle those elements vocally, feel free to skip that section. You are a unique individual, and I want you to still sound like yourself after training your voice. If you are new to singing rock, think of these exercises as tools in your toolbox and the resulting tone qualities as new colors on your painting palette. Take what you like and discard what you do not. As long as you can sell it to an audience, and it doesn't hurt, it is good!

Singing Rock

In traditional classical singing there are many established vocal norms. For example, when singing an opera aria by Mozart, it is expected that you will use pure Italian vowels, maintain a noble posture, and use a legato line to connect the words and phrases as well as maintain a certain operatic sound. In rock music, all bets are off. Bob Dylan, Elvis Presley, Rufus Wainwright, Axl Rose, and Randy Blythe would all take a different approach to singing the same rock song. That is not only acceptable, it is expected. Rock singers build careers on being unique. As you work through the exercises in this chapter, you will discover many new sounds that you may have never produced before. It is my hope that you will combine the sounds that you like with the stylistic choices outlined in chapter 5 to cultivate your own unique voice.

What You Hear versus What Everyone Else Hears

Before you work through these exercises it is important to understand that what you hear inside your head may differ dramatically from what your audience hears. We have two types of hearing—external hearing (sensorineural) and internal hearing (conductive) (McCoy, 2004). When you are listening to someone else sing, the sound waves of their voice will enter your ear canal and be transmitted to your brain for processing. When you sing, sound waves from the room will enter your ear canals, but your

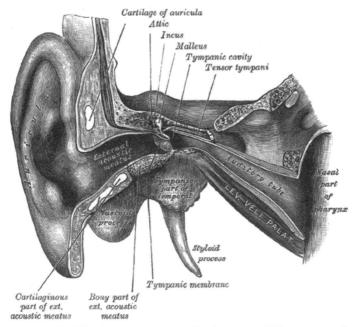

Figure 4.1   The bone structures that surround the ear canal.

ears will also respond to the internal vibrations of sound waves traveling through your bones (called bone conduction). Because you hear your voice both internally and externally, you will always hear yourself differently from how others hear you (see figure 4.1).

When you produce really powerful vocal sounds, there will be strong internal vibrations traveling through your cervical vertebrae and your skull. Sometimes bone vibrations will overpower the external sound waves entering your ear canal and you will hear your voice as being shrill, pointy, or ringy. While you may not like the sound, your audience could love it. If you are struggling to determine whether or not what you hear matches what the audience hears, record yourself when you practice and/or have a lesson. When you listen to the recording, you will only be hearing yourself with your external hearing and you will therefore hear what everyone else hears. Just remember that not all microphones reproduce sound accurately (see chapter 6). In order to determine whether or not the recording is an accurate representation of your voice, record a short track with a friend talking or singing in alternation with you. Listen to the recording and pay careful attention to what your friend's voice sounds like. If you believe that the recording accurately resembles the tone quality of your friend, then the recording probably accurately represents you as well. If you feel that the recording is not an accurate representation of your friend, then it is probably not an accurate representation of you either. Even if you believe a particular recording is inaccurate, do not completely disregard it. Evaluate the information that is available, such as pitch accuracy, rhythmic accuracy, diction, and musical and stylistic choices.

Experiment

If you are new to vocal study, it may be helpful to isolate what your voice sounds like on the inside. When you become accustomed to the sounds you hear vibrating through your bones, you may be less likely to be discouraged when you hear them while singing. Clean your hands thoroughly and then place your index fingers in your left and right ear canals. Do not push them all the way in; you are only trying to block your external hearing. Now sing with your ears blocked. Observe what you hear and feel. Now sustain a pitch and move your fingers in and out of your ear canals. See if you can notice the qualities of your internal hearing that mix with your external hearing when you sing.

Should You Really Feel Nothing?

Before we address the technical issues surrounding rock vocal production, it is important to cover one final concern. Some voice teachers will tell you that you should feel nothing in your throat when you sing. I disagree. Most voice teachers have been singing for years, if not decades. Their muscle memory is a deeply ingrained part of their being. When they sing, the physiological actions necessary for producing sound are second nature to them. Because they are not drawing direct attention to their vocal mechanism, they are often not aware of what they are feeling.

Think about your left ankle. Before I just told you to think about it you were probably not aware of that part of your body. Now that I have told you to think about your ankle, you are probably aware of what it feels like right now. You may notice that it is sore from playing sports or that it is comfortable because you are relaxing in your recliner. Only now that I have called your attention to your ankle are you aware of what you feel. The same concept holds true when training your voice. As you begin to sing rock, you will become aware of new sensations in your throat because you are being asked to pay careful attention to your vocal mechanism. You are experiencing new sensations, trying to distinguish the good ones from the bad, while also trying to process the verbal feedback you are receiving from others. It is completely normal and expected that you feel these things. However, the one thing you should never feel is pain.

It takes time to coordinate your body when learning a new technique. On your first few tries you might overexert your muscles or use muscles that should not be involved in a particular task. If that happens, you may feel slight discomfort (as if stretching a tight hamstring) and/or you may feel muscle fatigue (similar to what you would feel after spending time at the gym). Both of those sensations are normal and acceptable for a brief period of time. If you feel short-term discomfort or fatigue, it does not mean you should quit trying. Take a break for a day or two and then try again. You must be honest with yourself when assessing the sensations you feel while singing. If you really like a certain sound, but you know that it doesn't feel good, do not ignore that feeling. Almost every sound that you want to make can be achieved without damaging your voice. You just need to find the right technique for producing the sound. If you cannot find a way to produce a sound comfortably on your own, consider working with a voice teacher.

What Do *You* Experience?

As you work through these exercises, it may be tempting to focus on feeling or hearing something you have heard another singer mention. Trying to replicate the sensations that another person experiences while singing can impede your vocal progress. Everyone learns differently. Some people are visual learners, others learn by hearing, and others learn by the feelings that they experience while doing an activity. This is why learning from a teacher who only uses imagery can be problematic. As you work through the exercises in this chapter, trust your own experiences. Do not try to force yourself into experiencing your voice in the same way that others do (LoVetri, 2009).

Basic Patterns

Vocal exercises can seem silly and/or boring at times. If you are going through the motions just to make noise, they aren't going to be very productive. If you were to work with a personal trainer, you would find yourself doing all kinds of new and sometimes strange physical movements to stabilize and strengthen the muscles in your body. When used correctly, vocal exercises should do the same for your voice. To be a successful professional performer you need to build vocal stability, strength, flexibility, and stamina. You do not need fancy patterns to accomplish these objectives. The pattern is not nearly as important as understanding your objective and focusing your attention on achieving that objective. Appendix B in the back of this book and SoYouWanttoSing.org, found at the National Association of Teachers of Singing website, http://www.nats.org, provides ten patterns that you can use with nearly every exercise in this book. If you see a reference in this chapter to a pattern you are not familiar with, see Appendix B and SoYouWanttoSing.org for more information.

While the basic patterns in Appendix B are the best for learning new techniques, sometimes repeating the same major scale patterns over and over again can become boring. For some singers the boredom may eventually become a barrier to practicing. To help mix things up, I have included several of my own exercises that are built around the scale patterns discussed in chapter 5. If you like these alternative patterns, I encourage you to compose your own as well. If you like singing the exercises, you will be more likely to do them.

In general you should begin every exercise in a comfortable part of your range (see figure 4.2). If you reach a note that is difficult for you, go backward by one to two half steps and then work your way back to the pitch that you struggled with. Bounce around that pitch until it is comfortable, and then try moving beyond the pitch (LoVetri, 2009). This is similar to the process an athlete would use when training to bench press two hundred pounds six times in a row. If you had never lifted that much weight before, you would not just do it until you got it right. Instead, you would slowly build up to that weight, increasing the reps a little at a time and moving down in weight if lifting was too difficult. Use the same approach as you are building your voice.

Figure 4.2. "Bouncing."

Physical Preparation

Before you begin practicing, it is a good idea to warm up your body. Football players do not run out on the field and start playing right away, and neither should the vocal athlete sing without a proper warm-up. The exercises below will help you warm up your body for singing.

1. Using small circles, gently massage around your temples.

2. Then use your index fingers to find the joint of your jaw, which is positioned directly in front of your ears. As you open your mouth you will feel a space open in the joint. Drop your jaw, take in a relaxed breath, and focus on releasing any tension you are holding in that joint. You can also massage small circles in that area to help relax the muscles.

3. Next, place your fingers on your cheekbones and slowly slide your fingers down toward your jawline as you simultaneously allow your jaw to drop.

4. Now place both of your thumbs underneath your chin and gently massage this area, which is the base of the tongue. First try massaging this area with your tongue in your mouth and then try massaging it with your tongue extended over your bottom lip.

5. Using your right hand, massage the muscles that connect your left shoulder to your neck. After thirty seconds to a minute, switch hands and work on your right side.

6. Now stretch your right arm across your chest as if reaching for an object to your left. Then stretch your left arm in the same manner.

7. Finally, slowly drop your forehead forward and, vertebrae by vertebrae, allow your spine to release until you reach a hanging position. Hold this position for at least thirty seconds and then slowly work your way back up to a standing position.

Posture

If you are new to vocal training, you will want to take some time to explore "ideal" alignment. You do not need to maintain this alignment at all times when singing. However, it is helpful to become familiar with postural alignment to help you identify any unnatural physical tension that could interfere with your singing.

One of the easiest ways to find your body's natural alignment is to lie on the ground. In this position, allow your body to relax into the floor. Flex your feet forward and back several times, rocking your body into the ground. Next move your feet left to right and allow that motion to work its way through your body. Lying still, close your eyes and mentally assess what your body feels like. Pay attention to your head, jaw, neck, ribs, hips, and legs. Slowly come to a standing position and try to maintain the alignment that you found while lying on the ground.

When upright, your feet should be shoulder-width apart, your knees should be comfortably relaxed (not bent and not locked), your hips should be straight, your arms should be free and loose, your shoulders relaxed, your neck long, and your head should be free to move easily in all directions (Borch, Sundberg, Lindestad, & Thalén, 2005). When standing, your body should be tall, relaxed, and commanding. You should feel as though you take up space above you, below you, in front of you, behind you, and to both of your sides.

If you have been taught to sing in one uniform position, you should know that there are many ways you can position your body and still sing well. If you come from such a background, it would be beneficial for you to experiment with nontraditional postures to see how changing your body position can affect your voice. Begin by singing an /a/ vowel in your default stance. Now experiment with the following movements while singing /a/ and notice what happens. These are not necessarily ideal positions, but they could help you discover something new about your voice:

- Move your chin forward and back.

- Lift your chin up and down.

- Sit on the edge of a chair and shift between sitting up straight and slouching over.

- Sing with your body perfectly straight, with your chin tucked down and in. Then relax your body, allowing your lumbar spine to slightly curve inward and your chin to shift slightly forward and up.

What changes did you notice in your vocal quality as you moved between these various positions? Did some allow your voice to release? How could you use these various positions in your rock singing?

As you continue to experiment with your technique and posture, consider the following:

- Tilting your head backwards will help you release your throat so it doesn't constrict. In this position you might find that your voice takes on a brighter tone quality.

- Lowering your chin might add warmth to your sound, but it might also lead to throat and tongue constriction.

- Shifting your chin forward might brighten the sound.

- Bringing your chin back might artificially darken the sound.

- Maintaining an upright posture with a slightly elevated rib cage will allow you to use your full lung capacity.

- Collapsing your chest will limit your rib cage mobility and will reduce your lung capacity.

Anatomy of Singing

A Nonlinear System

Many singers think of the voice as a linear system where sound production begins with the breath, followed by the vocal folds, the resonators, and then the articulators, as shown in figure 4.3. Research suggests that the system is actually less linear than we thought, as shown in figure 4.4 (Guzman, Laukkanen, Krupa, Horáček, Švec, & Geneid, 2013; Cookman & Verdolini, 1990).

For instance, the action of the vocal folds impacts the respiratory system, so singers must adjust their breathing strategy accordingly. Resonance can affect vocal fold closure and therefore must be considered when working on

Figure 4.3. A linear system.

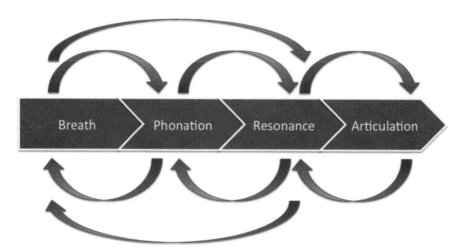

Figure 4.4. A nonlinear system.

registration. Since the vocal mechanism is a nonlinear system, you should not approach this chapter in a linear manner. After you have read this chapter and you begin working through the exercises, you should feel free to jump backward or forward in the chapter. Working on registration may help your resonance, which may require you to change the way you manage your breath. Try every exercise and take what you can from each. You never know what may lead to a breakthrough. For more information about how the components of the voice interact with each other, I recommend *Vocology: The Science and Practice of Voice Habilitation* by Ingo R. Titze and Katherine Verdolini Abbott.

Respiration—the Power Source

Our respiratory system controls both breath pressure and flow rate. Breath pressure is the pressure that builds up beneath closed vocal folds (often called subglottic pressure). If you fill your lungs with air and hold your breath, you will feel significant subglottic pressure in your throat below and around your vocal folds. The term "Flow rate" describes the way that air passes through the vocal folds. If you are singing light and airy, you will have a high flow rate and lower breath pressure because a lot of air will be passing through your vocal folds. If you are belting, you will have a lower flow rate and you might feel greater pressure because less air will be passing through your vocal folds. These parameters are controlled by the closure of the vocal folds (see "Registration" below). If you are trying to belt, but the vocal folds are not in a chest-voice dominant position, you can manipulate your respiratory mechanism in every possible way, but you will still fail to achieve the desired result. As stated above, the vocal mechanism is nonlinear. Breathing is only one part of the system. If the vocal folds are not in the proper configuration for the desired tone quality (e.g., chest register for belting), making corrections to the respiratory mechanism will not solve your problems.

If you are new to voice training, familiarize yourself with the basics of breathing for singing by working through the steps below and practicing them until they are comfortable.

The Basic Steps

1. Begin with your mouth in a relaxed position, lips together or slightly apart. Inhale through your nose and imagine that the air is moving down into the bottom of your abdomen as if you are filling a water balloon.

2. At the same time that you feel your abdomen expanding, allow your lower ribs to expand to the sides. You may also feel some forward and backward movement in your torso. Slight vertical movement in the sternum is acceptable, but resist the temptation to heave your rib cage up and down.

3. Exhale on a gentle /s/.

4. As you sustain /s/, try to maintain a steady volume level and air stream. Keep your rib cage expanded and your abdominal muscles released in order to resist the inward collapse of your rib cage and abdominal cavity. As you sustain the /s/, your abdominal wall will gradually return to a relaxed position while your rib cage collapses. The goal of this exercise is to allow the respiratory system to slowly return to its natural resting state without using muscular force to get there.

5. Repeat the exercise above with a /z/ instead of a /s/. Then try it with an /i/ or /u/ vowel on a sustained pitch in a comfortable part of your range.

If you are having difficulty coordinating the movement of your rib cage and abdominal wall, try the following:

- Place one hand just below your collar bone (clavicle) and one hand on your belly (see figure 4.5). As you inhale, concentrate on relaxing these two areas. Repeat this exercise until you are able to successfully keep both of these areas relaxed during inhalation.

- Place your hands on your ribcage with thumbs toward the back and elbows out to the sides as if they are wings (see figure 4.6). As you inhale, concentrate on allowing a comfortable expansion in the mid part of your rib cage.

Advanced techniques for breath control are discussed in Appendix C. If you are an experienced singer, it may be helpful to read Appendix C before reading the rest of this chapter. If you are new to vocal study, continue reading this chapter and work through the exercises that follow. When you feel

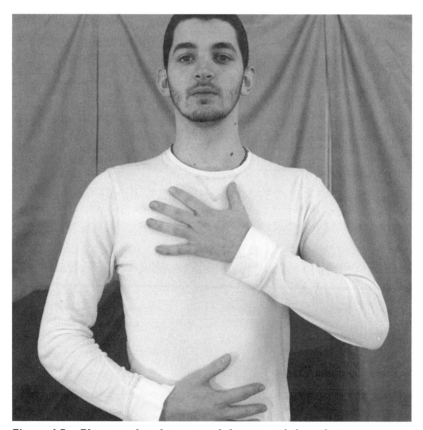

Figure 4.5. Place one hand on your abdomen and the other on your upper chest as you inhale to monitor your movement during respiration.

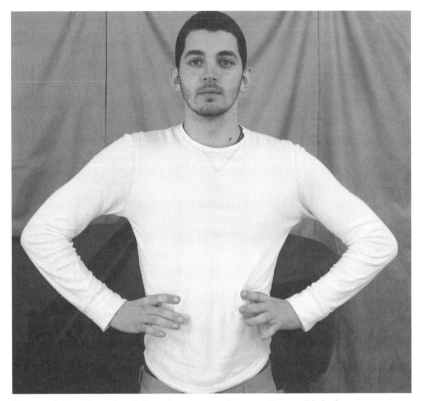

Figure 4.6. Place both hands on your lower ribs and inhale.

comfortable singing simple songs, read Appendix C and try applying those concepts to your work.

Warming Up and Cooling Down

Whenever you practice or perform, you need to take a few minutes to warm up your voice. Vocal warm-ups are different from vocal exercises. Whereas vocal exercises are designed to accomplish specific technical goals, vocal warm-ups are solely meant to warm up the muscles and awaken your mind-body connection for singing. See the video at SoYouWanttoSing.org.

1. Sing a sustained pitch in a comfortable part of your range on /ng/. Do this three to five times, holding each repetition for at least fifteen seconds.

2. Sing a 1-2-3-2-1 pattern (ascending then descending) in a comfortable part of your range on /ng/.

3. Sing a sustained pitch in a comfortable part of your range on a hum. Do this three to five times, holding each repetition for at least fifteen seconds.

4. Sing a 1-2-3-2-1 pattern (ascending then descending) in a comfortable part of your range on /ng/.

5. Place your first finger vertically against your lips in the hum position. Open the hum to a /u/ vowel, and sustain a single pitch at a medium volume level, allowing your breath to flow in the same manner as it does when humming. The resulting sound will be similar to a kazoo. Do this three to five times, holding each repetition for at least ten seconds.

6. Sing a descending five tone scale on /u/, allowing your breath to flow as in step number 5, at a moderate volume level, in the middle of your range. Work upward by half steps and then descend.

7. Slowly glide from your low range to your upper range and back down on /a/ at a moderate volume. Each glide should last at least ten seconds. Do this three to five times.

When you are finished practicing or singing, you need to cool down your voice. Use the same exercises above, but begin with number 7 and work backward to number 1.

Singing Like You Speak

Most rock singers use a tone quality that is similar to their speaking voice. If you come from a choral, classical, or music theater background, this may be a foreign concept to you. Classical singers often train with Italian vowels, which are different from the vowel qualities used in conversational English. Therefore, they often need to be retrained to use elements of their speaking voice quality when singing. Work through the exercises below to teach your body to speak on pitch.

1. Speak through the first verse of "Mary Had a Little Lamb" without trying to add any excessive inflection to your voice: "Mary had a little lamb, little lamb, little lamb. Mary had a little lamb; its fleece was white as snow."

2. Now speak the text in rhythm with the accompaniment track on SoYouWanttoSing.org.

3. Next speak through the text as if you were a radio announcer, allowing your voice to rise and fall in pitch as you speak.

4. Now do the same in rhythm with the accompaniment track on SoYouWanttoSing.org.

5. Speak through the words again using your radio announcer voice, but this time allow the pitch of your voice to rise and fall in approximation to the pitches of the vocal line. I call this process "tracing."

6. Now trace the pitches in rhythm with the accompaniment track on SoYouWanttoSing.org (see figure 4.7).

7. Now it is time to add the exact pitches. Your goal in this step is to sing the words on the notes without any attempt at musicality. Do not worry about your vocal tone; simply speak the words on pitch.

8. After you have mastered this process with "Mary Had a Little Lamb," try the same approach with other simple religious and/or folk songs.

Mary Had a Little Lamb

Sarah Josepha Hale   Lowell Mason

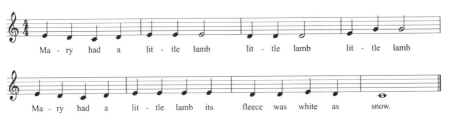

Figure 4.7. "Mary Had a Little Lamb." Sarah Josepha Hale (1788–1879).

Phonation and Registers

Anatomy Review

Before I begin addressing the specifics of vocal function at the vocal-fold level, let us first review some of the basics. The vocal folds are located in the larynx directly behind the laryngeal prominence of the thyroid cartilage, which is commonly known as the Adam's apple. The vocal folds vibrate as air from the lungs passes over them. The vocal folds can be elongated, making a pitch higher, or shortened, making a pitch lower. Singers can also control the thickness of the vocal folds, which affects registration (see page 102). The muscle responsible for lengthening the vocal folds is the cricothyroid (CT) muscle. As this muscle contracts, the thyroid cartilage tilts toward the front of the neck. If breath pressure beneath the folds builds to a high level as the larynx tilts, the larynx may rise up toward the root of the tongue. Though classical singers avoid laryngeal rise, research suggests that contemporary commercial music singers can benefit from the resonance changes that accompany a slightly elevated larynx. Follow the steps below to explore your own laryngeal movement.

1. Touch your chin with your index finger and lightly slide it down your neck, beginning at the tip of your chin. In the middle part of your neck you should feel a slight bump. That is your thyroid cartilage.

2. Lightly place your index finger and thumb on both sides of your thyroid cartilage and swallow. When you swallow you will feel your larynx rise from its resting place and then return.

3. Now say "gee gee gee." When you say this, you should feel your larynx rise.

4. Now say "ho ho ho" with a deep Santa Claus voice. When you do this, you should feel your larynx lower.

When you sing high and bright sounds in rock 'n' roll, it can be helpful to allow the larynx to slightly rise from its neutral position. If your larynx feels like it is always in a high position while singing, you should probably work on lowering it. To explore a higher laryngeal position while singing, stick your tongue out. To explore a lower laryngeal position while singing, try using your Santa Claus or Barry White voice (LoVetri, 2009).

Phonation

Phonation refers to the action of the vocal folds that creates the vibrations necessary for speech and singing. There are several muscles within the vocal mechanism that control phonation. When you sing a melodic line, there are muscles that stretch your vocal folds for higher pitches and relax your folds for lower pitches. There are also muscles that regulate the thickness of the folds. These muscles respond to changes in pitch and volume and affect registration. While voice scientists have many different terms to describe the delicate interactions between these muscles, as singers and singing-voice teachers, it is easier to broadly label the resulting tone qualities. The most commonly accepted term for the resulting tone qualities of various vocal fold configurations is "register" or "registration" (discussed later).

Vocal Range

Your vocal range is as unique as you are. The traditional terms for vocal ranges are "bass" (low-voiced male), "baritone" (medium-voiced male), "tenor" (high-voiced male), "mezzo" or "alto" (medium-voiced female), and "soprano" (high-voiced female). Sing through the pitches below and determine your lowest and highest comfortable pitch. Then use these ranges as a guide when determining the pitches you should cover when exercising your voice. While you can easily find men who fit each of the male categories, it is rather unusual to find sopranos in rock. Sopranos can learn to sing rock, but they must develop their lower register and mic voice. Even the mezzos you find will have an upper range that is usually lower than notated in figures 4.8 and 4.9. However, exercising only the notes you sing in your material will prevent you from developing the entire vocal mechanism. These guidelines will help ensure that you work the entire voice and not just the portion you are currently comfortable performing in (see figures 4.8 and 4.9).

Rock voices are unique; they do not fit into a box. In rock 'n' roll there are basses and baritones with both bright and warm voices and tenors with

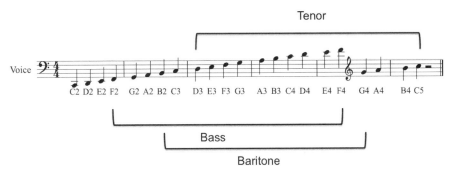

Figure 4.8. Vocal ranges, female.

101

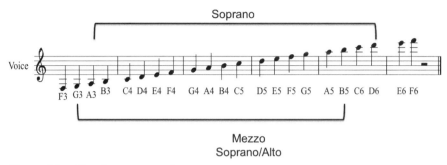

Figure 4.9. Vocal ranges, male.

dark gravely voices. There are male and female singers whose ranges defy traditional descriptions. Unless you are attempting to make a career covering the songs of other artists, you should not worry about labeling your vocal range. Instead, focus on developing your voice to its full potential and writing songs that work for you.

Timbre

Timbre is a term that is used to describe the unique tonal qualities of a voice that are separate from range. Whereas classical and music theater performers have a more formal system of timbre classification, rockers are more informal, using terms like smoky, earthy, gritty, edgy, and soulful to describe vocal qualities. Rock singers are not limited by expectations of their vocal timbre; in fact, trying to fit a rock singer's voice into a box can take away the unique attributes that make them successful. Embrace your sound and own it. There is only one "you" and your timbre is part of what makes you special.

Registration

There are two primary muscles that control registration—the thyro-arytenoid (TA) muscle, which is the main body of the vocal folds, and the cricothyroid (CT) muscle, which acts upon the main body of the vocal folds to stretch them thus raising the pitch. When the TA muscle is dominant, the vocal folds are thick and the resulting quality is called "chest voice" or chest register (mode 1). When the CT muscle is dominant, the vocal folds are stretched and thin and the resulting quality is called "head voice" or head register (mode 2). See figure 4.10.

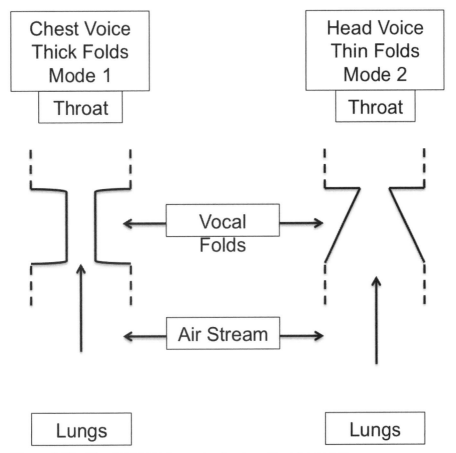

Figure 4.10. Vocal fold thickness in chest and head register.

The interaction of these two muscles controls the thickness of the vocal folds so that you can produce a wide variety of tone qualities on the same pitch. To visualize the differences in vocal fold thickness, put the palms of your two hands together in front of you with all four fingers touching. Separate your fingers from each other one at a time, starting with the pinky, then the ring finger, then the middle, then the index. When all of your fingers are separated, bring your pinkies back together, then the ring fingers, then the middle fingers, and finally the index fingers. As soon as the index fingers touch, repeat the movement.

This hand motion simulates the movement of the vocal folds when vibrating. When all four fingers are touching (thick vocal fold vibration/mode

1), the tone quality will have a lot of buzz and very little airflow. This is chest voice, which is produced by contraction of the thyroarytenoid muscle. Repeat the finger motion without allowing the pinkies to come together. This is like chest-mix. The resulting tone quality will have a little less buzz than chest voice. Next repeat the hand motion with only the middle and index finger touching. This is like head-mix. There is only a little buzz left in the voice at this point. Finally, repeat the motion with only your index fingers touching, this is pure head voice (thin vocal fold vibration/mode 2). There is little if any buzz in head voice and a lot of excess air might escape as you phonate. No matter what register you are singing in, both the TA and CT are involved. Therefore it is extremely important to train both registers equally. Weight lifters would never exercise their triceps while ignoring their biceps. Likewise, singers should never neglect training either the TA or the CT. Doing so will leave you with an unbalanced voice.

Chest Voice (Mode 1)

The chest voice, used in speech when a person yells, shouts, or calls for someone across a room, adds power and ring to the voice. Almost all men and many women habitually speak in chest voice. People with higher speaking voices are usually speaking in a mix. For men and women, the chest voice should be easily accessible below E4, the E above middle C (see figures 4.8 and 4.9). Try the exercises in figure 4.11, starting on C3 (an octave below middle C) for men and A3 (A below middle C) for women on an /a/ or /o/ vowel.

Figure 4.11. Chest voice exercises.

Head Voice (Mode 2)

In head voice, the vocal folds are vibrating on their thin upper edge. The voice will usually have a soft quality and may lack ring and power. Head voice is the quality often found in a parent trying to calm a fussy infant in the middle of the night. Men often identify the quality as falsetto. For men and women, the head voice should be easily accessible above F4. Try the exercises

Figure 4.12. Head voice exercises.

above (figure 4.12) using /i/ and /u/, beginning on C5 for men and E5 for women. Spend some time practicing in both chest and head voice using the patterns above. Also practice with three-note and five-note patterns. Be sure to explore your range of possibilities by singing each exercise with different combinations of dynamics.

Belting

Author Daniel Zangger Borch describes the belt voice as a tone with high breath pressure, high pitch, and volume with an elevated larynx (Borch, 2005). Anne Peckham, a voice teacher at Berklee College of Music, describes the belt voice as chest voice dominant, full, loud, and emotional. Both men and women belt but with slightly different approaches, both resulting in the same type of loud, exciting tone quality that electrifies audiences time and time again. There are two types of belt, chest belt and mix belt (often called mixing).

Use the exercise in figure 4.13 to explore your chest belt. Sing the first pitch in chest and then slide up to the second note carrying your chest voice all the way up (LoVetri, 2009). Imagine that your vocal folds are in the four-finger position, described above, the entire time. As you ascend, they might move toward a three-finger position, but be careful not to flip over to a head-dominant production. Successful navigation of these exercises depends on a singer having already developed a dependable chest register. Sing only as high as you feel comfortable. Most singers will carry a chest belt no higher than A4 before beginning to mix. Try the exercise in figure 4.14.

Figure 4.13. Glides.

Figure 4.14. "Hey yeah, yeah, yeah, yeah."

Mix Coordination

Coordinating the mix can be difficult. If the head voice and chest voice are not equally balanced in strength and coordination, you don't have a whole lot to mix together. The mix can be further divided into chest-mix and head-mix. Chest-mix combines head and chest tonal qualities, with chest quality being dominant. The vocal folds close firmly and the tone quality has significant buzz and power. This is the registration used in mix belting. Head-mix also combines head and chest qualities, with the head quality being dominant. The vocal folds are vibrating almost along their uppermost edge, but there is still some tension thanks to the involvement of the TA. Finding your own mix can be difficult, so most singers see the best results by working under the guidance of a voice teacher. If you are unable to work with someone, try experimenting with the following exercises, but be aware that it can be difficult to evaluate your own sound to determine whether or not the mix you are achieving is ideal.

- Begin by awakening your chest voice. Sing an /a/ or /o/ vowel on a three-note pattern.

- Next, awaken your head voice with a five-note pattern on /i/ or /u/. Carry your head voice as low as possible and pay close attention to what you experience as you move past the traditional register transition between head and chest (E4-F4).

- Now bring your head voice down with a descending five-note pattern on /i/ with a small buzzing quality, like a nagging child or irritating bug.

- Next, beginning in your chest voice at the bottom of your range, vocalize upward on /i/ using a 1-3-5-3-1 pattern.

- Alternate between taking your head voice down with a five-note descending pattern and carrying your chest voice up with a 1-3-5-3-1 pattern on /i/. Pay attention to what is happening in the middle part of your range when descending and ascending (LoVetri, 2009).

- Next use a five-note descending pattern to combine head voice and chest voice qualities. Men should begin on an A major chord (A3-E4). Women should begin on an E major chord (E4-B4). First sing the upper pitch of the pattern in your head voice on /i/. Then sing the bottom pitch in your chest voice on /i/. Repeat this two to three times. By singing the highest pitch and lowest pitch in both head and chest register, you are telling your body where you want to start and where you want to go. Next, using the vowel /i/, sing slowly down the pattern beginning in head voice and ending in chest voice. If you have difficulties, repeat the process of singing the upper note in head, the lower note in chest, and then try transitioning from head to chest. Repeat this process throughout your range.

- When you are able to successfully blend from head to chest, try experimenting with a mix that has more chest voice than head voice quality. Then try singing with more head voice than chest voice quality.

- After mastering /i/, try the same with /e/, then /ae/, then bright /a/, then /o/, then /u/.

- If the mix is weak and airy, it does not have enough chest voice in it. To find a better balance, work on carrying /ae/ up on third or fifth glides. If the mix feels stuck and/or shouty as you ascend, it doesn't have enough head register in it. Work on bringing your head voice down on /i/ with a descending fifth glide and delay the onset of full chest. Then try an ascending fifth glide with the same vocal quality you found while descending. Then repeat the process with the vowels /e/, /ae/, and /a/ (see figure 4.15).

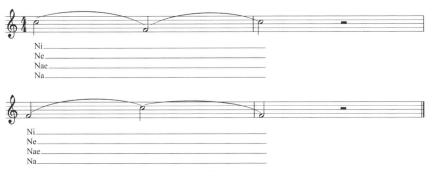

Figure 4.15. Ascending and descending glides.

Figure 4.16.   Descending blues scale, practice blending from head to chest.

For a challenge, try singing the minor-scale pattern, blending from head to chest (see figure 4.16).

Using Nasality to Find Your Mix

Nasalized vowels can be useful when trying to bridge the gap between chest and head. Just remember, nasality is a tool, it is not the desired end result (unless that sound appeals to you). To use nasality as a tool in finding your mix, begin with the exercise in figure 4.17. The vowel sound is a French nasal /o/. Once you are able to create a nasalized vowel on a single pitch, try vocalizing on a three- or five-note pattern. Be careful not to constrict when singing nasal vowels. It is normal to feel your larynx rise slightly as if you are saying "goog," but you should not feel as though you are straining. If you find imagery helpful, imagine that half of your voice is escaping through the nose and the other half through your mouth. Once you are able to successfully find your mix, slowly begin opening the French nasal /o/ to an American /o/ and eventually an /a/. The goal is not to sound like Pepe Le Pew but rather to learn how to maintain a mixed quality at the vocal fold level when singing any repertoire that you choose (see figure 4.17).

Figure 4.17.   Exercises for nasalized vowels.

Register Use in Rock

In many ways, men and women exchange registration strategies when moving from classical singing to rock. In classical singing, men learn to carry their chest voice into their upper range while women learn to lighten their voices toward a head dominant mix as they ascend. In rock, men move toward chest dominant or head dominant mix as they ascend while women carry their chest voice or a strong chest mix to the upper extremes of their range. In many ways the men learn to sing like women and the women to sing like men. If you are a classically trained baritone and you are struggling to get high notes, there is a very good chance you are carrying your classical registration strategy into your rock singing. You will want to work on bringing more head voice into your mix in order to successfully navigate your upper range. If you are a classically trained soprano and you cannot bring power into the notes below C5, you are probably bringing down too much head quality. You will need to work on developing your chest voice and then work on adding more chest to your mix. When you sing high and bright sounds in rock 'n' roll it can be helpful to know that your larynx may slightly rise from a neutral position. Don't be concerned if it does not hurt. However, if the sound feels stuck when you sing, it could be that your larynx is stuck in a high position and cannot move down. In that case, try the constriction exercises starting on page 122.

Flexibility

Flexibility is a vital component of fitness training. If you lift weights without ever working on flexibility, your muscles will become stiff and your range of motion will decrease. Failing to work on flexibility as a singer can lead to vocal stiffness. To help improve your flexibility, use the exercises in figure 4.18 as well as the exercises in chapter 5 and Appendix C. Begin at a comfortable tempo and try increasing your speed over time, but only go as fast as you can while maintaining pitch accuracy.

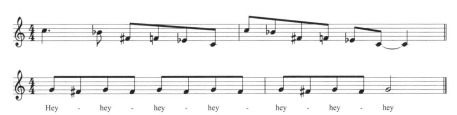

Figure 4.18. Flexibility exercises.

Throwaway High Notes

Operatic and music theater high notes are typically written to be loud and glorious. Rock singers also use high notes to convey intense emotions, but sometimes the high notes are written high because that's just where the melody took them. When you encounter high notes in a song, try to determine whether they are high because they are meant to be epic, or if they are high "just because." If the notes are epic, then you will probably want to sing them with a big ringing tone quality. But if the high notes occur on short rhythms, in speech-like sections of up-tempo songs, there is a good chance that they are what I like to call "throwaway" high notes. Throwaway high notes do not require perfect technical execution, intense tone quality, or loud volume levels. You should instead sing them in the most comfortable way possible and move on. Listen to the examples on the SoYouWanttoSing.com website for more information and try the exercises in figure 4.19.

Figure 4.19. Throwaway high notes.

Onsets

In order to sing a pitch, your body must learn to coordinate the closure of the vocal folds with the acceleration of the breath. There are several ways to do this and each will result in a different attack quality that we call "onset" (the beginning of the tone). The primary types of onset are clean, glottal, and aspirate. Work through the exercises below to explore these onset types.

Clean Onsets

Clean onsets are produced when the vocal folds are set into vibration at the exact moment that air is released from the lungs. The resulting sound quality has neither harshness nor breathiness. The clean onset is found in speech when one sighs on the word "Oh." As in "Oh, those are great shoes" (Kayes, 2004). Try the exercise in figure 4.20 on the vowel /o/. Your goal is to begin vibrating the pitch at the same time that your breath begins to flow.

Figure 4.20. Clean onsets.

Glottal Onsets

When the vocal folds come fully together before air is released, air pressure builds up behind them. If you initiate phonation with closed vocal folds, the excess pressure below the folds will create a slight popping sound alongside the vowel. This is called a glottal onset. Take a deep breath, hold it for a moment and then say /i/. The resulting quality at the beginning of the sound is a glottal attack. Try the following exercise in figure 4.21 with staccato articulation on the vowel /i/. You should feel as though breath pressure builds up before you begin to sing each note.

Figure 4.21. Glottal onsets.

Aspirate Onsets

Aspirate onsets are produced when air is released before the vocal folds come together. These onsets sound as if a /h/ has been added before the vowel. Hold your hand in front of your mouth and sarcastically say "ha, ha, ha" at a low-to-moderate volume level. You should feel warm air flowing on each attack. Try the exercise in figure 4.22 with your hand in front of your mouth and let your air flow on the initial /h/ of each attack.

Figure 4.22. Aspirate onsets.

Vocal Fry

Sing a note in the upper part of your head voice range (falsetto) and slowly glide down, being sure to carry your head voice all the way down to the absolute lowest pitch you can sing. As you reach the bottom of the slide, your vocal folds should pull apart and begin vibrating sporadically without an exact pitch. The resulting sound is what we call vocal fry. It's the sound used by the child in *The Shining* when he is repeating "redrum" over and over again while carrying a large knife around his mother's bedroom. Try the following exercises:

- Work on gliding your head voice down until you can create a fry comfortably (LoVetri, 2009).

- Close your lips into a /m/ position and sustain a vocal fry on a comfortable pitch without opening your lips.

- Once that is comfortable, alternate between the /m/ position and an /a/ (Cross, 2005).

- When you are comfortable with producing the /a/ vowel, try beginning on the vowel without the /m/. Then try incorporating a fry onset on words that begin with an /a/ vowel.

Vocal fry is safe as long as you do not do it too loudly or for too long. I once worked with a student who had nodules that went away while he was learning to "scream" death metal (an extended vocal fry technique). It can be done, but you must take your time, eliminate all constriction, master your breathing mechanism, and only sing as loudly as you need to in order to amplify your voice with a microphone (see chapter 6). For more information on vocal fry and other distorted vocal techniques, I highly recommend Melissa Cross's *Zen of Scream* DVD series.

Releases

You have the same choices when it comes to ending a note as you do for onsets. In a clean release, vocal folds stop vibrating at the same time airflow ceases. In a glottal release, vocal folds suddenly stop vibrating, allowing breath pressure to build up beneath them. In an aspirate release, the /h/ sounds after the pitch. In an aspirate release (which I call "airing it out") vocal folds open in order to stop vibration while air continues to move through the vocal tract. The result is that you end your vocal line with air instead of tone. In a vocal fry release, you will allow the pitch to drop, the air pressure to decrease, and the vocal folds to vibrate sporadically so that you end with the gravelly quality of a vocal fry. As you work through your songs, experiment with the various types of onsets and releases. As long as you like the result and it does not hurt, it is the right choice for you.

Vowels and Consonants: Controlling Your Mouth, Lips, and Tongue

Articulation is the process of forming vowels and consonants when singing. Rock singers sing in their native dialect unless that dialect interferes with their desired sound quality. For rock singers, learning formal vowels, especially Italian ones, can end up doing more harm than good. If you spent two years hitting a baseball off of a tee, you would most likely find it rather difficult to hit moving balls that varied in speed. That task would be difficult because your brain had programmed itself to focus on hitting a stationary object. Training your voice to sing Italian vowels in order to improve your rock singing would be the same as training your body for hitting a baseball off of a baseball tee and expecting to be able to jump into a fast-pitch game without further training.

Are there instances where learning formal vowels can be beneficial? Occasionally. For instance, let's say you have a thick Southern drawl and you are interested in cultivating a richer and warmer sound with a more neutral accent. Working on formal vowels could possibly help you unlearn the muscular coordination that you are accustomed to using when speaking with your Southern accent. However, if you dwell on formal vowels for too long, you may take yourself far beyond the point of achieving a neutral American accent. When learning to sing, it is often useful to explore the extremes. However, you will almost always want to land somewhere in the middle. Never dwell on the extremes for so long that they become your new default position.

The Tongue

Functional exercises that address the musculature of the articulators can help correct vowel and articulation problems. When a singer focuses on freeing and coordinating the muscles used in articulation, the body will be able to respond to neurological commands without requiring overthinking while singing. Use the exercises below to begin training your articulators. Even if you are an experienced singer, these exercises can be very beneficial. I myself return to these quite often since, like most people, I talk more than I sing. These exercises are the equivalent of physical training for an athlete. I would venture to say that most athletes would prefer to play the game than spend time in the gym working with a personal trainer. Yet they do it because they know it will make them play better. These exercises offer the same benefits for singers. They prepare your body so that when it's time to sing, you can just focus on rocking out.

Lower Tongue Release

Place your thumb under your chin and very lightly push up between your jawbones. Swallow. As you swallow you should feel several muscles flex and push against your thumb. These muscles are involved in swallowing and will often try to engage while you are singing. With your thumb in this position, you can easily detect and monitor tongue tension (McClosky, 2011). Sing the vowels at the end of this paragraph in order, on a single pitch, in the lower part of your range. If you feel your tongue pushing down as you sing, you probably have tongue tension. Working on only one vowel at a time, move your tongue up and forward until you find a position that releases the downward pressure. The first seven vowels can be formed without tensing. The final two vowels, /u/ and /i/ will require the tongue to slightly flex downward. The movement should only be slight; it should not mimic the movement felt when swallowing.

/ ʊ /-/æ/-/a/-/ ɛ /-/e/-/ɪ/-/o/-/u/-/i/

After you have mastered all of the vowels on one pitch, try them on three- and five-note patterns. As you cross register transitions and reach the upper part of your range, you will feel some shifting and flexing on the underside of your tongue. Slight movement and flexing is acceptable, just avoid tensing that is comparable to what you would feel when swallowing.

Tongue Stretching and Isolation

To get the greatest benefit of any stretch, you need to hold it for at least ten to thirty seconds. To do this with your tongue, begin by stretching it across your bottom lip. Maintain this position for thirty seconds, then release. Now try extending your tongue as far as comfortable and hold for at least thirty seconds. If your tongue tries to retract, you can use your fingers to hold it in place (Kayes, 2004). You may feel some shaking in your tongue as you hold this position, which is normal. Now close your mouth around your tongue. In this position, sing a sustained pitch in a comfortable part of your range. Do this a few times and then try vocalizing on a three-note pattern. Once you are able to keep your tongue relaxed on a three-note pattern, try a five-note pattern, and then a 1-3-5-3-1 arpeggio. Next work through what I like to call the "Ultimate Tongue Workout":

- Sing the word "glockida" as shown in figure 4.23. Allow your tongue to move freely in your mouth and take note of what you experience as you sing throughout your range (LoVetri, 2009).

- Next sing the words "huckleberry struckleberry po" using the pattern in figure 4.24. Take note of what you experience (Griffel, personal communication, 2004).

- Next sing the words "diddle daddle deedle daddle do" as seen in figure 4.25. Take note of what you experience.

- Next we will try to isolate the movements of your tongue and jaw. In normal speech the jaw and tongue move together. When singing rock, you will want to separate the movement of the two so that you can adjust both to produce various tone qualities. Return to the "glockida" exercise, but now place a finger on your chin and try to keep it as still as possible while your tongue does all of the work. Try the same thing with the "diddle daddle deedle daddle do" exercise.

- Your final challenge is to alternate between the vowels /i/ and /a/ without moving your jaw. To do this exercise, drop your jaw and raise your tongue to your upper molars as if saying "he." Drop your tongue from that position and move to /a/. Alternate between the high tongue /i/ vowel and the lower tongue /a/ vowel on one pitch. Once you have mastered alternating the vowels on a single pitch, try intervals of a third and then a fifth. Then try the exercise on arpeggios. See figure 4.26.

Figure 4.23. "Glockida."

Figure 4.24. "Huckleberry struckleberry po."

Figure 4.25. "Diddle daddle deedle daddle do."

Figure 4.26. Tongue isolation.

Open and Closed Vowels

Vowels can be formed with an open mouth or closed mouth. Closed-mouth vowels can be made edgier than open-mouth vowels and are better for up-tempo songs. Open mouth vowels will have more depth and power and are better for ballads and epic vocal lines. Using the five basic vowels /a/-/e/-/i/-/o/-/u/, try the following exercise.

- Place the tip of your pinky finger horizontally between your front teeth and gently bite down. In this position, pronounce each of the five basic vowel sounds with your lips in a wide smile with very little opening between your lips. Try to find a tone quality that is extremely bright, as if you had turned up the treble on your stereo. If you are having difficulty adding brightness to your voice, try arching your tongue while forming the vowels. After negotiating this position in speech, chant the five basic vowels on several comfortable pitches. Then try singing the vowels on a three-note and five-note pattern. See figure 4.27.

- Now try the same exercise, placing your thumb vertically between your teeth, with round lips. Use a speech-like or moderate treble quality in this position. See figure 4.28.

Figure 4.27. Closed vowel mouth position.

Figure 4.28. Open vowel mouth position.

- Now sing through the exercises below using both the closed and open positions. When you begin to feel comfortable, remove your fingers. See figure 4.29.

Figure 4.29. Closed/open vowel exercise.

In a fast up-tempo song or a breathy ballad, you may find that the closed-mouth vowels work best. In a big power ballad, you will probably find that the big open vowels work best. Sing through the exercise in figure 4.30, first with closed vowels, then open vowels. Then sing the first measure closed and open up in the second measure. Sing through the exercise several times and think about how you can use this concept in your own songs.

Figure 4.30. Sing this exercise with both open and closed vowels.

Flat Tongue and High Tongue Vowels

You can also adjust the tone quality of your vowels by raising your tongue. While this is not very useful on the lower- to mid-range pitches in your voice, it can be very helpful on extreme high notes and squeals. To find the high-tongue-vowel positions, start by adding an /h/ before each vowel you sing. Sing the following exercise first with the /h/ and then take the /h/ away (see figure 4.31). The high tongue position will add a treble quality to your voice, but it may also raise your larynx. A raised larynx will not harm your voice as long as you do not sing too high, too loudly, for too long. If it feels uncomfortable, take your time and/or consult a voice teacher.

Figure 4.31. High tongue exercise.

Unifying Your Vowels

Depending on the style of rock that you sing, you may also want to work on unifying your vowels to achieve a specific tone quality. This is very much a matter of choice, not necessity. If you are trying to strengthen your voice, working on unifying your vowels might help stabilize your instrument. If you are trying to change over from a classical vowel strategy to a rock strategy, this exercise (figure 4.32) may also be useful for building consistency with the new vowel qualities you have discovered. In this exercise, try to match the second vowel to the first. As you go back and forth between the two vowels, pay close attention to the movements of your jaw and tongue. Try to unify the tone quality by minimizing the movement of your tongue, jaw, and lips. Experiment with open, closed, and high tongue vowels on each of these patterns.

Figure 4.32. Vowel unification exercises.

Vowel Morphing

If your voice is already strong, you might want to change your vowel sounds up so you have more than one way to sing each vowel. In the English language, vowel sounds exist in a single syllable either alone or in combination with one or more vowels. A diphthong contains two separate vowel sounds within the same syllable, for instance "low." Pronouncing the word correctly requires the inclusion of both an /o/ and an /u/ vowel. Tripthongs contain three vowel sounds combined in one syllable. For example in the word "our" there is a three-vowel series of /ɑ/, /ʊ/, /ə/ in the first syllable.

Whereas classical singers sustain one vowel for the majority of any one note, rockers switch between multiple vowels on a sustained pitch and even change a vowel that is not a diphthong into a diphthong for musical effect (see figure 4.33). I call this technique "vowel morphing." Vowel morphing uses both the tongue and the lips. In the first exercise (figure 4.34), sustain one of the vowels and move your lips between a smiley /a/, an /o/, and an /u/. Pay attention to how those lip changes affect the sound (see figure 4.34). In this exercise (figure 4.35), you will practice singing both vowels of the exclamation "wo" as you descend the melodic line. In this exercise (figure 4.36) you will practice moving between the /e/ and /i/ vowel sounds in the word "hey."

Figure 4.33. Diphthongs: classical vs. rock.

Figure 4.34. Vowel morphing exercise, lips.

Figure 4.35. Vowel morphin exercise, "wo."

Figure 4.36. Vowel morphing exercise, "hey"

Consonants

Vocalizing with consonants can not only raise awareness of what your body does to produce these sounds, but it can also help release tongue tension. Since rock singers perform in their native dialect, it is not usually necessary to improve consonant pronunciation. However, in order to sing fast lyrics with strong rhythmic attacks, you need to have a free and flexible tongue. As you work through the following exercises, pay attention to what you feel, hear, and/or visualize.

- Dental consonants are formed by using the tip of the tongue and the back of your upper teeth. The dental consonants are /d/, /l/, /n/, /t/, and /th/.

- Labials are formed with the lips. The labial consonants are /w/, /b/, /m/, /p/. There are two other consonants that are formed with the lips with the aid of the teeth; they are /f/ and /v/.

- The consonants /s/, /z/, /sh/, /y/, and /r/ are formed with the front of the tongue and the hard palate.

- The consonants /g/, /k/, and /q/ are formed with the back of the tongue and the soft palate.

- Consonants can also be divided into voiced (those that have pitch) and unvoiced (those that do not have pitch).

  - Voiced: /b/, /d/, /g/, /v/, /z/, /w/, /m/, /n/, /l/, /r/, /j/ (as in "yesterday"), and /th/ as in "this."

  - Unvoiced: /p/, /t/, /k/, /f/, /s/, /h/, and /th/ as in "thought."

Sing through the exercises in figure 4.37. Start slowly and focus on articulating each consonant clearly. Then speed up the tempo. Listen to the songs "All Star" by Smash Mouth and "Two Princes" by Spin Doctors. Learn the lyrics and then practice singing both of the songs. Keep your consonants crisp and

Figure 4.37. Consonant exercises.

120

rhythmic. Not every song will require strong consonants; in fact many songs will require you to largely ignore the consonants. As with all other aspects of your voice, exploring the extremes will help you master your instrument.

Constriction—Your Worst Enemy

The constrictor muscles surround your larynx and work in tandem with your tongue to move food down your esophagus when you swallow (see figure 4.38). When you sing, the back of your tongue will often tighten

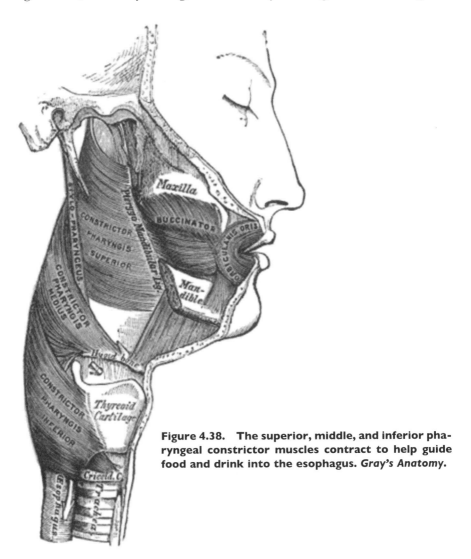

Figure 4.38. The superior, middle, and inferior pharyngeal constrictor muscles contract to help guide food and drink into the esophagus. *Gray's Anatomy.*

and the larynx will rise. These two muscular actions resemble those that are involved with swallowing, and therefore our body will often engage the rest of constrictor muscles when we sing (Caldwell & Wall, 2001). When these muscles engage, they limit the ability of the larynx to tilt and stretch the vocal folds. When the constrictors are engaged, the voice may be sharp, flat, have an uneven vibrato, an edgy sound, and/or a forced quality. Consistent constrictor involvement may also eventually lead to vocal damage.

These muscles can be difficult to separate from the act of singing and can take months or even years of work to release. For the self-taught singer, it can be very difficult to tell whether or not the constrictor muscles are engaged. Even if you discover that they are engaged, it can be rather difficult to relax them without professional guidance. The most effective way to address constriction on your own is to combine the exercises that follow with the tongue exercises in figures 4.23 through 4.26.

As you work on balancing your registration and releasing your tongue, you should have less difficulty with constriction. Remember, the voice is a nonlinear system (see pages 94–95). Addressing one part of the mechanism will often affect another.

Identifying the Sensation of Constriction

- If your sound feels squeezed, grabbed, tight, muffled, restricted, stuck, or tense, your throat is likely constricted. You will notice this by what you hear, feel, or see. Call out the word "no" and pay attention to what you hear, feel, or visualize. Next call out the word "what" and pay attention to what you experience. If while calling out "no," you notice that the outside veins of the neck are sticking out and/or turning blue, you are likely constricting. When calling out "what" your constrictors should relax, you will hopefully see the neck muscles relax, and your throat should open (Borch, 2005).

- Place the four fingers of your left hand on the left side of your neck and the four fingers of your right hand on the right side of your neck (see figure 4.39). Now swallow. Do this several times and pay very close attention to what you feel underneath your fingers. Now stick both of your thumbs underneath your chin and do the same. The muscles that you feel engaging in these ex-

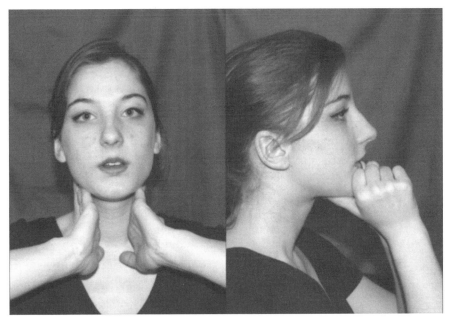

Figure 4.39. Monitoring constriction.

ercises are all part of the swallowing mechanism that contributes to constriction when singing.

- Next I want you to sing "goog" with a small and edgy tone quality on a 1-3-5-3-1 arpeggio (Love, 1999). Then I want you to take in a big open breath, lift your chin up, stick out your tongue, and sigh (LoVetri, 2009). Pay attention to any differences that you experience between singing "goog" and sighing with your chin up and tongue out. If you notice your throat closing in when singing the word "goog," you are most likely feeling the action of your constrictors. If you feel release when you look up and sigh, you are most likely experiencing the sensation of an open throat that occurs when your constrictors release.

Constriction Release

To work on releasing and relaxing your constrictor muscles, try the exercises below. These exercises may be mentally difficult, but they should feel relaxing in your throat. You may or may not notice an immediate change, but if you work on these exercises each day, you should eventually notice a difference.

When performing these exercises, you should be singing at a volume level somewhere between four and six on a ten-point scale (see "Dynamics" below). Only after you have mastered the release of these muscles at a medium volume level should you increase your volume. When your voice is free, it will naturally become louder over time with continued training (Vennard, 1967). Trying to force your voice to be louder than it naturally wants to be will often engage your constrictor muscles and make things worse.

Covered Mouth Singing

First open your mouth and place your fingers across the opening. The fingers should be close together, but you need to leave some space between them for the sound to escape (see figure 4.40). Sustain a comfortable pitch in this position. The vowel is not as important as the sensation of an open throat, with a strong and steady airflow and a buzzy sound quality. Next sustain a comfortable pitch on /a/ at a moderate volume level. As you sustain the pitch, remove your hand and try to maintain the sensation of a free and open throat (Behlau & Oliveira, 2008). Next try singing a five-note pattern alternating between a covered and uncovered mouth. This exercise can also be very helpful on the text of a song.

Figure 4.40. Cover your mouth with either hand and allow some space between your fingers for air to escape.

Silent Laugh

One simple way to relax your constrictors and open your throat is to imagine a silent laugh. Smile, inhale, and recall the sensation of laughing (Kayes, 2004). Now maintain that position and sigh. Then try to sustain a comfortable pitch. Next try the exercises in figure 4.41. As you sing the first exercise, you should feel as though you are laughing on /a/, /i/, and /o/. In the first measure of the second exercise, begin with a laugh and then try to keep the laugh position while you sustain a single vowel in the second measure (see figure 4.41).

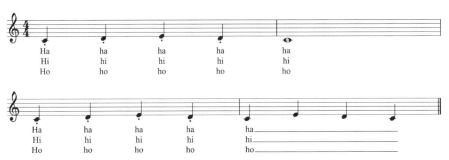

Figure 4.41. Silent laugh exercise.

The Drinking Position

Look up at the ceiling and try to swallow. More than likely you cannot because in this position the constrictor muscles elongate to the point that they can no longer function. This is called stretch weakness. Try the following experiment: Find a heavy object to do a curl with (left or right arm). Extend your arm fully, so that it is straight and parallel to your body. Lift the heavy object from this position. Now start with your arm at a ninety-degree angle to the floor, in front of your body, and lift the same object. Notice a difference? When your bicep is stretched, it is weak and has difficulty engaging. When you phonate while looking up, your constrictors are in a state of stretch weakness and are therefore less likely to interfere with your singing. This position allows your vocal folds to learn to function independently of the constrictor muscles. After building muscle memory in this position, you should be able to begin phonating in a level position without their involvement.

In the upward position, sing /a/ on a three-note pattern and pay attention to the feelings, sounds, and visuals that you experience as you vocalize. Do not tilt your head back any further than you would while taking a drink of water from a bottle (LoVetri, 2009). You may notice that in this position the larynx is somewhat elevated. An elevated larynx is not problematic unless you try to sing too loud or too high. Especially for a classical singer who has trained with a low laryngeal position, learning to allow the larynx to rise can be very beneficial when learning to sing rock. Do not be afraid of a high laryngeal position. Just know that it may create different sensations from those to which you are accustomed.

Resonators

The Equalizer

Your vocal tract (see figure 4.42) is the parametric equalizer for your voice (see chapter 6 for more information about equalizers). Narrowing and expanding the various parts of your vocal tract will enhance the low (bass), mid, and high (treble) tone qualities of your voice. In order to make your voice blend with various types of instruments, for example electric guitar or acoustic guitar, you will need to make minor adjustments to your tone

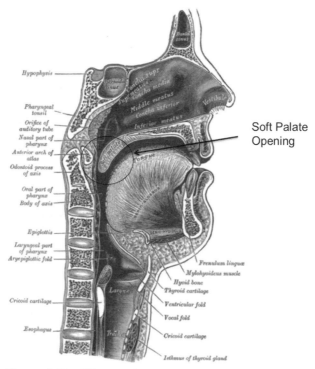

Figure 4.42. The vocal tract can be adjusted to alter the tonal quality of the voice. *Gray's Anatomy*.

quality. Refer back to figure 4.39. A relaxed throat in a neutral position around point "A" will help you produce clear mids. If you narrow that space, the tone quality will be brighter; if you expand that space the tone will get warmer. Opening around point "B" will add warmth to your voice, narrowing will brighten the voice. The distance between your tongue and the roof of your mouth controls point "C." If you decrease that space, your voice will brighten; if you increase that space, it will darken. The opening of your lips is identified by point "D." In the neutral position, the opening at "D" will complement the mids. If you spread and open the lips, you will brighten the sound; if you round the lips, you will darken the sound. The distance between points "A" and "D" also has an effect on vocal tone. Shortening the distance between "A" and "D" will brighten the sound while lengthening the distance between "A" and "D" will darken the sound (see figure 4.43).

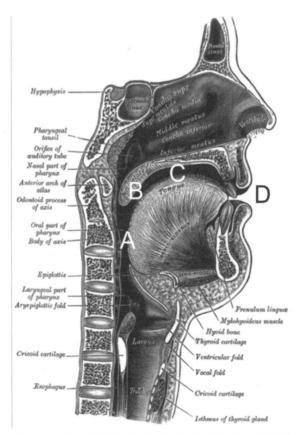

Figure 4.43. Points A, B, C, and D can be altered for specific tonal adjustments. *Gray's Anatomy.*

So how do you use this knowledge to improve your singing? These changes are essentially micromanagements of vowel shapes. The easiest way to achieve results is to think about general sound qualities when singing. Qualities like warm, dark, bright, and brassy can sometimes be enough to coax your body into adjusting the resonator on its own. If thinking about tone quality is not enough, explore the variations listed below while sustaining a vowel.

- Rounding the lips will produce a warmer and/or darker tone. This position increases the distance between A and D.

- Spreading the lips in a smile will brighten and/or make the tone brassier. This position shortens the distance between A and D.

- Raising your tongue will brighten the tone.

- Lowering the tongue will warm the tone.

- Lifting the soft palate as if saying a British /a/, will increase the space in zone B and add warmth to the tone.

- Lowering the soft palate as if using French nasal vowels will decrease the space in zone B and add brightness to the tone.

If you are sustaining a high /i/ vowel in a song and the tone is too dark, you can try lifting your tongue, lowering your palate, and spreading your lips, all of which will accentuate the highs in your voice. If your voice is too bright in a ballad, you could try rounding your lips and lifting your palate while keeping a relaxed tongue to add mids and lows. Try the exercise below (see figure 4.44).

/i/   /e/   /a/   /o/   /u/

1) Round your lips and lift your palate. This will accentuate the mids and lows.
2) Spread your lips and lower your palate. This will accentuate the highs.
3) Decrease the space between your tongue and the roof of your mouth. This will increase the highs.
4) Increase the space between your tongue and the roof of your mouth. This will decrease the highs.

Figure 4.44. Equalization exercise.

Soft Palate

If you are a classical singer or music theater performer, you have most likely worked on lifting your soft palate at some point during your training.

If you have never had voice lessons before, this will be a new concept. Look inside your mouth using a mirror and a flashlight. In the back you will see your uvula hanging down toward your tongue. The flexible tissue in front of your uvula forms what we call the soft palate. When the soft palate is low, sound can enter the nasal cavity resulting in a nasal tone quality. When the soft palate is lifted, your nasal cavity is closed off, eliminating nasality. In addition to controlling nasality, you can also think of the soft palate and tongue as barriers that can regulate the flow of air and vibration exiting your mouth from your vocal folds. If your tongue and uvula nearly touch, as in photo A in figure 4.45, the sound does not have an open pathway out of your throat. The additional backed up air pressure will interfere with what your vocal folds are doing and could cause unwanted tension. When you configure the vowel in a way that the soft palate automatically moves, there will be more space between your palate and your tongue and it will be easier for your vocal fold vibrations to move through the vocal tract. When you are doing this work, you must only focus on whether or not there is an opening in the back. Do not try to associate palatal lift with any specific tone quality.

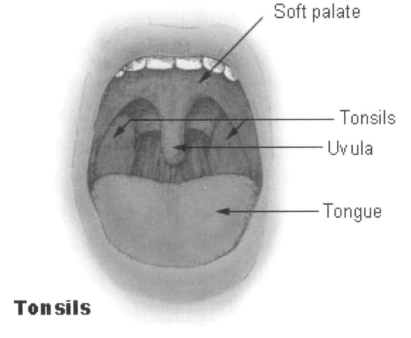

Figure 4.45. Basic anatomical features of the mouth. U.S. National Cancer Institute.

Grab a flashlight, go back to the mirror, and try the following experiment. Drop your jaw and say /a/ while pointing the flashlight in your mouth and looking in the mirror. Does what you see look more like picture A or picture B in figure 4.46? Picture A shows what it looks like when the palate, tongue, and uvula come together to form a barrier. In picture B, the soft palate and uvula are lifted out of the way so that there is no barrier between the mouth and throat. If your voice is nasal, lacking power, or you would like to cultivate a warmer quality, you will need to learn how to create an opening in the back. Each person will experience this lift differently. Some will feel a stretch, and others will feel nothing. Some may respond to the imagery of a lightbulb in the back of their throat, while others will only notice a difference in sound. It is also very possible that you will not immediately be aware of anything different between lifting and not lifting. To improve your awareness of the movement in the back of your mouth, try these exercises.

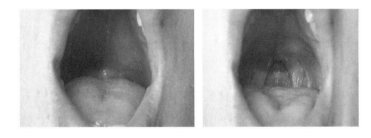

A   B

Figure 4.46. A lowered soft palate (left) and elevated soft palate (right).

Soft Palate Control Exercise

1. Look in in a mirror and see if your soft palate is lifting when you say /a/. If it lifts, skip this exercise.

2. If it does not lift, put a tongue depressor on your tongue, and breathe in. You should see the palate lift in the back. If not, breathe in again and imagine that you are saying /a/ so that a doctor can give you a strep-throat test.

3. Try to hold the inhale position as long as possible. The soft palate will more than likely try to fall back down toward your

tongue. If you have a strong gag reflex, it may kick in as you do this exercise. Do several reps of these palate lifts, holding each lift as long as you can, up to thirty seconds.

4. Next add a sigh after you've inhaled and lifted the palate. Repeat this until you are able to keep the palate high while sighing.

5. Next add a sustained pitch on /a/ /ae/ /ʊ/ or / ɛ / while holding the palate high. Begin with sustained pitches in your mid to low range and then try singing a three-note pattern.

6. Next try a five-note pattern and a 1-3-5-3-1 arpeggio.

7. Once these exercises feel comfortable, try adding lift to your songs.

When you are learning to control your soft palate, it is not uncommon for the back of your throat to feel a little dry or sore as if you were coming down with a sinus infection or strep throat. This is completely normal. You are stretching the tissue in the back of your throat and working muscles that are not accustomed to being stretched or worked. The tenderness should go away in one to two weeks. You should not be going hoarse.

Soft Palate Lowering Exercise

If you are a classically trained singer who is accustomed to lifting the soft palate, you may need to learn how to sing without lifting. This exercise begins with a low palate position and then moves toward a mid-level position.

1. Take a very small breath with your lips slightly open and lift your tongue to the soft palate as if saying "ng." Resist the urge to also lift your soft palate. In this position, sing a pitch and try to keep your palate from lifting. Try lowering the tongue from the palate and find an /a/ vowel. Alternate between the "ng" and /a/. This is easiest to accomplish with a breathy, earthy tone quality.

2. Now try singing through different vowels in this position, still at a soft to moderate volume.

3. After you are comfortable with the first two steps, slowly increase your volume and experiment with the sounds you can make in this new position.

4. If you are still having difficulty lowering your soft palate, experiment with French nasal vowels.

5. After you have found a nasalized quality, try applying it to the exercise in figure 4.47.

Ev' - ry   time   I   see   you   it's   pul - lin'   me   do - wn

Figure 4.47. Try applying a French nasal vowel quality to this exerpt.

Monitoring the Palate Opening

You are capable of singing with your palate lifted, lowered, and somewhere in the middle. An easy way to tell which position you are in is to pinch your nose. If you have sound escaping through your nose when you pinch it shut, you will notice a change in the sound and perhaps a physical sensation of the sound being stuck. When you pinch your nose shut with a lifted palate, nothing will change (Kayes, 2004). Try this exercise to become familiar with the nose pinching technique for monitoring palate lift:

- Sustain a pitch on /ng/. In this position your soft palate is lowered. Pinch your nose as you sustain a pitch. When you pinch your nose, you will feel as though your voice is immediately shut off. This is because all of your vocal tone is traveling through your nasal cavity, and it has nowhere to escape.

- Sustain a British /a/ on a single pitch (think Julia Child). Now pinch your nose. If your British /a/ is spot on, you will notice no difference in your tone or airflow when you pinch your nose.

Finally, sustain a French nasalized /o/ (think of the "Les Poissons" song from *Little Mermaid*). When you pinch your nose in this position, you should feel a slight sensation of the sound being shut off, along with a change in your tone quality. However, the difference in this position should be less drastic than in the /ng/ position (Kayes, 2004).

Vocal Stunts

Once you have taught yourself to sing with a relatively comfortable vocal production that covers approximately a two-octave range and you can produce a reasonable amount of volume with control over pitches, vowels, and consonants, you might be ready to explore vocal stunts. Understand that producing these effects can be harmful if you do not do them carefully. When you experiment with these sounds, be sure not to do anything that makes your voice feel tired or hoarse. You must also remember that most of these sounds require the assistance of amplification, so be sure to read chapter 6.

It would be impossible to account for all of the various tricks that singers have developed and worked into their styles, but to get you started I have put together several exercises that explore sounds that some may consider "nontraditional." Just remember that when it comes to rock, "traditional" doesn't exist and anything goes, as long as it works with your style.

Healthy Breathy Singing

Breathy singing is an essential element of rock style. One of the most common issues that I notice with self-taught rock singers is the use of constriction when attempting to sing breathy. These singers use the swallowing muscles to tighten their throat to suppress the vibrancy of their voice. Instead of suppressing vibrancy, use the natural function of the head voice mechanism to enhance breathiness. Because head register uses a thinner closure of the vocal folds, more air can escape and the voice will naturally take on a breathy quality. Try the following exercise for finding a healthy breathy tone.

Grab a Straw. In this exercise you are going to use a drinking straw to cultivate a steady airflow while singing. Place the straw between your lips as if taking a drink. Sing a sustained pitch in a comfortable part of your range at a soft volume level. You should feel a great deal of air flowing through the straw if you are doing this correctly. If you do not feel air moving through the straw, you are constricting in your throat. If that is the case, work on the constriction release exercises first. After you feel comfortable singing through the straw with free flowing air, remove the straw and sustain an /a/ vowel. Try this exercise on all of the basic patterns in Appendix C and with songs that you are working on that should have a breathy quality. First sing through the pattern or song using the straw and then remove the straw while maintaining the feeling of free flowing air.[1]

Reinforced Falsetto

This vocal quality is also sometimes called "squeal." It's the sound that you hear in the climax of Aerosmith's "Dream On." This tone quality is produced with a strong head-mix, bright vowels, a high tongue, a slightly raised larynx, and high subglottic pressure. If you are not yet comfortable with your head voice, work on that first. Try this exercise: Begin in a comfortable part of your upper head voice range. Place the tip of your tongue behind your bottom lip and arch your tongue in the back so that it is touching your upper molars. Smile and sing the exercise below. Use a slight inward contraction of your abdominal wall to add power to the sound (see figure 4.48).

Figure 4.48. Reinforced falsetto exercise.

Intentional Vocal Distortion

I have already mentioned Melissa Cross in regard to vocal fry onsets. The vocal fry quality is also appropriate for sustained singing in styles such as death metal, screamo, and hard rock. To properly teach you how to make those sounds would take more than a small subsection in a book. However, there are a few things that can be briefly discussed to help clarify the validity of these techniques.

A common question is whether or not vocal fry will cause vocal damage. Any extreme vocal behavior carries an inherent risk. Singing a chest-voice high C for a tenor used to be anathema but is now an expected behavior. Vocal fry is a part of rock style, so a singer needs to learn to do it in a way that minimizes the risk. Singers also need to understand that electronic amplification plays a big part in the power of vocal fry sounds. Digital distortion effects can help a singer achieve a nearly identical sound quality when recording and performing live. If you want to use distorted sound qualities but would like to preserve your voice for undistorted singing, investigate digital voice processors that offer such effects.

Finally, singers need to know that much of what is presented on YouTube about this type of singing is not only misinformed but also possibly dangerous. Most of the videos are self-taught singers, and what worked for them may or may not work for you. Remember, their anatomy is different than yours. Melissa Cross is the authority on this type of singing, and I trust her work. She works alongside medical professionals not only in the rehabilitation of clients who come to her with existing vocal damage but also with clients looking to improve their understanding of how the vocal mechanism works in extreme settings. Online at MelissaCross.com.

Uvula Trill

Uvula trills are one of the safer ways to add distortion to a single pitch. Depending on your anatomy, this technique may or may not work for you. I have found that students with larger tonsils are able to produce this sound more easily than those who have had their tonsils removed. This sound is basically produced in the same manner as when you are attempting to clear phlegm out of the back of your throat. Try flexing the sidewalls of your throat toward your uvula. Now blow air through the remaining space. First practice making this sound without bringing your vocal folds together. After you feel comfortable making these sounds without pitch, try adding pitch with the exercise in figure 4.49. The uvula trill happens on the onset of "I" before gliding up to the B♭.

Figure 4.49. Uvula trill exercise.

Intentional Tongue Tension

In the section on articulation, we worked on freeing the muscles in your tongue, but sometimes you may want to activate those muscles in order to achieve specific tone qualities. When the tongue retracts, as when pronouncing /r/, the resulting tone quality is often what judges on television singing competitions like to call "unique." In classical singing, tongue tension is never considered "unique"; it is something that you want to get rid of. However, if you like the sound qualities produced by tongue retraction, you can use the exercises below to explore the possibilities.

1. First say the words "red," "ray," and "read," allowing the tongue to tense in the back.

2. Instead of releasing the /r/ position before the vowel, try to maintain that position for the remainder of the word.

3. Now sing the three words above on a three-note pattern at a moderate volume level in a comfortable part of your range.

Singing with a tense tongue may feel uncomfortable. If that is the case, do not try pushing it. It may be a sound that your body does not want to make, you may be overdoing it, or this exercise alone may not be enough to guide you to where you need to go.

Dynamics

Students who come to my private studio often want to know if they are loud enough. In rock 'n' roll, if you are singing as loudly as or louder than you speak, you are loud enough. You have to remember that rock singers use a microphone 99 percent of the time. The reason singers often think they need to be louder is that they listen to music through their headphones several hours a day and they have a skewed sense of what unamplified singers sound like. Sound is measured in decibels. Table 4.1 displays sound-pressure levels, measured in decibels, of common sounds and vocal dynamics.

Researchers at Kennesaw State University found that students were listening to their headphones at volumes as loud as 110.7 dB. On average,

Table 4.1. Sound pressure levels, measured in decibels, of common sounds and vocal dynamics.

	Decibel Level	Examples	Singing Equivalent
Quiet	0		
	10	Rustling leaves	
	20	Whisper	
	30	Quiet conversation	
	40	Library	
Moderate	50	Inside of the average home	
	60	Normal conversation	Soft singing
Loud	70	Vacuum cleaner or loud conversation	Medium-low singing
	80	Garbage disposal, hair dryer	Medium-high singing
Very Loud	90	Blender, subway tunnel	Loud singing
	100	Snowmobile, impact wrench	Very loud singing
Uncomfortable	110	Car horn at one meter, crying baby	Extreme singing (belters and opera singers)
	120	Thunder, rock concert	
Painful	130+	Jet engine, fireworks at one meter	

students were listening at 94.8 dB (Alarcon & Jones, 2009). Studies of rock, country, and music theater singers have reported decibel readings of between 62 and 101 dB (Borch, Sundberg, Lindestad, & Thalén, 2005; Björkner, 2008). The data seems to suggest that many students are listening to music delivered directly into their ear canals at volume levels that exceed the actual amplitude of many professional singers. You do want to have a range of dynamics available to you, but the range should be within your own limits and not determined by your perceptions of other singers' voices.

Vocal dynamics are controlled by registration, vowel shape, breath pressure, airflow, and the space within the throat and mouth. A small palatal opening with head voice registration, a dark vowel, and low to medium breath pressure will not create a loud sound. A large palatal opening with chest voice, a bright vowel, and significant breath pressure will produce a loud sound. The traditional terms for dynamic levels are "pianissimo" (very soft), "piano" (soft), "mezzo piano" (medium soft), "mezzo forte" (medium loud), "forte" (loud), and "fortissimo" (very loud). Instead of trying to make your voice fit into a defined set of dynamics, I suggest that you think of your dynamic range on a numeric scale from one to ten, with one being the softest and ten being the loudest (LoVetri, 2009).

Working through the exercises in this book should help you expand your range of dynamic possibilities. Play around with various combinations of the different variables to explore your voice. There are of course more variations than represented in this chart. For instance, you can sing loud with a round vowel and you can sing soft in your chest voice. However, this chart will at least give you a starting place from which you can explore all of the possibilities. The chart in table 4.2 shows how registration, vowel shape, breath pressure, and palate opening can affect vocal dynamics.

Table 4.2. How registration, vowel shape, breath pressure, and palate opening can affect vocal dynamics.

	Volume 1–3	Volume 3–7	Volume 7–10
Registration	Head	Head mix to chest mix	Chest mix to chest
Vowel shape	Round	Neutral	Spread
Breath pressure	Low	Medium	High
Palate opening	Small	Medium	Large

Musicality

Composers and songwriters have four tools available to them to control energy—pitch, dynamics, rhythm, and harmony. As a singer, you only have control over pitch, rhythm, and dynamics. If you are singing a cover song, you only have control over dynamics and how you accent the rhythms you are given. There are some basic assumptions about music that listeners expect. As the pitch gets higher, the listener expects that the volume will get louder. As the pitch descends, the listener expects that the volume will get softer. If the rhythm section is accentuating the rhythm on beats one and three, we expect the singer to lock into the first and third beat. If the rhythm section is accentuating the rhythm on beats two and four, we expect the singer to lock into beats two and four. If a singer makes a musical choice that goes against our expectations, it creates excitement and changes the energy of the song. The list below describes a few of the most basic options for shaping the energy in a melody.

- Sing high notes softer than expected

- Sing lower notes loud and the higher notes soft

- Sing the lower notes soft and the higher notes loud

- Start a phrase loud, fade into a softer volume, and then crescendo the end.

- Start a phrase soft, crescendo into a louder volume, and then taper off to silence.

- Sing a phrase beginning with closed vowels and progressing to open vowels.

Sing through the exercises in figure 4.50 with the dynamics that are indicated. The < symbol is called a crescendo and it directs you to gradually get

Figure 4.50. Dynamics exercise.

louder. The > symbol is called a decrescendo and it directs you to gradually get softer. Registration is another ingredient that we can use to build excitement. Follow the dynamic markings in the exercise in figure 4.51, but also follow the registration suggestions.

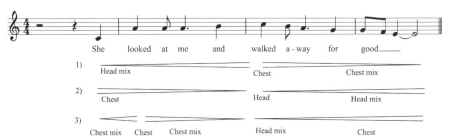

Figure 4.51. Registration and dynamics exercise.

Conclusion

As I mentioned at the beginning of this chapter, learning to sing solely from an instructional text is difficult if not impossible. However, if you practice daily with these exercises, you are bound to learn something new about your voice. Practice must be regular and diligent. You cannot simply sing in your car and expect results. You need to set aside a specific time and place to sit down with this text and work through each exercise until it becomes comfortable. Always remember: If it hurts, it's wrong.

Note

1. Dr. Ingo Titze also uses straw phonation as a method for semi-occluded vocal tract work. For more information on his use of straws, consult *Vocology: The Science and Practice of Voice Habilitation* by Ingo R. Titze and Katherine Verdolini Abbott.

Bibliography

American Academy of Teachers of Singing. (2008). NATS visits AATS. *Journal of Singing*, 65(1), 7–11.

Alarcon, R., & Jones, S. (2009). Measurement of decibel exposure in college students from personal music devices. *International Journal of Academic Research*, 1(2), 99–107.

Behlau, M., & Oliveira, G. (2008). Hand-over-mouth. In A. Behrman & J. Haskell (Eds.), *Exercises for voice therapy* (pp. 35–36). San Diego: Plural Publishing.

Björkner, E. (2008). Musical theater and opera singing—why so different? A study of subglottal pressure, voice source, and formant frequency characteristics. *Journal of Voice*, *22*(5), 533–40. doi:10.1016/j.jvoice.2006.12.007

Borch, D. Z. (2005). *Ultimate vocal voyage: The definitive method for unleashing the rock, pop or soul singer within you*. Mediagallerian: Notfabriken Music Publishing.

Borch, D. Z., Sundberg, J., Lindestad, P. A., & Thalén, M. (2005). Vocal fold vibration and voice source aperiodicity in "dist" tones: study of a timbral ornament in rock singing. *Logopedics, phoniatrics, vocology*, *29*(4), 147–53. doi:10.1080/1415430410016073

Brown, W. (1957). *Vocal wisdom: The maxims of Giovanni Battista Lamperti*. Malboro: Taplinger Publishing Co.

Caldwell, R., & Wall, J. (2001). *Excellence in singing*. Redmond: Caldwell Publishing Company.

Cleveland, T. F., Stone, R. E., Sundberg, J., & Iwarsson, J. (1997). Estimated subglottal pressure in six professional country singers. *Journal of Voice*. *11*(4), 403–9.

Cookman, S., & Verdolini, K. (1999). Interrelation of mandibular laryngeal functions. *Journal of Voice*, *13*(1), 11–24. Retrieved from http://www.sciencedirect.com/science/article/pii/S0892199799800575.

Cross, M. (producer), & Korycki, D. (director). (2005). *The zen of screaming* (DVD). Loudmouth, Inc.

Edwards, M. (2013, June). Pop/rock singers' attitudes towards professional training. Poster session presented at the Voice Foundation Annual Symposium: Care of the Professional Voice, Philadelphia, PA.

Guzman, M., Laukkanen, A. M., Krupa, P., Horáček, J., Švec, J. G., & Geneid, A. (2013). Vocal tract and glottal function during and after vocal exercising with resonance tube and straw. *Journal of Voice*, *27*(4), 19–34.

Kayes, G. (2004). *Singing and the actor*. New York: Routledge.

Love, R. (1999). *Set your voice free*. New York: Little, Brown.

LoVetri, J. (2013). The necessity of using functional training in the independent studio. *Journal of Singing*, *70*(1), 79–86.

LoVetri, J. (2009, July). Somatic Voicework levels I–III. *Contemporary Commercial Music Voice Pedagogy Institute*. Lecture conducted from Winchester, VA.

McClosky, D. B. (2011). *Your voice at its best*. Long Grove, IL: Waveland Press.

McCoy, S. (2004). *Your voice: An inside view*. Princeton, NJ: Inside View.

Miller, R. (1996). *The structure of singing: System and art in vocal technique*. New York: Schirmer.

Stark, J. (1999). *Bel canto: A history of vocal pedagogy*. Toronto: University of Toronto Press.

Vennard, William. (1967). *Singing: The mechanism and the technic* (5th ed.). New York: Carl Fischer.

BLUE SUEDE SHOES
Singing with Style

Create your own style . . . let it be unique for yourself and yet identifiable for others.

—Anna Wintour

Developing your own style may or may not come easily, but regardless of your musical background, a basic understanding of rock music history (see chapter 1) and the musical language will help you find your own artistic voice. If you have previously studied music, you are probably already familiar with many elements of musical language. If you are new to the study of music, this may be the first time you've encountered some of these concepts, but you can probably identify many of the traits by ear. No matter what musical background you come from, it is helpful to consider how vocal music has evolved through the centuries and how and why rock styles are different than classical styles.

Transitioning from Bach to Rock

As vocal demands evolved from elevated speech, in the early days of church music, to volume levels needed to compete with a large orchestra, classical singers had to adapt their voices to match the new styles. In the same way, singers of popular music such as rock have had to adapt to evolutions in the music they sing.

Important differences between the instrumentation of classical and rock music further explain the differences in tonal quality that have influenced vocal style. Most instruments found in the orchestra are not strummed; they are bowed and plucked (strings) or use air (brass and wind). These instruments create long legato lines where rhythm, while important, is not usually the dominant feature. If percussion is included, the typical instruments include tympani, bass drum, gong, bells, and other forms of hand percussion; rarely will you see a full drum set on the stage. Even then, the percussion instruments are not there to drive the rhythm but rather to accent it at specific places in the score.

The underlying, driving force in rock is rhythm. The drummer sets the beat[1] and tempo for the song, while the bass guitarist lays the ground structure for the harmonic content and accents the downbeat of each measure at the same time. The rhythm[2] guitar fills in the rest of the chord established by the bass and often accents the back beat (beats two and four). The singer, with the possible addition of a lead guitarist or keyboardist, is usually solely responsible for supplying the melodic material (Everett, 2009). Because the instruments in a rock ensemble are rhythmically driven, the singer cannot focus solely on creating flowing melodic lines. The singer must also connect to the rhythmic drive of the song to be effective.

Musical Structure in Rock 'n' Roll

Rock songs feature beat, melody, and harmony. Connecting a variety of carefully selected pitches with various rhythmic values that support the lyrics creates melodies. Combining pitches that complement each other to create a thick texture that supports the melody creates harmony. There are four base structures for creating harmonies in songs: the major chord, the minor chord, the diminished chord, and the augmented chord. Before we learn how to spell the various chord types, we need to cover scales and intervals. If you are unfamiliar with musical notation, I suggest you consult Amy Appleby's *You Can Read Music*.

Scales

Scales are the building blocks of melody. The four basic scales you will encounter in rock 'n' roll are: the major scale, the natural minor scale, the harmonic minor scale, and the melodic minor scale.

The major scale is perhaps the most recognizable of the four. Most of the simple songs our parents sang to us as children are composed using the major scale. Examples include "Twinkle, Twinkle Little Star," "Hush Little Baby," and "Itsy Bitsy Spider." The major scale consists of eight notes that we can number 1 through 8. (See figure 5.1.) The distance between the notes changes as you ascend the scale. When you are first learning to count the distance between notes, it is easiest to refer to a piano keyboard. On the piano keyboard (as in figure 5.2) you will find the notes laid out in black and white. The distance from one note to the next closest note is called a half step. Skipping a note and going to the next note equals a whole step. The pattern for a major scale beginning from any note is whole, whole, half, whole, whole, whole, half (see figure 5.1).

Figure 5.1. Major scale pattern.

When writing a scale, you must use every note of the musical alphabet: A, B, C, D, E, F, and G. As you move from key to key, you will find yourself landing on black keys on the piano. When you encounter a black key, you will need to use a flat or a sharp in order to utilize every note name within the musical alphabet. There are four notes that you will encounter on the piano that only have a black key on one side, these are E, F, B, and C. When you encounter one of these notes, you will use E as F♭, F as E♯, B as C♭, and C as B♯ (see figure 5.2).

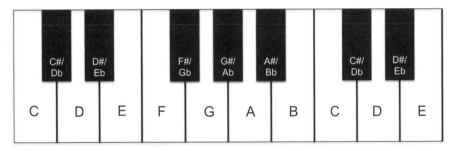

Figure 5.2. The musical alphabet as found on a piano keyboard

The minor scale also consists of eight notes; however, the distance between the notes is different from that in the major scale. The pattern for this scale is whole, half, whole, whole, half, whole, whole (see figure 5.3).

Figure 5.3. Minor scale pattern.

There are also two variations of the minor scale. The first is the harmonic minor. In the harmonic minor scale, the seventh scale degree is raised
a half step. For instance, in a minor key you would raise the G to a G♯
(see figure 5.4).

The minor melodic scale raises both the sixth and seventh scale degree
by a half step. For instance, in the key of A minor, the F and G would be
raised a half step to F♯ and G♯ (see figure 5.5).

Figure 5.4. Harmonic minor scale.

Figure 5.5. Melodic minor scale.

Creating Melodies

Melodies move between the notes of a scale by stepwise motion, leaps,
and skips. For instance, a stepwise pattern from C to D to E to F could
function as the structure for a simple melody. You could also leap across
notes, for instance from C to A, or skip across notes, for instance from C
to E. Combining stepwise motion, leaps, and skips will give you even more
possibilities, for instance C-A-F-G-D-E-C. Differences in rhythmic values
create variations from melody to melody, enabling two songs with identical
pitches to sound different (see figure 5.6).

Figure 5.6. Melodic variations.

The Language of Style

There are many different ways to make a song your own. Vocal coloring and dynamic changes are two of the most common tools, but sometimes you will want to do a little more. The next step is experimenting with altering the melodic and rhythmic material. This type of styling requires an in-depth understanding of musical structure and a lot of practice. The best way to learn how to embellish a melodic line is through practice and experimentation. As you experiment with the various patterns below, you will begin to discover licks, riffs, and runs that connect to your personal style. Record yourself when you practice so, if you come up with a great idea, you will be able to remember it and perhaps use it as the basis for a song.

The Blues Scale

When Africans were taken from their homeland and brought to America for slavery, they carried their musical language and traditions with them. One of the most noticeable traits of their vocal styling was the use of "blue notes," ♭3, ♭5(♯4), and ♭7 (Crawford, 2001). The blues scale integrates those notes while dropping the second and sixth scale degrees. The pattern for the scale is 1–♭3–4–♯4–5–♭7–8 (see figure 5.7).

Figure 5.7. The blues scale.

Experiment with the blues scale in every register of your voice, with every possible vowel, and every possible volume level. Experimenting will help you explore the range of possibilities so when you begin to improvise, you will already have plenty of tools to work with.

Pentatonic Scale

The pentatonic scale is the most common scale that you will encounter in rock 'n' roll. It comes in two types: major and minor. The major pentatonic scale consists of scale degrees 1–2–3–5–6 (see figure 5.8). The minor pentatonic scale consists of 1–3–4–5–7 (see figure 5.9).

Figure 5.8. The major pentatonic scale.

Figure 5.9. The minor pentatonic scale.

Intervals

"Interval" is a term used to describe the distance between two notes. The first interval, unison, is created when two different instruments are singing or playing the same pitch. The succeeding intervals can be played on one or two instruments. The qualities of each interval are identified above the staff in figure 5.10.

Figure 5.10. Major intervals.

The intervals listed above consist of notes found within the major scale and are therefore called major intervals. There are three exceptions: The fourth and the fifth intervals are called "perfect" and the interval following the major seventh is called an "octave." Intervals that are one half step lower than a major interval are called "minor intervals." The only exception is the flat perfect fifth, which is called a "tritone." The major and minor intervals are notated in figure 5.11.

Figure 5.11. Major and minor intervals.

The study of intervals should not only be an intellectual exercise but also a vocal one. The exercise below (figure 5.12) is designed to take you through the major and minor intervals, both up and down the scale, with your voice. Practice this exercise daily until you can sing it in tune without the use of a piano. Then try singing it backwards (see figure 5.13).

Figure 5.12. Interval exercise ascending.

Figure 5.13. Interval exercise descending.

Your Vocal Options

Through vocal tone color, and melodic and rhythmic variations, a singer can uniquely cover any song or spice up his or her own songs. Let's take a look at some of the basic vocal technique options at your disposal.

Tone Color Variations

In CCM (contempory commercial music) styles such as rock 'n' roll, a unified tone quality throughout the voice is not necessarily the goal. CCM styles represent the music of the people, so singing with vocal qualities of the common man is often the most appealing. The qualities of rock singing are:

- breathy tones

- exploitation of either bright or dark colors

- vowels that are often bright, ringy, and "spread"

- glottal stops

- little if any vibrato at all

Vocal Registers

As mentioned in chapter 3, there are four registers of the voice, or group-ings of pitches that have similar tone qualities. While terms such as "chest voice" do not necessarily represent the physiological action that is involved in producing these registers, these terms do represent a common vocabulary most singers and singing teachers understand; therefore, the following terms will be used throughout the remainder of this chapter: chest, chest-mix, head-mix, and head (see chapter 4 for more information on registers).

Some singing styles expect a performer to sound as if there are no regis-ter shifts at all, but no such expectations exist in rock 'n' roll. CCM perform-ers often exploit the breaks between registers to create unique vocal qualities. For example, the yodeling quality one might hear in country music comes from encouraging a strong break between chest and head registers. Rock singers use a less extreme flip over register breaks to create unique effects (for example, "What's Up?" by 4 Non Blondes). Experiment with flipping across your break by trying the following exercise (see figure 5.14). Pick a comfortable pitch to begin with and alternate back and forth with a pitch a perfect fifth higher on the vowel [a]. Allow your voice to feel as though it is wobbling back and forth between the two pitches. As you move up the scale, allow your voice to break as it crosses registers.

Figure 5.14. Wobbles.

When practicing a new song, experiment with variations in registration. If a note in the song is too high, instead of just screaming it out, try blend-ing into the next register to create a "mixed" vocal quality. If that does not work, try flipping across the break into a lighter registration as you ascend, and then flip back as the melodic line descends (for example Adele's "Rolling in the Deep"). As long as you are making an artistic choice to do so, your audience will probably not notice the difference. However, if you look timid and scared as you flip your voice over into a lighter place, you are essentially letting everyone know that you made the choice to change registrations due to your own technical issues. Never broadcast to the audience what you are not capable of doing yet; everyone has weaknesses. Instead, sell any vocal choices that you make as artistic choices.

Rhythmic Singing

While European-based singing styles favor a long vocal line over strict rhythmic delivery, rock 'n' roll alternates between melodic and rhythmic singing. While classical music usually puts the emphasis on beats one and three, rock 'n' roll emphasizes beats two and four. While the classical artist usually sticks to the rhythm on the page, the rock artist may take liberties with what is written. Rhythmic tools such as anticipation (coming in before the beat), back phrasing (coming in after the beat), and syncopation (creating rhythms that go against the beats) are all tools that are part of the rock singer's toolbox.

Vowel Shading

In rock music, singers usually sing with the vowel qualities of their native dialect. American speech has five main vowels but approximately sixteen different vowel sounds are possible (Deterding, 2004). Those vowels may be dark, bright, or somewhere in between, and the rock singer usually makes no effort to alter the natural tonal quality of the vowel, except for artistic effect.

When singing vocal exercises and songs, experiment with bright (smiley/ spread lip vowels), dark (round-lip vowels), and neutral (speech-like) vowels. Play with volume levels as well and see what options you can discover. Just as a painter uses various shadings and colors to create unique pictures of the same scene, you can use colors and shadings of your voice to create your own unique painting of a song. If consciously making adjustments to vowels and volume levels seems too mechanical, see chapter 8.

Vibrato

Vibrato is perceived when the listener hears fluctuations above and below a sustained pitch. Typical vibrato rates fall somewhere between four and seven fluctuations per second (see figure 5.15). Consistent vibrato was not a component of classical singing until the mid-nineteenth century when operatic productions had grown to such extraordinary sizes that vibrato-filled, oversized, bigger-than-life voices were the only ones capable of filling the opera house. Operas by composers such as Mozart and Handel did not require those types of voices, and singers of that era used vibrato only occasionally as an expressive tool (Salzman, 2000). It can therefore be argued that vibrato is not a necessary ingredient of free and healthy singing and that it is actually a stylistic choice. At loud volumes it can be useful; but it is not necessary at softer volumes of moderate vocal range.

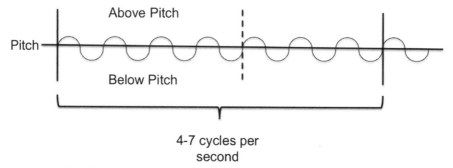

Figure 5.15. The squiggly line depicts vibrato.

Vibrato usage in rock 'n' roll is the source of much controversy. Some teachers and coaches say that vibrato is never present in rock, while others insist that vibrato is a necessary ingredient of healthy singing. Early rock 'n' roll singers who sang acoustically often had vibrato, most likely a by-product of needing to sing loud enough to be amplified by primitive microphones. As microphones evolved and became more sensitive, vibrato became less pronounced, since loud singing was no longer required in order to be heard. Now that audio engineers can auto-tune vibrato out of sustained notes (Hurwitz, 2007), many commercial recordings appear to be vibratoless.

When trying to minimize or eliminate vibrato from your sound, begin by singing no louder than 50 percent of what you are capable of without making any special efforts at breath control. Breathe for this exercise with only as much air as you would need if you are preparing to speak. By singing softly, with reduced air flow, you are taking away some of the breath energy that propels the vocal folds, which will often make it easier to steady your tone.

When adding vibrato to your voice, the reverse is not necessarily true. Attempting to sing louder will often cause beginning singers to sing in a more effortful way, squeezing the muscles surrounding the larynx. This constriction can inhibit the vocal folds from vibrating freely and actually prevent vibrato from finding its way into the sound. In order to cultivate a vibrato, first work on finding an open throat with a steady flow of air between the vocal folds (see chapter 4). As your throat relaxes, slowly increase the volume of your voice. Only sing as loud as you can with a free and open throat. While some books endorse belly pulsations to induce vibrato, I do not support such techniques. Since vibrato rates range between four and seven pulsations per second, singers would need to generate belly pulsations at those rates in order to achieve a normal vibrato. In my experience, this is a feat that is nearly impossible to achieve, even by skilled belly dancers.

Vibrato is a prickly subject and can be a difficult technique to learn. Some teachers believe that vibrato must always be present in a healthy voice. Others believe that vibrato should never be involved in rock singing. If one takes the view that vibrato is just one of many elements of an artistic palette for singers, then its inclusion or exclusion becomes the choice of the performer.

Tongue Tension

Even though, in traditional classical training, habitual tongue tension is an undesirable physiological trait, in rock 'n' roll, intentional tongue tension can create interesting sound qualities that may be useful. The back, lower part of your tongue attaches to the epiglottis, a flap that folds over the top of your vocal folds to prevent food from entering your lungs when you are swallowing (see chapter 3). If your tongue retracts when singing, the epiglottis will slightly fold over the vocal folds and affect your sound. For many singers, this produces a sound that is unwelcome, but in some instances the tone quality may be desirable: for example, when a singer is covering a song by Dave Matthews or Eddie Vedder.

Even if a tongue tension quality is desirable, tongue tension should never cause physical discomfort or excessive tightness that leads to voice loss. If you are struggling with fatigue or voice loss, find an experienced voice teacher who can help you identify and release tongue tension. Once you have learned to release tongue tension, you will be able to add it back in as wanted. However, when you add it back in, it will be a stylistic choice and not because it is the only way you are able to sing.

Intended Vocal Distortion

In the past, the raspy, gravelly sounds that hard rock singers made were often considered hazardous to a singer's vocal health. However, contemporary voice teachers have begun to explore new techniques for singing these styles that have helped revolutionize our understanding of these sound qualities. Heavy metal voice teacher Melissa Cross uses the term "intended vocal distortion," which I believe accurately describes the tone qualities these artists make. Harsh, growling sounds are indicative of intense emotions, such as anger and hate, that artists use to convey intense emotional messages to their listeners. Cross has produced a DVD series called *The Zen of Scream*, which instructs singers on how to develop intentionally distorted sounds with their own voice. If this tone quality is something that interests you, I highly recommend checking out Melissa Cross's work.

Gang Shouts

Gang shouts are typically found in heavier styles of rock 'n' roll. They generally occur in short bursts with several members of the band shouting the same lyrics at the same time. When integrating shouting in your work, it is important to use a free throat without any excess tension. Extremely sensitive recording studio microphones can easily make vocal sounds seem louder than they actually are (see chapter 6). When practicing any aggressive style of singing, always work with a microphone so that you can avoid the temptation to sing louder than necessary, which could eventually lead to vocal damage.

Musical Options

Bends

If you have ever watched a guitar player perform live, you may have noticed that during the course of a solo they often bend their strings upward to affect the pitch and tone of their solos or riffs. When adding vocal bends to a song, you are essentially imitating a guitar (see figure 5.16).

Figure 5.16. Bends.

Turns

Turns are pitch movements above and below a sustained note. See figure 5.17 for examples of two different types of turns. Turns usually happen quickly on a single vowel within a word.

Figure 5.17. Turns.

Fall-Offs

Fall-offs are notes that descend from a sustained pitch as the voice tapers off in volume (see figure 5.18). Fall-offs are always at the end of a word and often at the end of a vocal line. Otherwise, if a fall-off were sung at the same volume and in the middle of a vocal line, we would simply consider it to be part of the melody or a lick.

Figure 5.18. Fall-off.

Scoops

Scoops are slides from a lower pitch to a higher pitch (see figure 5.19). Scoops can be slow or fast. Usually, the notes between the bottom note and the top note are indiscernible as the singer glides from one to another.

Figure 5.19. Scoop.

Dips

Dips are slides from a higher pitch to a lower pitch (see figure 5.20). Dips do not hit exact notes but rather slide through the passing tones of the scale.

Figure 5.20. Dip.

Licks

Licks are short and fast ascending or descending patterns (see figure 5.21). The difference between licks and runs is length. Licks are short segments used to convey a specific emotional feeling on a single word. Technically, bends, turns, and fall-offs could all be considered licks. Try not to get caught up in the terminology. These terms are being presented as an analytical tool to help you make sense of common musical patterns that artists use. The goal is to be able to improvise spontaneously without thinking about the details.

Figure 5.21. Licks.

Runs

Runs are extended ornamental passages used to improvise on a vocal line and add emotional strength. Runs may contain elements of bends, turns, fall-offs, dips, and scoops (see figure 5.22). However, what makes runs unique is the extended length that they use to progress through an ascending or descending line.

Figure 5.22. Runs.

Working with Your New Vocal Vocabulary

Learning to improvise requires practice and discipline to achieve 100 percent accuracy at full tempo. If vocal improvisation is relatively new to you, begin with riffs that someone else has already written. The sheet music of artists such as Christina Aguilera and Mariah Carey often contain written-out vocal riffs that are perfect for practice. When learning new riffs, it can be helpful to break them down into smaller sections. Work each of the smaller sections one at a time until you can sing them perfectly in tune. Then combine the individual sections and work on the riff as a whole. When you begin practicing the individual sections, start at a slow tempo using a metronome (click-track) to help you avoid rushing. The sooner you get comfortable with singing with a metronome, the better off you will be when you go to work in a studio. As you perfect the riffs at a slower tempo, start increasing the speed incrementally, but only push yourself as far as you can handle the riff while staying in tune. Eventually you will be able to move up to full tempo and maintain complete accuracy.

While an artist can sometimes get away with imperfect riffs in live performance, in the recording studio, sloppy riffs are particularly noticeable. If you cannot sing a riff perfectly in front of the recording studio microphone, the recording engineer will have to resort to graphical auto-tune to fix your intonation issues. This will not only affect the final tone quality of your vocals, but it can also become quite expensive, since the engineer will bill you for the additional studio time it will take to make the edits.

Once you have studied other artists' riffs, you are ready to begin creating your own. To begin, pick one of the scales from figures 5.7, 5.8, or 5.9 and select three to four random notes. First practice skipping between those notes, then add scoops and dips. Next, experiment with upper neighbors (a half step or whole step above the primary pitch) and lower neighbors (a half step or whole step below the primary pitch). Experiment with several different patterns within the same scale and then move on to one of the other scales. In addition to attempting various note patterns, try varying rhythmic values.

When you are ready to push yourself a little bit further, try playing a major or minor chord on a keyboard or guitar and improvise vocal riffs over the chord. Once you have mastered riffing over a single chord, try riffing over a two-chord progression. After you've mastered that, try adding a third chord. When you first begin working with multiple chords, it can be helpful to outline the chord tones first (these are also called target notes). Singing each note of each chord before beginning to riff will help program the target notes of each chord into your memory (see figure 5.32). Then, as you begin to experiment with skips, leaps, turns, and runs, you will know where the target notes are.

Figure 5.23. To practice the "changes," sing the chord tones of each chord.

Listening Examples

The categorization of rock subgenres is very subjective. For the purpose of this book, I have included selected subgenres in order to give a general overview while specifically addressing some of the vocal style differences. For further reading, I suggest *What's That Sound?* by John Covach.

Listening

The best way to learn new vocal styles is through listening and imitating. Early rock 'n' roll performers regularly imitated others while developing their own style. The Rolling Stones learned the songs of artists such as Chuck Berry and Muddy Waters and combined traits of those artists to develop their own style (Ward, Stokes, & Tucker, 1986). Listening and copying others as you attempt to create your own unique style is not cheating. In fact, it would be impossible to not be influenced by other artists, since you have been surrounded by music since you were born. When a student learns a foreign language, the textbook provides sentences to study and repeat, both verbally and in written form. Once the student has learned the sentences provided in the textbook, they are instructed to begin combining the various grammatical elements to form their own sentences. This is the same process that will help you find success in integrating these vocal styles into your singing.

Ideally, you should purchase both audio recordings and printed sheet music of songs. Sit with the musical score and listen to the recording several times through. Listen to one instrument at a time and make notations on the sheet music about when those instruments enter, when they exit, and when they change tonal qualities (for instance, turning distortion on and off). Look at the chord structures that have been used and mark any repetitions in the verse, bridge, pre-chorus, and chorus. When you are listening to the voice, make notations about vocal colors, registrations, volume levels, bends, scoops, dips, etc. When you begin to sing the song yourself, you will look at it differently than if you had only imitated what you heard on the recording.

It is important to remember that when the original performers recorded the song, they were actively participating in the writing process. The more connected you are with the creative process, the more effectively you can present the song. By extensively studying the audio recording and written sheet music, you are changing roles from hearer to creator, effectively inserting yourself into the creative process. Not only will you begin to learn what goes into creating a great vocal part, but you will also begin to notice specific elements of songwriting that may help you with your own songwriting.

Rockabilly

Rockabilly was formed in the earliest days of rock 'n' roll by the melding of country western music and rhythm and blues. Both country western and rhythm and blues styles were built around I-IV-V chord progressions with slight differences. While blues artists sang songs about being down–and-out in a general way, country artists sang story-driven songs. At first, country singers wrote for voice and acoustic guitar only, but Fred Maddox eventually added an upright bass played rhythmically by snapping or slapping the strings (called slap bass). The slap bass not only helped drive the rhythm but also began to set blues styles and country styles apart.

Rockabilly came into its own when musicians began combining twangy electric guitar with the slap bass and rhythm guitar. Only after 1956 did rockabilly groups begin to add drums to the mix, which pushed the genre even further away from its singing-cowboy roots (Walser, 2014b). The exciting upbeat tempo of rockabilly was the first venture of white audiences into exploring the rhythmic and lyrical traits of rhythm and blues. It was also the first style to make rock 'n' roll accessible and acceptable to the average white American. Because of its roots in the acoustic singing styles of country and western, the voices in rockabilly music are acoustically powerful as in the vaudeville tradition and often contain hints of vibrato. Examples: "That's Alright" by Elvis Presley and "Great Balls of Fire" by Jerry Lee Lewis.

Folk Rock

Folk rock applies the story-telling traditions of American folk music to rock 'n' roll music styles. One of the most recognizable elements of folk rock is the singable and memorable chorus delivered with clear vocal harmonies. Folk rock looked to the past for its inspiration and thus carried on acoustic singing traditions. Men sang with resonance similar to that found in theater singing, and women sang in a mixed registration with either head-mix or chest-mix. Even though performers sang with tonal qualities of earlier generations, the voices still conveyed the feeling of listening to an everyday person, not a commercialized, perfected voice. Popular artists include Peter, Paul, and Mary; Arlo Guthrie; and Bob Dylan. Examples: "Mr. Tambourine Man" by The Byrds and "Black Day in July" by Gordon Lightfoot.

Hard Rock

The characteristic sound of music in the hard rock genre includes loud, aggressive guitar parts with deep drums and loud cymbals (Moore, 2014b). Distinct from its subgenres heavy metal and punk, hard rock is not as loud or aggressive. With its strong backbeat, epic choruses, and larger-than-life guitar riffs, hard rock unabashedly aims to please commercial audiences. Male performers are known for putting on displays of masculinity when on stage.

The band Black Sabbath acts as a dividing point because, after them, bands with darker thematic material were considered "heavy metal" bands. Other differences surface in the guitar parts where heavy metal riffs function as stand-alone melodies and hard rock riffs outline the chord progression of the chorus. Heavy metal and hard rock both influenced the music of the mid-1960s when psychedelic bands and performers, such as Cream, Jimi Hendrix, and The Jeff Beck Group, merged the musical traits of heavy metal, hard rock, and blues rock bands to create a new sound. Examples: "Crazy Train" by Ozzy Osbourne and "Born to Be Wild" by Steppenwolf.

Psychedelic Rock

Psychedelic rock evolved during the 1960s as bands began to break the verse-chorus patterns previously heard in rock 'n' roll and instead moved toward more free-flowing song structures. Many psychedelic bands embraced beliefs from Eastern religions and began to flavor their work with those new beliefs. Additionally, many artists began regularly using mind-altering drugs such as marijuana and LSD while composing and performing. One of the most notable traits of psychedelic rock is the extended and often improvised middle section, which often explores variations in instrumental textures, scales, and harmonic progressions to create an otherworldly feeling. These bands also took advantage of technological innovations to electronically enhance their instruments and voices while working in the recording studio. Examples: "White Rabbit" by Jefferson Airplane and "In-A-Gadda-Da-Vida" by Iron Butterfly.

Heavy Metal

Heavy metal developed in the late 1960s with bands such as Iron Maiden, Led Zeppelin, Alice Cooper, Black Sabbath, and Deep Purple. Typical traits include heavily overdriven guitars, heavy bass, and large drum kits with multiple cymbals, and toms. The musical structure abandons the twelve-bar blues progression and instead alternates back and forth between a few power chords[3] (Wilton). Heavy metal fans were known to bang their heads back and forth while dancing to the music, which spawned the term "head bangers" (Covach, 2009). Examples: "Ride the Lightning" by Metallica and "Fear of the Dark" by Iron Maiden.

Progressive Rock

Sometimes called "art rock," progressive rock represents an attempt to lift rock 'n' roll to a higher level of artistic credibility. Progressive rock tends to be influenced by classical instrumental technique, melodic vocal lines, and literary lyrics often based on a narrative storyline. Many progressive rock bands experimented with concept albums, albums recorded in order to present a complete storyline or deal with one continuous theme. Progressive rock became mainstream in the early 1970s with bands such as Emerson, Lake, and Palmer; Yes; Genesis; and Pink Floyd. Soon the music became too complex and pretentious, and bands were forced to adapt their style in order to remain relevant to audiences (Moore, 2014c). Examples: "The Wall" by Pink Floyd and "Aqualung" by Jethro Tull.

Arena Rock

Arena rock shares many traits with progressive rock. Arena rock bands recorded albums with high production values and lavish, memorable choruses. These bands were more commercial, receiving generous airplay and touring extensively, playing huge arenas to support their albums. Arena rock bands include Journey, REO Speed Wagon, Foreigner, Styx, and Boston (Arena Rock, 2014). Examples: "Hell's Bells" by AC/DC and "Come Sail Away" by Styx.

Glam Rock

Glam rock was a British invention that became popular in the first half of the 1970s. Glam rock music was elementary; distorted guitars played simple chord progressions to support catchy melodies while the rhythm section added early rock 'n' roll rhythms. What really made this style stand out from other rock genres was the showmanship in live performance. Glam rock performers often took the stage in androgynous costumes with heavy makeup. Artists such as David Bowie, T. Rex, and New York Dolls are examples of the style (Moore, 2014a). Examples: "Bang a Gong (Get It On)" by T. Rex and "Tight Pants" by Iggy Pop and the Stooges.

Punk

Punk developed in the 1970s as a reaction to the excess displayed by commercial rock bands. Punk music is not known for its lush harmonic content. In fact, most songs consist of no more than three chords played aggressively with no regard to traditional ideas of musicality. Instead, the focus is the message, the attitude, and the anti-commercial lifestyle. In the United States the earliest punk bands included Patti Smith, the Ramones, Lou

Reed, and the Velvet Underground (Shaw, 1982). Vocals are simple, sometimes shouted, and often difficult to understand. Punk bands that pushed the genre into edgier territory became known as "hard core," which later influenced screamo and emo. Examples: "Blitzkrieg Bop" by the Ramones and "Holiday in Cambodia" by Dead Kennedys.

Alternative Rock

Alternative rock describes the anti-commercial bands that were formed between the mid-1980s and the mid-1990s, after the fall of punk style. Though alternative rock contains multiple subgenres, they are all tied together with the common thread of existing outside of commercial studios and mainstream radio. The movement was a reaction to the flashy performance style of the heavy metal bands and the visually driven choices of MTV artists (Covach, 2009).

The band Nirvana provides a dividing point for alternative music. Before "Smells Like Teen Spirit" broke onto the national scene in 1991, independent labels were the primary producers of alternative bands. After Nirvana's success, many major record labels took notice of alternative bands and began signing them to record deals. However, once those labels put their commercial influence on the style, it became less "alternative." Examples: "Smells Like Teen Spirit" by Nirvana and "Bullet with Butterfly Wings" by The Smashing Pumpkins.

Death Metal

Death metal pushed the boundaries of subject matter. As its name implies, death metal is about death and related subjects, such as pain and suffering. The lyrics are often morbid and are supported by angry guitar riffs that drive the rhythm forward. Stage performances of death metal bands also embodied death and antireligious themes that sometimes included gruesome stage antics. GWAR donned theatrical masks and splattered fake blood across the stage and audience by attacking onstage props with various torture devices during live performances (GWAR, 2014). Death metal neither sought nor attained mainstream success. And while heavy metal bands such as Metallica, Kiss, and Guns N' Roses catered to the mainstream, death metal bands such as Slayer, Sepultura, Megadeath, Anthrax, and GWAR were happy to please a more independent audience (Walser, 2014b). Examples: "Now You've Got Something to Die For" by Lamb of God and "We Will Rise" by Arch Enemy.

Emo

A subgenre of punk, Emo began as a largely underground movement following the anti-commercial philosophy of punk and hard core. Most artists signed with small labels and released albums in small numbers. Lyrics in emo music have deep personal connections to the artists and often come from personal experiences. Vocals are frequently delivered with breathy tones high in the singer's range as a means of conveying a heightened emotional state. Whereas hard core bands often resort to screaming vocal lines, emo artists favor melodic and expressive vocals with only occasional screams. The emotional content often drives and flavors the vocals with a slightly nasal and almost whiney vocal quality. Ornamentation is minimal and the vocals are heavily processed and reliant on audio technology for both tone quality and projection (Arena Rock; Cateforis). Examples: "Helena—So Long & Goodnight" by My Chemical Romance and "Misery Business" by Paramore.

Screamo

Screamo is a hybrid of emo and hard core. Screamo bands usually alternate between soft emotional singing and loud screaming, often using two vocalists to achieve such extremes. The lyrics are often introspective, though some also deal with violent imagery. Otherwise, the musical traits are very similar to emo as described above, with the addition of aggressive guitar parts in the screaming sections of songs. Examples: "This War Is Ours" by Escape the Fate and "Relentless Chaos" by Miss and I.

Industrial Rock and Metal

Industrial rock combines synthesizers and electronic noise with rock and punk elements. The movement gained momentum in the mid-1980s, with bands surfacing in Great Britain and Australia as well as the United States. Some groups continued to use acoustic drums while others converted to digital drums, resulting in an aural texture where the only acoustic instrument present was the voice. This was the first genre in rock to favor technology over live musicians. Bands of note include Chrome, Killing Joke, Big Black, and Swans. An outgrowth of the industrial rock movement, industrial metal bands used a combination of synthesizers and more traditional instruments, such as the heavy metal guitar, to direct their rage. Bands of this genre include Nine Inch Nails, Ministry, KMFDM, and Marilyn Manson (Kirk,

2013). Examples: "March of the Pigs" by Nine Inch Nails and "The Dope Show" by Marilyn Manson.

The Impact of Technology on Rock Styles

When learning to sing in various styles, one must also consider technological evolutions through the decades. Vocal qualities that worked well with early rock 'n' roll, which was amplified but not heavily distorted, may not work well with electric guitars and heavy digital distortion. Similarly, vocal colors that work well with natural acoustic instruments may not sound appropriate when accompanied by an electric synthesizer. Perhaps the most influential technological element is the microphone (see chapter 6). Songs written to be performed with a microphone will need a microphone in order to sound appropriate, but songs written without a microphone in mind will need an acoustically projected voice in order to sound appropriate.

For example, if you were singing a Buddy Holly song written when microphones were still relatively new, you would sing with vocal resonance more akin to that found in early music theater.[4] Music theater artists sang without the use of wireless microphones until the production of *Hair* in 1968, so early music theater performers had to sing in a manner that produced a bright and ringing tone quality that could be heard over the orchestra accompanying them in performance. If you are singing a Bob Dylan song from the 1960s when microphones were commonplace, that quality would not be as important. Instead, you would focus on adapting your vocal tone to match the timbre of the acoustic guitar. If you sing a Led Zeppelin song, your vocal quality must match the sound of the instruments in that piece. For example, in "Hair of the Dog," you would use a gritty voice with intentional vocal distortion, but the beginning of "Stairway to Heaven" would require a lighter, breathier quality.

Guitars in the 1980s became even more distorted in guitar solos, often played in the extreme upper range of the instrument. Therefore, in order to match the quality of that sound, your vocal quality should be just as shrill when singing songs from that era. For example, the lead singers of Guns N' Roses, Aerosmith, and Poison all have bright and edgy vocal qualities.

The 1990s combine acoustic and electric guitar instrumentation, so when singing songs from this era, you will need to adjust your voice to match the acoustic or electrical sounds as you move through the various sections of each song.

Music of the late 1990s to the present is frequently heavily processed. You will need to utilize digital vocal processing to produce these tone qualities without causing vocal fatigue (see chapter 6 for more information on audio technology).

Conclusion

Though all of the information in this chapter can be overwhelming at first, the main point is that there are no rules. These artists did not follow standard conventions of the day but cut their own paths in reaction to the world around them. When the music evolved in reaction to social issues and technological developments, the quality of the voice evolved as well. Learning to sing rock 'n' roll is all about finding your own voice, your own tone quality, and your own technical approach (with vocal health in mind). So, do not despair if your voice doesn't sound the same as someone else's. In many ways that's a good thing. This is a genre that is all about who you are and what you bring to the table.

Notes

1. The beat is the steady pulse of the music that drives it forward.
2. The rhythmic figures played by the guitar coincide with the beat to create rhythmic variety.
3. Power chords are chords that are constructed with only the root and the perfect fifth. Power chords are popular among punk and alternative musicians because they require only two fingers and two strings to play, yet they deliver a powerful tone.
4. Early musical theater was an outgrowth of English operetta, which was an outgrowth of European opera. In the early days of musical theater there were no microphones and singers had to project their voices like opera singers in order to be heard.

Bibliography

Appleby, A. (1995). *You can read music*. New York: Music Sales America.

Arena Rock. http://www.allmusic.com/subgenre/arena-rock-ma0000012329

Cateforis, T. Emo. Grove Music Online. Oxford Music Online. Oxford University Press, accessed January 4, 2014, http://www.oxfordmusiconline.com/subscriber/article/grove/music/A2240803.

Covach, J. (2009). *What's that sound? An introduction to rock and its history*. New York: W. W. Norton.

Crawford, R. (2001). *An introduction to America's music.* New York: W. W. Norton.

Deterding, D. (2004). How many vowel sounds are there in English? *STETS Language & Communication Review, 3*(1), 19–21. Retrieved from http://www.ubd .edu.bn/academic/faculty/FASS/staff/docs/DD/STETS-vowels.pdf.

Emo. (2014). http://www.allmusic.com/style/emo-ma0000004447.

Everett, W. (2009). *The foundations of rock from Blue Suede Shoes to Suite: Judy Blue Eyes.* New York: Oxford.

Fine, S. (2007). *Violence in the model city: The Cavanagh administration, race relations, and the Detroit race riot of 1967.* Lansing: Michigan State University Press.

Grout, D. J. A., & Palisca, C. V. A. (1996). *A history of western music.* New York: W. W. Norton.

GWAR. (2014). In *Encyclopedia of Popular Music,* 4th ed. Oxford Music Online. Oxford University Press, accessed January 4, 2014, http://www.oxfordmusicon-line.com/subscriber/article/epm/48800.

Hurwitz, M. (2007, October). Memory: Track by Track. MixOnline.com, 1–5.

Kirk, R. (2014). Industrial rock. In *Grove Music Online.* Oxford Music Online. Oxford University Press, accessed January 4, 2014, http://www.oxfordmusiconline. com/subscriber/article/grove/music/A2241536.

Moon, T. (2008). *1,000 recordings to hear before you die: A listener's life list.* New York: Workman Publishing.

Moore, A. F. (2014a). Glam rock. In *Grove Music Online.* Oxford Music Online. Oxford University Press, accessed January 3, 2014, http://www.oxfordmusic online.com/subscriber/article/grove/music/46248.

Moore, A. F. (2014b). Hard rock. In *Grove Music Online.* Oxford Music Online. Oxford University Press, accessed January 3, 2014, http://www.oxfordmusicon-line.com/subscriber/article/grove/music/46249.

Moore, A. F. (2014c). Progressive rock. In *Grove Music Online.* Oxford Music Online. Oxford University Press, accessed January 3, 2014, http://www.oxfordmusiconline .com/subscriber/article/grove/music/46255.

Olwage, G. (2004). The class and colour of tone: An essay on the social history of vocal timbre. *Ethnomusicology Forum, 13*(2), 203–26. Retrieved from http://www .jstor.org/stable/20184481.

Salzman, E. (2000). Some notes on the origins vof new music-theater. *Theater, 30*(2), 9–23. Retrieved from https://muse.jhu.edu/login?auth=0&type=summary&url=/ journals/theater/v030/30.2salzman01.html.

Shaw, A. (1982). Punk rock. In *Dictionary of American pop/rock.* New York: Schirmer Books.

Walser, R. (2014a). Rockabilly. In *Grove Music Online.* Oxford Music Online. New York: Oxford University Press. Retrieved January 3, 2014, from http://www .oxfordmusiconline.com/subscriber/article/grove/music/49141.

Walser, R. (2014b). Thrash metal. In *Grove Music Online*. Oxford Music Online. Oxford University Press, accessed January 4, 2014, http://www.oxfordmusiconline.com/subscriber/article/grove/music/49137.

Ward, E., Stokes, G., & Tucker, K. (1986). *Rock of ages: The* Rolling Stone *history of rock & roll*. New York: Rolling Stone Press.

Wilton, P. Heavy metal. The Oxford Companion to Music. Oxford Music Online. Oxford University Press, accessed January 3, 2014, http://www.oxfordmusiconline.com/subscriber/article/opr/t114/e3192.

CHAPTER SIX
I LOVE IT LOUD!
Using Audio Enhancement Technology

Any sufficiently advanced technology is indistinguishable from magic.

—Arthur C. Clarke

In the early days of blues, gospel, and country western music, musicians performed without electronic amplification. Singers learned to project their voices in the tradition of vaudeville performers with a technique similar to operatic and operetta performers, who had been singing unamplified for centuries. When the microphone began appearing on stage in 1930, vocal performance changed forever since the loudness of a voice was no longer a factor. All singers needed was an interesting vocal quality and an emotional connection to what they were singing, and the microphone would project it. One of the first singing styles that evolved alongside the microphone technology was crooning. Crooners sang with a breathy vocal quality that led listeners to fantasize about intimate conversations with the singer (Lockheart, 2003).

Using a microphone, a singer can produce tones that may sound unpleasant without it. The same singer can produces beautiful unamplified tones that sound terrible when filtered through a microphone. Understanding how to use audio equipment to get the sounds you want without hurting your voice when both recording and performing is crucial. The information that follows will provide a basic knowledge of common equipment.

The Fundamentals of Sound

In order to understand how to manipulate sound, you must first understand a few of its basics: frequency, amplitude, and resonance.

Frequency

Sound travels in waves of compression and rarefaction within a medium, which for our purposes is air. These waves travel through the air around us, into our inner ears via the ear canal, and are converted to nerve impulses that are transmitted to the brain and interpreted as sound. The number of waves per second is measured in Hertz (Hz)—the *frequency* of the sound that we perceive as pitch. For example, we hear 440 Hz (440 vibrations per second) as the pitch A above middle C (McCoy, 2004).

Amplitude

The magnitude of the waves of compression and rarefaction determines the amplitude of the sound that we hear as its volume. The larger the waves of compression and rarefaction, the louder we perceive the sound to be. Measured in decibels (dB), *amplitude* represents changes in air pressure from the baseline. Decibel measurements range from zero decibels (0 dB), the threshold of human hearing, to 130 dB, the upper edge of the threshold of pain (see figure 4.50) (McCoy, 2004).

Harmonics

As mentioned above, in order to create the pitch A above middle C, we must create 440 vibrations per second in the air surrounding us. The vibrating mechanism of an instrument is responsible for producing the vibrations necessary to establish pitch (the fundamental frequency). The vibrating mechanisms for a singer are the vocal folds. If an instrument produced a note with the fundamental frequency alone, the sound would be strident and mechanical like the emergency alert signal used on television. Musical sounds and most sounds found in nature consist of multiple simultaneous frequencies. The vibrating mechanism simultaneously produces a series of frequencies above the fundamental, called "overtones." For the purposes of this book, the overtones that we are interested in are called *harmonics*. Harmonics are whole-number multiples of the fundamental frequency. For example, if the fundamental is 220 Hz, the harmonic overtone series would be 220 Hz, 440 Hz (fundamental frequency times two), 660 Hz (fundamental frequency times three), 880 Hz (fundamental frequency times four), and so on. Every musical note contains both the fundamental frequency and a predictable series of harmonic overtones, each of which can be measured and identified as a particular frequency. This series of frequencies then travels through a resonator—for a singer, the throat and mouth (McCoy, 2004; Nair, 1999).

Resonance

As these sounds travel through the resonator, they are changed: Some sounds are amplified and some are muffled, depending on the resonator's shape. Different musical instruments have different resonating spaces and, therefore, different amplifying/muffling effects on the sound. We can analyze these changes with a tool called a spectral analyzer as seen in figure 6.1 (McCoy, 2004; Nair, 1999).

The slope from left to right in figure 6.1 is called the spectral slope. The peaks and valleys along the slope indicate amplitude variations of the corresponding overtones. The difference in spectral slope between instruments is what enables most people to aurally distinguish the difference between a violin and a trumpet playing the same note. Differences in spectral slope also account for two different singers sounding recognizably different when they are singing the same pitch (McCoy, 2004).

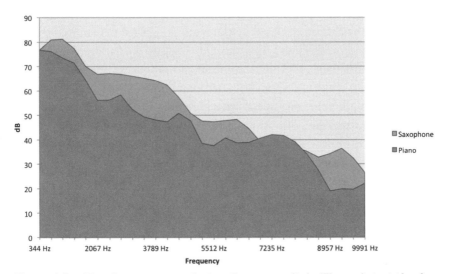

Figure 6.1. Two instruments playing the same pitch. The point at the far left is the fundamental frequency, and the peaks to the right are harmonics that have been amplified and attenuated by the instruments' resonator resulting in a specific timbre.

Because the throat and mouth act as the resonating tube in acoustic singing, changing their size and shape is the only option for making adjustments to timbre. In electronically amplified singing, the sound engineer can make electronic adjustments to amplify or reduce specific frequency ranges. For this and many other reasons we will discuss, it is vitally important for the rock singer to keep in mind how audio technology can affect the sound quality of the voice.

This section serves as a very brief introduction to the basics of sound enhancement. Thinking of sound as a collection and pattern of frequencies can be helpful to the rock singer for both improvements in vocal technique on an acoustic level and for ease of adjusting electronic sound. When applying this information to your own singing, first see what adjustments you can make in your own personal resonator within the bounds of healthy singing. Remember, if you try to replicate an electronically altered voice with your acoustic voice, you are attempting to accomplish the impossible. You can only replicate electronically enhanced singing with electronic equipment.

Signal Chain

The signal chain is the path an audio signal travels from the input to the output of a sound system. A voice enters the signal chain through the input, in most cases a microphone, which transforms acoustic energy into electrical impulses. The electrical impulses generated by the microphone are transmitted through a series of components that modify the signal before the speakers transform it back into acoustic energy. Audio engineers and producers understand the intricacies of these systems and can help make an infinite variety of alterations to your vocals. While some engineers strive to replicate the original sound source as accurately as possible, others use the capabilities of the system to alter the sound for artistic effect. Since more components and variations exist than can be discussed in just a few pages, this chapter will discuss only basic components and variations found in most systems and should serve as a starting point for understanding audio technology.

Microphones

Microphones transform the acoustic sound waves of the voice into electrical impulses. The three most common microphone types are "dynamic," "condenser," and "ribbon." Each offers advantages and disadvantages, depending on how you plan to use them. Before discussing the various types of microphones, let us first look at the basic specifications you will encounter when selecting a mic.

Frequency Response

"Frequency response" is a term used to define how accurately a microphone captures the tone quality of the signal. Each singer produces resonance variations that create unique tonal characteristics (see chapter 4). Alterations to the frequency output of a singer's voice can potentially alter its tone quality (Omori, Kacker, Carroll, Riley, and Blaugrund, 1996).

A "flat response" microphone captures the original signal with little to no signal alteration. These microphones are also sometimes called "measurement mics" since they are ideal for situations where accurate measurements of the audio signal are required. Most microphones that are not designated as "flat" have some type of attenuation or amplification, also known as "cut" or "boost," within the audio spectrum. For instance, the Shure SM58 microphone attenuates the signal drastically below 300 Hz and amplifies the signal in the 3 kHz range by 6 dB, the 5 kHz range by nearly 8 dB, and the 10 kHz range by approximately 6 dB (see figure 6.2). The Oktava 319 microphone

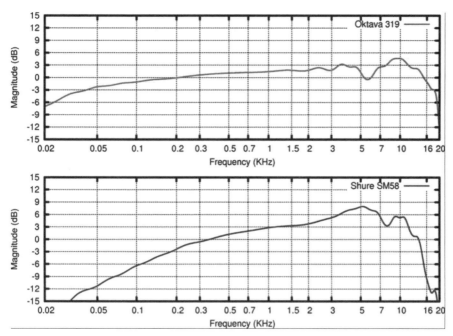

Figure 6.2. Example frequency response graphs for the Oktava 319 and the Shure SM58. Wikimedia Commons.

cuts the frequencies below 200 Hz while boosting everything above 300 Hz with nearly 5 dB between 7 kHz and 10 kHz (see figure 6.2). In practical terms, recording a bass singer with the Shure SM58 would drastically reduce the amplitude of the fundamental frequency, while the Oktava 319 would produce a slightly more consistent boost in the range of the singer's formant. Either of these options could be acceptable, depending on your needs, but the frequency response must be considered before making the recording.

Amplitude Response

The amplitude response of a microphone varies depending on the angle at which the singer is positioned in relation to the axis of the microphone. In order to visualize the amplitude response of a microphone at various angles, microphone manufacturers publish polar-pattern diagrams (also sometimes called a "directional pattern" or a "pickup pattern"). Polar pattern diagrams usually consist of six concentric circles divided into twelve equal sections. The center point of the microphone's diaphragm is labeled "0°" and is referred to as "on-axis," while the opposite side of the diagram is labeled "180°" and is described as "off-axis."

Although polar pattern diagrams appear in two dimensions, they actually represent a three-dimensional response to acoustic energy. Think of a round balloon as a real-life polar-pattern diagram. Position the tied end away from your mouth and the inflated end directly in front of your lips. In this position, you are singing on-axis at 0° with the tied end of the balloon being 180°, or off-axis. If you were to split the balloon in half vertically and horizontally (in relationship to your lips), the point at which those lines intersect would be the center point of the balloon. That imaginary center represents the diaphragm of the microphone. If you extended a 45° angle in any direction from the imaginary center and then drew a circle around the inside of the balloon following that angle, you would have a visualization of the three-dimensional application of the two-dimensional polar-pattern drawing.

The outermost circle of the diagram indicates that the sound pressure level (SPL) of the signal is transferred without any amplitude reduction, indicated in decibels (dB). Each of the inner circles represents a –5 dB reduction in the amplitude of the signal up to –25 dB. For example, look at figure 6.3. If the microphone's response circle crossed point A on this diagram, we would know that the strength of the signal received by the microphone at that point would be reduced by 10 dB. The examples in figures 6.4, 6.5, and 6.6 show the most common polar patterns that you will encounter.

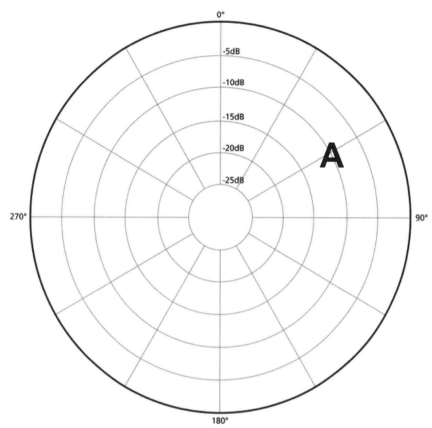

Figure 6.3. An example of a microphone polar-pattern diagram. Wikimedia Commons.

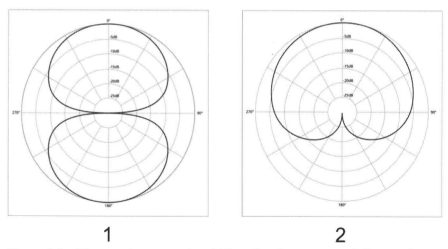

1

2

Figure 6.4. Diagram 1 represents a bidirectional pattern, and diagram 2 represents a cardioid pattern. Creative Commons.

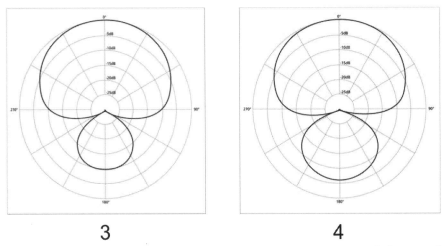

Figure 6.5. Diagram 3 represents a super-cardioid pattern, and diagram 4 represents a hyper-cardioid pattern. Creative Commons.

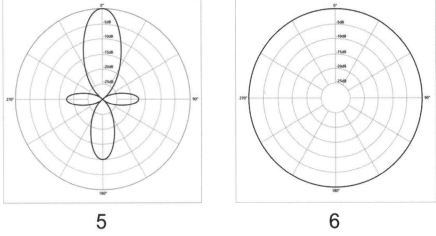

Figure 6.6. Diagram 5 represents a shotgun pattern, and diagram 6 represents an omnidirectional pattern. Creative Commons.

When you are using a microphone with a polar pattern other than omnidirectional (a pattern that responds to sound equally from all directions), you may encounter frequency-response fluctuations in addition to amplitude fluctuations. Cardioid microphones in particular are known for their tendency to boost lower frequencies at close proximity to the sound source, while attenuating those same frequencies as the distance between the sound source and the microphone increases. This is known as the "proximity effect." Some manufacturers will notate these frequency-response changes on their polar-pattern diagrams by using a combination of various lines and dashes alongside the amplitude-response curve.

Sensitivity

While sensitivity can be difficult to explain in technical terms without going into an in-depth discussion of electricity and electrical terminology, a simplified explanation should suffice for most singers. Manufacturers test microphones with a standardized 1 kHz tone at 94 dB in order to determine how sensitive the microphone's diaphragm will be to acoustic energy. Microphones with greater sensitivity can be placed farther from the sound source without adding excessive noise to the signal. Microphones with lower sensitivity will need to be placed closer to the sound source in order to keep excess noise at a minimum. When shopping for a microphone, you should audition several microphones, and plugged into the same soundboard, with the same volume level for each microphone. As you sing, you will notice that some models replicate your voice louder than others do. This change in output level is due to differences in each microphone's sensitivity. If your voice is naturally loud, you may prefer a microphone with lower sensitivity (one that requires more acoustic energy to respond). If you have a lighter voice, you may prefer a microphone with higher sensitivity (one that responds well to softer signals).

Microphone Types

When choosing a microphone, you will not only need to make a choice based on polar pattern (omnidirectional, cardioid, etc.) frequency response and sensitivity, but you will also need to choose a type of diaphragm. Singers will most often encounter three basic diaphragm types: dynamic, condenser, and ribbon.

Dynamic

Dynamic microphones use a Mylar diaphragm that moves within a magnetic field to turn acoustic vibrations into an electrical signal that can be amplified. The Shure SM-58 model provides the industry standard for live performance and is affordable, nearly indestructible, and easy to use. Dynamic microphones such as the Shure have a lower sensitivity than condenser microphones, which often makes them more successful at avoiding feedback. This feature makes them an excellent choice for rock singers performing on a loud stage, since the ability of this microphone to amplify sound dissipates as the distance between it and the sound source increases. In other words, this microphone is less likely to pick up other instruments on a loud stage. Softer voiced singers, such as crooners, who use dynamic microphones, must place their mouths extremely close to the microphone in order for it to respond to their singing. These singers often place their lips either almost or completely touching the metal screen. Even these singers will want to create some distance between themselves and the microphone at louder dynamic levels, but usually no more than two to four inches.

Condenser

Condenser microphones use two electrically charged thin metal plates separated by a layer of insulation to transform acoustic sound into an electrical signal. As acoustic vibrations send the anterior metal plate into motion, the distance between the two plates varies, which creates an electric signal that is then sent to the amplifier. These magnetic plates require a system called "phantom power." A component of the soundboard, phantom power sends a 48-volt power supply through the microphone cable to the microphone's diaphragm in order to power the magnetic field. If you are planning to use a condenser microphone, be sure that your sound system or recording console supplies phantom power (notated as "+48v"). Without a power source, standard condenser microphones will not work.

Some microphones on the market, called "electret condenser microphones" do not require phantom power. Usually found in smaller systems, electret microphones contain a permanently charged magnetic element within the diaphragm and thus eliminate the need for an external power source. Head-mounted microphones, laptop computers, and smart phones all utilize electret condenser microphones.

Recording engineers prefer condenser microphones for recording applications due to their high level of sensitivity. The higher sensitivity makes them a preferred choice in live performance by some jazz and folk singers, as well as in head-mounted microphones on Broadway stages. Using a condenser microphone, performers can sing at nearly inaudible acoustic levels and create a final tone that is intimate and earthy. While the same vocal effects can be produced with a dynamic microphone, they will not have the same clarity as those produced with a condenser microphone.

Ribbon

Ribbon microphones capture acoustic vibrations via a thin metal ribbon placed between two magnets. When the ribbon is set into motion by sound waves from the acoustic source, the magnetic field alters and creates an electric signal. Because of their fragility, early ribbon microphones did not enjoy the same popularity as condenser and dynamic microphones. Recently, advances in technology have enabled manufacturers to develop more durable products, which has led to a boost in their popularity. Use caution when connecting a ribbon microphone to your soundboard and never use phantom power. Phantom power will ruin a ribbon microphone and void the warranty.

Equalization (EQ)

Equalizers enable the audio engineer to alter the audio spectrum of the sound source and make tone adjustments with a few simple tweaks on an equalizer. Equalizers come in three main types: shelf, parametric, and graphic.

Shelf

Shelf equalizers cut or boost the uppermost and lowermost frequencies of an audio signal in a straight line (see figure 6.7). While this style of equalization is not very useful for fine-tuning a singer's tone quality, it can be very

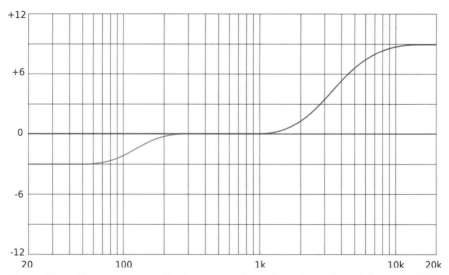

Figure 6.7. Frequency amplitude curves show the affect of applying a shelf EQ to an audio signal. Wikimedia Commons.

effective in removing room noise. For example, if an air-conditioner creates a 60 Hz hum in the recording studio, the shelf can be set at 65 Hz, with a steep slope. This setting eliminates frequencies below 65 Hz and effectively removes the hum from the recording.

Parametric

Parametric units simultaneously adjust multiple frequencies of the audio spectrum that fall within a defined parameter. The engineer selects a center frequency and adjusts the width of the bell curve surrounding that frequency by adjusting the "Q" (see figure 6.8). They then boost or cut the frequencies within the bell curve to alter the audio spectrum. Parametric controls take up minimal space on a soundboard and offer sufficient control for most situations. Therefore most live performance soundboards have parametric EQs on each individual channel. With the advent of digital workstations, engineers can now use computer software to fine-tune the audio quality of each individual channel in both live and recording studio settings without taking up any additional physical space. However, many engineers still prefer to use parametric controls during a live performance since they are usually sufficient and are easier to adjust mid-performance.

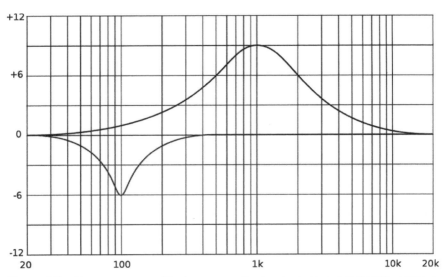

Figure 6.8. Frequency amplitude curves display two parametric EQ settings. The top curve represents a boost of +8 dB set at 1 kHz with a relatively large bell curve—a low Q. The lower curve represents a high Q set at 100 Hz with a cut of -6 dB. Wikimedia Commons.

Graphic

Graphic equalizers allow engineers to identify a specific frequency for boost or cut with a fixed-frequency bandwidth. For example, a ten-band equalizer gives the audio engineer the opportunity to adjust ten specific frequencies that typically include (in Hz): 31, 63, 125, 250, 500, 1 k, 2 k, 4 k, 8 k, and 16 k. Graphic equalizers are often one of the final elements of the signal chain preceding only the amplifier and speakers. In this position, they can be used to adjust the overall sound quality of the entire mix.

Utilizing Equalization

Opinions on the usage of equalization vary among engineers. Some more conservative engineers only use equalization to remove or reduce frequencies that were not a part of the original sound signal. Others will use EQ only if adjusting microphone placement fails to yield acceptable results. Some engineers prefer a more processed sound and may use equalization liberally to intentionally change the vocal quality of the singer. For instance, if the singer's voice sounds dull, the engineer could add "ring" or "presence" to the voice by boosting the equalizer in the 2 k–10 kHz range. Using equalization to its full effect, a singer can easily avoid constriction while still being able to alter the tone quality toward a brighter or darker timbre as needed in the studio or live performance.

Compression

Singers can create sounds that feature extremes in both frequency and amplitude levels, which can prove problematic for the sound team since dramatic volume shifts require adjustments at the soundboard. To help solve this problem, engineers often use compression. Compressors limit the output of a sound source by a specified ratio. The user sets the maximum acceptable amplitude level for the output, or the "threshold," and then sets a ratio to reduce the output once it surpasses the threshold. The typical ratio for a singer is usually between 3:1 and 5:1. A 4:1 ratio indicates that for every 4 dB beyond the threshold level, the output will only increase by 1 dB. For example, if the singer went 24 dB beyond the threshold with a 4:1 ratio, the output would only be 6 dB beyond the threshold level (see figure 6.9).

Adjusting the sound via microphone technique can provide some of the same results as compression and is preferable for the experienced artist, but compression tends not only to be more consistent but also gives the

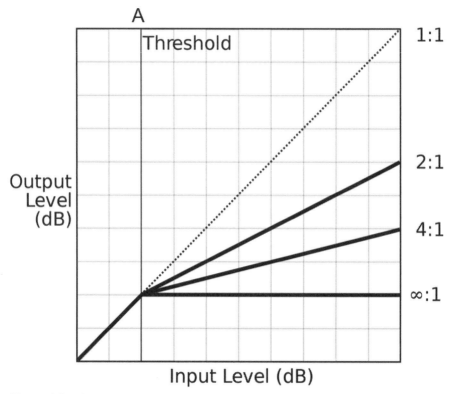

Figure 6.9. Graph representing the effects of various compression ratios applied to a signal. The 1:1 angle represents no compression; the other ratios represent the effect of compression on an input signal with the threshold set at line A. Wikimedia Commons.

singer freedom to focus on performing and telling a story. The additional artistic freedom provided by compression benefits music theater performers, singers using head-mounted microphones in performance, and singers new to performing with a microphone. Compression can also be helpful for classical singers whose dynamic abilities, while impressive live, are often difficult to record in a manner that allows for consistent listening levels through a stereo system.

Multiband Compression

If a standard compressor causes unacceptable alterations to the tone quality, engineers can turn to a multiband compressor. Rather than affecting the entire spectrum of sound, multiband compressors allow the engineer to isolate a specific frequency range within the audio signal and then set an individual compression setting for that frequency range. For example, if a singer creates a dramatic boost in the 4 kHz range every time they sing above an A4, a multiband compressor can be used to limit the amplitude of the signal in only that part of the voice. By setting a 3:1 ratio in the 4 kHz range at a threshold that corresponds to the amplitude peaks that appear when the performer sings above A4, the engineer can eliminate vocal "ring" from the sound on only the offending notes while leaving the rest of the signal untouched. These units are available for both live and studio use and can be a great alternative to compressing the entire signal.

Reverb and Delay

Reverb is one of the easier effects for singers to identify. An audience experiences natural reverberation when they hear the direct signal from the singer, and then milliseconds later, they hear the voice again as it reflects off the sidewalls of the performance hall. Many CCM venues and recording studios are designed to inhibit natural reverb. Without at least a little reverb added to the sound, even the best singer can sound harsh and even amateurish. Early reverb units transmitted the audio signal through a metal spring, which added supplementary vibrations to the sound. While some engineers still use spring reverb to obtain a specific effect, most now use digital units to add reverb. Common settings on digital reverb units include wet/dry, bright/dark, and options for delay time. The wet/dry control adjusts the amount of direct signal (dry) and the amount of reverberated signal (wet). The bright/dark control helps simulate the effects of various surfaces within a natural space. For instance, harder surfaces such as stone reflect high frequency tones and create a brighter tone quality while softer surfaces such as wood reflect lower frequency tones and create a darker tone quality. The delay time, which is usually adjustable from milliseconds to seconds, adjusts the amount of time between when the dry signal and wet signal reach the ear. Engineers can transform almost any room into a chamber music hall or concert stadium, simply by adjusting these settings.

Delay is an extreme version of reverb. Whereas reverb blends the wet and dry signals together to replicate a natural space, delay purposefully separates the two signals. With delay, you will hear the original note first and then a digitally produced repeat of the note several milliseconds to whole seconds later. The delayed note may be heard one time or multiple times, and the timing of those repeats can be adjusted to match the tempo of the song.

Auto-Tune

Auto-tune, first used in studios as a useful way to clean up minor imperfections in otherwise perfect performances, is now an industry standard that many artists use, even if they are not willing to admit it (WENN, 2012). Auto-tune has gained a bad reputation in the last few years, and whether or not you agree with its use, it is a reality in today's market. If you do not understand how to use it properly, you could end up sounding like T-Pain.[1]

Both Antares and Melodyne have developed auto-tune technology for both "auto" and "graphical" editing. "Auto" auto-tune allows the engineer to set specific parameters for pitch correction that are then computer controlled. "Graphical" auto-tune tracks the pitch in the selected area of a recording and plots the fundamental frequency on a linear graph. The engineer can then select specific notes for pitch correction. They can also drag selected pitches to a different frequency, add or reduce vibrato, and change formant frequencies above the fundamental. To simplify, the "auto" function makes general corrections while the "graphic" function makes specific corrections. The "auto" setting is usually used to achieve a specific effect (for instance, "I Believe" by Cher), while the "graphic" setting is used to correct small imperfections in a recorded performance.

Digital Voice Processors

Digital voice processors are still relatively new to the market and have yet to gain widespread usage among singers. While there are several brands of vocal effects processors available, the industry leader as of this printing is a company called TC-Helicon. TC-Helicon manufactures several different units that range from consumer to professional grade. TC-Helicon's premiere performer-controlled unit is called the VoiceLive 3. The VoiceLive 3 incorporates over twelve vocal effects, eleven guitar effects, and a multitrack looper with 250 factory presets and 250 memory slots for user presets. The VoiceLive 3 puts the effects at the singer's feet in a programmable stomp box that also includes phantom power, MIDI in/out, a USB connection, guitar input, and monitor out. Onboard vocal effects include equalization, compression, reverb, and "auto" auto-tune. The unit also offers µMod (an adjustable voice modulator), a doubler (for thickening the lead vocal), echo, delay, reverb, and several other specialized effects (VoiceLive 3).

One of the most impressive features of digital voice processors is the ability to add computer-generated harmonies to the lead vocal. After the user sets the musical key, the processor identifies the fundamental frequency of each note sung. The computer then adds digitized voices at designated intervals above and below the lead singer. If you are using the VoiceLive 3, you can plug your instrument into the unit, and the processor will determine key-appropriate harmonies for you. The unit also offers the option to program each individual song, with multiple settings for every verse, chorus, and bridge.

The Basics of Live Sound Systems

Live sound systems come in a variety of sizes, from small practice units to state-of-the-art stadium rigs. Most singers only need a basic knowledge of the components commonly found in systems that have one to eight inputs. Units beyond that size usually require an independent sound engineer and are beyond the scope of this chapter.

Following the microphone, the first element in the signal chain is usually the mixer. Basic portable mixers provide controls for equalization, volume level, auxiliary (usually used for effects such as reverb and compression), and on some units, controls for built-in digital effects processors. Powered mixers combine an amplifier with a basic mixer, providing a compact solution for those who do not need a complex system. Since unpowered mixers do not provide amplification, you will need to add a separate amplifier to power this system.

The powered mixer or amplifier then connects to speaker cabinets, which contain a "woofer" and a "tweeter." The "woofer" is a large round speaker that handles the bass frequencies, while the "tweeter" is a horn-shaped speaker that handles the treble frequencies. The crossover separates high and low frequencies and sends them to the appropriate speaker (woofer or tweeter). Speaker cabinets can be either active or passive. Passive cabinets require a powered mixer or an amplifier in order to operate. Active cabinets have an amplifier built in and do not require an external amplifier.

Monitors

Arguably the element most important to a singer in a live sound system, the monitor is simply a speaker that faces a performer. Onstage volume levels can vary considerably, with drummers often producing sound levels as high as 120 dB. Those volume levels make it nearly impossible for singers to receive natural acoustic feedback while performing. Monitors can improve aural feedback and help reduce the temptation to oversing. Powered monitors offer the same advantages as powered speaker cabinets and can be a great option for amplification when singers are practicing. They are also good to have around as a backup plan in case you arrive at a venue and discover they do not supply monitors. In-ear monitors offer another option for performers and are especially useful for those who frequently move around the stage.

The threat of hearing damage should be a concern for all musicians. Hearing damage starts at exposure to 80 dB, but many bands surpass that level, reaching 100 to 110 dB on stage. Hearing damage is irreversible, so do your own research and take steps to protect yourself.

How Pros Use Electronic Enhancement

Three main approaches to vocal processing include doing as little processing as possible, using processing to enhance, and finally, using processing for effect. The first approach makes the fewest adjustments possible, using microphone placement alone to capture the natural sound of the singer. The engineer may slightly tweak the equalizer, add a hint of reverb, and use minimal compression but generally tries to leave the sound as true to the live acoustic sound as possible, flaws and all (for example John Cougar Mellencamp's album *No Better Than This*). The second approach uses vocal processing to enhance the natural tone quality of the voice and correct slight imperfections. The engineer may use equalization, reverb, delay, compression, and graphical auto-tune to correct slight mistakes so that the final product has a cleaner but still natural sound (for example Joss Stone's *Soul Sessions: Volume 2*, discussed below). In the third approach, the engineer and the singer consciously decide to use vocal processing for effect, adding liberal equalization, reverb, delay, compression, auto-tune, and other vocal effects to create a unique and sometimes unnatural tone quality (for example Foster the People's track "Pumped Up Kicks"). These decisions on how much processing is acceptable are part of the artistic process that helps give each artist a unique sound. To help you gain a better understanding of the possibilities, let's look at a few recordings and the approach used to capture the artist.

Joss Stone

Engineer Steve Greenwell of S-Curve Records recorded Joss Stone's *Soul Sessions: Volume 2*, which was released in July of 2012. Paul Tingen of *Sound on*

Sound interviewed Greenwell about the process behind recording the album. To begin, both Greenwell and Stone listened to approximately fifty different songs and chose the best selections for Stone to cover. The band then experimented with different keys until they found the best one for Stone's voice. When it came time to record, Stone was positioned inside an isolated vocal booth, while the rest of the band played live in the main room. The goal was to reproduce the feeling of a live performance. Stone sang each song straight through four to five times. She sang a few of the takes conservatively and then a few times full-out. (Greenwell tried to record no more than ten takes a day in order to prevent Stone's voice from getting tired.) Greenwell and Stone then listened to the takes and selected the portions from each take they liked. Together, they then edited them and rerecorded small sections, if it was necessary, to fix any mistakes. Finally, Stone went back into the recording booth and sang her own background vocals (Tingen, 2013b).

Stone's vocals were recorded with a Telefunken Elam 251 microphone, a vintage tube condenser mic, which has a high level of sensitivity and adds warmth, due to the vacuum tube design. The microphone signal was then sent to a Neve 1073 vintage equalizer (to make adjustments to the audio spectrum), an Avalon 737 tube compressor (to even out her dynamic levels), and then a Teletronix LA-2A leveling amplifier (another dynamics processor). The vocals were enhanced with Audio Ease's Altiverb plug-in and Sound Toy's Echo Boy (to add reverb and echo). The background vocals were processed with the Waves De-esser (to remove sibilant consonants such as /s/, /z/, and /sh/), the Bomb Factory BF76 Classic 1176 compressor emulator plug-in (for dynamic control), and the FilterBank equalization plug-in (for equalization adjustments) (Tingen, 2013b). As you can see, even though the goal was to capture a natural sound, the engineer still used a generous amount of processing in order to successfully transfer a natural sound to a digital recording.

Fun

Engineer Jeff Bhasker took two weeks to record and mix the group's four-minute-long hit song "We Are Young." Building the track from the bottom up, Bhasker first created a synthesized beat with an Akai MPC3000, then added bass with his Moog and Roland Juno 106 synthesizers. He then added vocals and piano. Lead singer Nate Ruess overdubbed his vocals repeatedly until there were forty-five total vocal tracks. Phil Spector first created this "wall of sound" approach in the 1960s by layering multiple takes by the same artist (Szatmary, 1996). The technique creates massive and larger-than-life instrumental and vocal parts and is still used today.

After the tracks were recorded, Bhasker used several effects to enhance the vocals. The lead vocals were treated with Waves Renaissance EQ and compression (to alter the audio spectrum and smooth out dynamic levels). Reverb and delay were added with the Audio Ease Altiverb, a digital plug-in that uses reverb patterns from actual spaces, including the Sydney Opera House, Wembley stadium, and the ancient caves of Malta (Altiverb 7). The backing vocals were processed with Waves MetaFlanger phaser effect (an effect that creates random peaks and drops in the audio spectrum) and the Waves Maserati VX1 plug-in to add air and presence (equalization adjustments in the 12–14 kHz range for "air" and 3–5 kHz for presence) (Tingen, 2013a). Clearly, reproduction of a natural sound was not the goal. Rather, the enhancements create specific effects as an artistic choice. Singers must understand that it is impossible to replicate the sound of forty-five simultaneous tracks without the assistance of digital enhancement.

Paul McCartney

David Kahne recorded McCartney's 2001 album *Driving Rain*. In 2007, Matt Hurwitz interviewed Kahne for MixOnline.com and uncovered some of the secrets behind McCartney's album. Kahne used Violet Design microphones, Federal AM-864 and Fairchild 670 tube compressors/limiters (for dynamic control), and recorded the tracks with Cubase Studio 4 (digital recording software). The album was not recorded with the same overall approach on each track but changed with the needs of each song. For example, on "You Tell Me," the lead vocal was recorded in one sing-through with background vocals performed by the band members. On "Feet in the Clouds," Kahne stacked thirty-six tracks of McCartney's vocals, then used Melodyne software to clean up the pitch while also removing vibrato from some of the tracks (Hurwitz, 2007). On this album, the listener will find a combination of simplistic and complex recording techniques.

Live Performance Effects

New technology makes it possible to carry many of the effects previously limited to the recording studio into live performance. Here's a look at how some of the pros set up their rigs.

Green Day

Lead singer Billie Joe Armstrong performs live with a Telefunken M80 dynamic microphone running into a Maselec MPL-2 high-frequency limiter that is often used as a de-esser (Maselec MPL-2). Finally, the signal runs through a Distressor, an ultra-high-quality digital compressor that emulates analogue units without distorting the sound (Distressor model EL8), which outputs to a John Hardy 990 preamp (to boost the signal) (Jennings, 2013). Armstrong's rig is relatively simple, and all of the components are used only to enhance the natural sound of his voice.

Paul McCartney

When Paul McCartney went on tour in 2011, he put together a set list of over fifty songs that spanned the entirety of his career. Paul "Pab" Boothroyd took advantage of digital technology to perfect McCartney's sound. Digital boards allowed the engineer to pre-program unique equalization, reverb, delay, and compression settings that could be instantly changed with the press of a button. In order to mimic the tone quality of McCartney's voice when each song was originally recorded, Boothroyd pre-programmed tailored-effect chains for each song. With a click of a button, McCartney could sound youthful while performing "Yesterday" or more mature when performing "From a Lover to a Friend" (Benzuly, 2011).

Mastodon

Mastodon, a heavy metal band from Atlanta, Georgia, mixes clean vocals with growls and screams in its recordings. To replicate the recording studio sounds, engineer Rob Lightner used a wide range of gear. The mixing board was a Yamaha PM5D-RH, which includes X-hall reverb, X-hall plate reverb, Voice Doubler (an effect that replicates Phil Spector's "wall of sound" approach), and Reverb Flanger effects (that add sweeping/ pulsing). Outboard effect units include the TC-Helicon D-2, a unit that produces vocal delays with specific rhythmic figures (D-Two), and the M-One, a processor that combines reverb, delay, chorus (a combination of a clean signal with two or more duplicated versions that are slightly delayed and out of pitch), a flanger (a combination of a dry signal and a delayed signal whose delay changes over time), and compression (M-One XL). He also uses the Yamaha SPX-990, which includes harmony, phaser, distortion (an effect that emulates a distorted electric guitar), delay, chorus, flanger, pitch change, and pan effects that shift the signal between the left and right speakers (SPX-990). By combining these units, Lightner is able to recreate the brutal otherworldly vocal sounds of the albums to keep the band's fans satisfied night after night (Jennings, 2011). If done well, this can allow a singer to use conservative vocal production and sound as if they are pushing their vocal limits.

Backing Tracks

Another way bands can reproduce the sounds captured in the recording studio is by the use of backing tracks. Backing tracks are audio files from the original recording session that are digitally synced with the live performers. With the development of reliable in-ear monitors, the use of backing tracks has become quite common. When bands record in a studio, they often synchronize with a click-track to maintain a steady tempo. In live performance, the click-track is piped only into the drummer's in-ear monitor. As long as the drummer stays with the click-track, the prerecorded tracks can be seamlessly mixed with the live instruments.

Microphone Technique

The microphone is part of the rock singer's instrument, and just as there are techniques that improve singing there are techniques that improve microphone use. Understanding what a microphone does is only the first step to using it successfully. Once you understand how a microphone works, you need hands-on experience.

Practicing with a Microphone

The best way to learn microphone technique is to experiment with one. As discussed above, each microphone has unique properties that can affect tone quality. Working with a condenser microphone is different from working with a dynamic mic. The same is true for microphones of different sensitivity levels. If you don't already have a microphone and amplification system, you can purchase a simple setup at a relatively low cost through online vendors, such as Sweetwater.com and MusiciansFriend.com. A dynamic microphone and a powered monitor are enough to get you started. If you would like to add a digital voice processor, Digitech and TC-Helicon both sell entry-level models that will significantly improve the tonal quality of your system.

- Position the microphone directly in front of your mouth, no further than one centimeter away. Sustain a comfortable pitch and slowly move the microphone away from your lips. Listen to how the sound quality changes. When the mic is close to your lips, you should notice that the sound is louder and has more bass response. As you move away from the mic, there will be a noticeable loss in volume and the tone will become brighter.

- Next, try sustaining a pitch while rotating the handle down. You should notice that the sound quality changes in a fashion similar to when you moved the mic away from your lips.

- Now try singing breathy with the microphone close to your lips. How little effort can you get away with and still sound good?

- Try singing bright, at a medium volume level, with a closed mouth and spread lips, with the microphone only one to three centimeters from your mouth. In this position you should be able to create aggressive sounds without oversinging.

- Next, cup both of your hands around the microphone and then sing into your hands. Try using a vocal fry in this position and experiment with death metal–style sounds. You should notice that the cupping of your hands increases the bass response and helps boost your vocal power without excess effort.

- Also, experiment with variations in your diction. Because the microphone amplifies everything, you may need to under-pronounce certain consonants when singing on a mic.

Conclusion

It's easy to get overwhelmed by all the technical information. Since this is primarily an overview, seek other resources to increase your understanding of these technical elements. Many great explanations are available online and can help clarify some of these difficult concepts. Check out your local library, as well, for any books about audio recording or live sound. Most importantly—experiment. The more you play around with equipment on your own, the better you will understand it.

Note

1. For example, listen to T-Pain's track "Buy You a Drank (Shawty Snappin')."

Bibliography

Altiverb 7. Retrieved from http://www.audioease.com/Pages/Altiverb/ [retrieved October 28, 2013].

Benzuly, S. (September 1, 2011). Sir Paul McCartney tour profile. MixOnline.com. Retrieved from http://mixonline.com/live/tourprofiles/sir_paul_mccartney_tour/.

Distressor model EL8. Retrieved from http://www.empiricallabs.com/distressor .html [retrieved November 4, 2013].

D-Two. Retrieved from http://www.tcelectronic.com/d-two/ [retrieved November 4, 2013].

Eskow, G. (April 1, 2008). New York's Met in HD. MixOnline.com. Retrieved from http://mixonline.com/post/features/audio_new_yorks_met/.

Federman, J., & Ricketts, T. (2008). Preferred and minimum acceptable listening levels for musicians while using floor and in-ear monitors. *Journal of Speech, Language, and Hearing Research*, 5, 147–59.

Hurwitz, M. (October 1, 2007). Memory: Track by track. MixOnline.com. Retrieved from http://mixonline.com/recording/tracking/audio_paul_mccartney/.

Jennings, S. (May 1, 2013). All access: Green Day. MixOnline.com. Retrieved from http://mixonline.com/live/tourprofiles/all_access_green_day//index.html.

Jennings, S. (December 1, 2011). Mastodon all access. MixOnline.com Retrieved from http://mixonline.com/live/tourprofiles/mastodon_all_access/.

Lockheart, P. (2003). A history of early microphone singing, 1925–1939: American mainstream popular singing at the advent of electronic amplification. *Popular Music and Society*, 26(3), 367–85. doi: 10.1080/0300776032000117003.

Maselec MPL-2. Retrieved from http://vintageking.com/Maselec-MPL-2 [retrieved October 29, 2013].

McCoy, S. (2004). *Your voice: An inside view.* Princeton: Inside View.

McCracken, A. (1999). "God's gift to us girls": Crooning, gender, and the re-creation of American popular song, 1928–1933. *American Music*, 14(4), 365–95. Retrieved from http://www.jstor.org/stable/3052656.

M-One XL. Retrieved from http://www.tcelectronic.com/m-one-xl/ [retrieved November 3, 2013].

Nair, G. (1999). *Voice-tradition and technology: A state-of-the-art studio.* San Diego: Singular Publishing Group.

Omori, K., Kacker, A., Carroll, L. M., Riley, W. D., & Blaugrund, S. M. (1996). Singing power ratio: Quantitative evaluation of singing voice quality. *Journal of Voice, 10*(3), 228–35. Retrieved from http://www.ncbi.nlm.nih.gov/pubmed/8865093.

SPX-990. Retrieved from http://usa.yamaha.com/products/live_sound/processors/spx990/?mode=model [retrieved November 3, 2013].

Szatmary, D. P. (1996). *A time to rock: A social history of rock and roll.* New York, NY: Schirmer Books.

Tingen, P. (2013a). Jeff Bhasker on mixing "We Are Young." *Sound on Sound.* Retrieved from http://www.soundonsound.com/sos/oct12/articles/it-1012.htm. (Original work published October 2012).

Tingen, P. (2013b). Steve Greenwell discusses Joss Stone. *Sound on Sound.* Retrieved from http://www.soundonsound.com/sos/nov12/articles/it-1112.htm (Original work published November 2012).

VoiceLive 3. Retrieved from http://www.tc-helicon.com/products/voicelive-3/ [retrieved February 1, 2014].

WENN.com. (July 4, 2012). Bieber admits studio vocal help. *Toronto Sun.* Toronto. Retrieved from http://www.torontosun.com/2012/07/04/bieber-admits-studio -vocal-help.

CHAPTER SEVEN
WHO ARE YOU? WHO-WHO, WHO-WHO?

To be yourself in a world that is constantly trying to make you something else is the greatest accomplishment.

—Ralph Waldo Emerson

In chapter 5 we talked about the vocabulary of vocal style and how different artists apply that vocabulary. While musical language is important, artistry requires more than great technical skills. Songs communicate the human experience by sharing stories of loss, hope, joy, grief, love, anger, and countless other life moments. They connect people of diverse backgrounds by sharing common experiences that audiences can easily identify with. However, if the performance is inhibited by a performer's emotional wall, the song can easily come across as cold and heartless, leaving the listener with little more than a catchy tune and rhyming words. Even though it can be difficult to expose your soul on the stage in front of others, this business demands it.

Actors are professional storytellers who have codified techniques, both for exploring their deepest inner thoughts and feelings and for using those thoughts and feelings to make a connection with their audience. When I first begin to talk about "acting" with rock performers, a look of discomfort often flashes across their faces. Whether they associate acting with being fake or with an overly "emo" style, the rock singer may not be eager to apply acting techniques to a performance. However, if we remember that the most successful rock songs make an authentic connection with a listener, using proven techniques for achieving that purpose seems wise.

Unlike the acting training of beginners that uses improvisation games and other presentational style exercises to help them break out of their shells and feel comfortable on a stage in front of others, advanced acting training avoids that kind of insincere and overly active performance. Professional actors bring their own life experiences into their work and allow those experiences to influence their creative process. When preparing to perform a script, they read it, analyze it, and make connections between the character and themselves. Many of the tools used by professional actors allow rock singers to make the same kinds of connections. This chapter will help you create a more authentic and engaging performance by applying tools that actors commonly use when preparing for a role.

Discovering Your Artistic Voice

Personal life experiences form the lenses through which we see life, and they influence our interpretations of what we see, feel, and hear. A child who grew up in housing projects will likely see the value of a college education differently from a child who grew up in Beverly Hills, and each would sing the lyrics "we don't need no education" from Pink Floyd's "Brick in the Wall" differently. Some performers access their life experiences easily and naturally bring them into the performing process, while others need guidance to help bring their artistic message into focus. Answer the following questions:

- What has been the most exciting event of your life thus far?

- What has been the most disappointing event of your life thus far?

- What do you want people to know about you that they may not see on the surface?

- What is your greatest wish? Your greatest fear?

- Do you have strong social or political beliefs that you want to share with others?

- Do you want your music to move your listeners to do something (for instance, move them to stand up for a cause, rebel, find love, etc.)?

- What does the way you dress tell others about you? Is that how you want to dress onstage, or do you want to show a different side of yourself when you perform?

After you have answered the questions, look for an underlying theme that propels everything you do in life. This kind of deep inner exploration can be difficult, but it is essential when trying to develop your artistic voice. Here is an example of what I am looking for. Casey, female, age 21:

- Most exciting life event—meeting her half-sister.

- Most disappointing life event—losing her high school sweetheart in a fatal car crash.

- What she wants other people to know—that beneath her tough exterior is an aching heart.

- Greatest wish—to meet her father.

- Greatest fear—that she never will meet her father.

- Beliefs that she wants to share with others—stop the hate and love one another.

- She wants her music to compel others to—commit themselves to their families and their partners.

- The way she dresses says—I don't care about what you think.

If you read carefully, you will notice two underlying themes—fear and loss. Casey has lost her father (by never meeting him) and has lost a lover due to a tragic accident. She is fearful of never meeting her father and she is fearful of letting others in, which is why she dresses the way that she does and admits that others may see a tough exterior. Those viewpoints likely drive her in everything she does. If she were to sing "Every Breath You Take," and she drew from the inner-self that she identified above, she would likely perform an emotionally powerful rendition of the song that differs significantly from the version performed by Sting. However, if she ignored her deepest feelings and only sang the words superficially, the performance would come off as disconnected and insincere.

Take your time to think about the questions above and to answer them honestly. For some, the answers will come easily. For others, it will take time. The answers are only for you; no one else needs to know what you discover. See if you can identify underlying themes that influence the choices that you make in your everyday life. Then think about how those underlying themes influence you as an artist and how you can draw from them in performance. As you work through the rest of this chapter, refer back to the answers to your questions above and make sure that your choices are reflective of the authentic you. When you know the underlying forces that drive your creative process, it becomes easier to pass on songs that do not align with what you have to say.

Visualizing

Visualizing helps an imaginary scenario become more realistic. Try this exercise and use an audio or video recorder, so you can review your work. First, I want you to think of a dream vacation destination that you have never visited and deliver a thirty-second sales pitch on why I should go there. Don't think about it, just pick a destination and start talking. Next, I want you to pick a vacation destination that you have visited before and know well. Repeat the same exercise and give a thirty-second sales pitch. Review the recordings. Did you notice a difference between the two? When I do this exercise in a presentation, I always see the same differences. The description of the dream vacation lacks specificity. For instance, when describing the dream vacation, the participant may say, "Rome has great Italian food, everything is old, and you can see the Pope." However, when describing a favorite destination that they have actually visited, the description is much different. "Petoskey is right next to the Little Traverse Bay. The air is crisp and fresh, the water glistens in the sun. The downtown is full of little clothing shops and cafes." Notice the difference? The first is generic. The second is very specific and you can feel the excitement in it just by reading the words because the person giving the pitch has actually been to Petoskey and can immediately visualize it. Since they have never been to Rome, they cannot immediately visualize the experience.

Visualizing brings a story to life in your mind and makes it real for you. Learning how to make the delivery of every song as full of detail and excitement as Petoskey is vital if you want to consistently capture your audience's attention. When trying to visualize the story of a song, it can be helpful to think about the music video you would direct, rather than the music video someone else has already produced. Work through the following process for each of your songs:

- Using a blank sheet of paper, sketch where the story of your song takes place. You can also look for related pictures online and attach them to the sketches.

- After you have created a sketch, close your eyes and imagine walking through the space that you have drawn. What time of day is it? Is it light or dark? Is it cold or warm? What is above you? What is below you? What surrounds you? If there are other people in the space, where are they? Is the space inviting or oppressive? Do you want to be there or do you want to leave? Write out a short narrative of your answers to the questions.

Getting Specific

Now that you have a better idea of where your song takes place, get specific with the details about the exact situation. Answer the following questions:

- Who are you talking to? It is not enough to say, "My friend"; you need to define who that friend is and use their name. Sometimes we sing songs to ourselves. If that is the case, decide if you are talking to your current self, a better version of you, or a lesser version of you.

- Why do you need to sing this song? Examples: "I need to stop my lover from leaving me." "I need to win his or her heart." "I need to destroy these memories."

- What is your goal in singing this song? Examples: I want to make him or her say, "I love you." "I want to make them surrender." "I want to punish them."

- How will you know if you succeed? Examples: "I want him to kiss me." "I want them to leave." "I want her to push me."

Finding Active Verbs

Now that we have identified where this song takes place and to whom you are singing, it is time to develop actions that will help you get what you want out of this song. Russian acting teacher Michael Chekhov developed a "psychological gesture" technique that many actors use to find the underlying action of a scene or song. Chekhov believed that a desire to do a physical action was behind every line an actor read. For example, if I tell an annoying salesman to get off my front porch, I may have an underlying desire to grab him by his shirt collar and physically throw him off the porch. However, I choose not to complete that gesture because it would get me arrested. Refusing to follow through on the gesture doesn't mean that the desire does not exist within my being. Instead of physically grabbing and throwing him, I may use a forceful hand gesture that belies my internal desire to act. Chekhov believed that exploring various actions and connecting them to the text would create a more realistic performance (Brestoff, 1996). The Michael Chekhov Acting Studio in New York City suggests five basic gestures: push, pull, throw, lift, crush (Petit, 2004) that I find especially useful for helping rock singers connect to the underlying action of their songs. The five movements are as follows:

Push. Take a step forward while using both hands and arms to push forward as if moving a heavy object.

Pull. Use both hands to grab onto an imaginary rope, take a big step back, and pull.

Throw. This is the same as pitching a baseball.

Lift. Do this action with both hands and arms. Bend down to the floor and lift your arms and hands upward toward the ceiling, like lifting a heavy box over your head.

Crush. Use both of your hands in front of the center of your body and pretend to crush a soda can.

Let's apply these actions to the lyric "I said I loved you but I lied." Let's assume we have already performed the visualization work above and decided on the scenario as follows:

- Who are you talking to?

  You are singing this song in a large and moderately noisy coffee shop, with patrons sitting at tables in front, behind, and to both sides of you. It is in the middle of the day and it is cold outside. You have decided that you are singing this song to a partner whom you have been dating for three months.

- Why do you need to sing this song?

One week ago you said you loved them, and yesterday you found out they were making out with someone else at a party.

- What is your goal in singing this song?

  You need to sing this song to end this relationship.

- How will you know if you succeed?

  You will know you succeed when they get up from the table and leave the coffee shop.

Say "I said I loved you but I lied" several times with each action—push, pull, throw, tear, lift, and crush. Which action seems to work best for you? Since each person will respond differently to the actions, there is no "correct" answer. Choose an action that you think is the best fit for the situation and the text and repeat it several times. Then drop the motion and speak the text. You should feel a deeper inner connection to the text than before doing this work. When you add your singing voice to this work, you should find that you sing differently as well. If you are singing with a mic and a stand, you can pull, lift, and push the stand while singing but also allow your chosen action to influence your musical choices. If you are playing the piano and you have selected pull, then imagine pulling the chords out of the piano as you sing. If you selected "crush" and you are a guitarist, then crush your power chords.

Choose one of your own songs and do this exercise with each line of text. Write the action verbs that you think best fit the lyrics on your lyric sheet or in your music. Sing the song while doing the actions several times until you have memorized the actions along with the words. While you are doing this part of the exercise, allow any emotions that naturally occur as a result of the movement to become integrated into your work. Finally, drop the motions and sing the song. If you've spent enough time actually doing the action, you will notice a natural inclination to physically move in a manner that is appropriate to what you are saying.

Applying and Experimenting

Growing as an artist requires you to perform as often as possible to receive and react to feedback. If you are already performing on a regular basis, the advice below may not apply to you. However, if live performance is still relatively new to you, the following information may help you make the move from performing in your garage to performing on a professional stage.

Cover Songs

If you are not already an experienced songwriter, creating your own work can be frustrating. Many beginning performers do not understand the inherent value of covering the songs of other artists and think the only way to be authentic is to create their own work. Remember that in the earliest days of rock, many artists found success reworking the songs of other performers. Elvis's first hit, "That's Alright Mama," was a cover song. Pat Boone covered songs by performers such as Fats Domino and Little Richard. Recently, singers such as Karmin, Boyce Avenue, and Sam Tsui have taken advantage of YouTube to make a name for themselves as cover artists.

First, find a few songs you really like and start experimenting with variations. Try speeding the song up, slowing it down, singing it light and airy or big and belty. Experiment with vocal improvisation as discussed in chapter 5. If you play an instrument, experiment with the rhythm and instrumentation. Add a drum machine beat or substitute hand percussion for the drums. Try using a piano instead of a rock band or substitute a synthesizer for the guitars. This type of experimentation is perfect for those who are new to song writing. If you play an instrument and want to really experiment, check out Beck's *Song Reader*, a collection of twenty songs published only in sheet music form. Beck wrote these songs specifically to be interpreted by others and made no original recordings. Experimenting with your own interpretations of other artists' songs and playing around with a collection like Beck's provide great opportunities to be creative without having to write your own material. Learning the music of other artists also helps you learn how a song is structured, which can help you learn to write or improve your work if you are already writing.

Karaoke and Open-Mic Nights

After you've worked up a few cover songs, go try them out in a low-pressure setting. Most towns have venues that offer open-mic nights or Karaoke. In these environments you can try out new interpretations, experiment with new vocal techniques, and get feedback on your performance. Movie studios regularly test their movies out with select audiences to get feedback before releasing the final version because they realize that those closely involved in the creative process can often have a skewed perception of the final product. Performing at an open-mic or Karaoke night can provide the same opportunity as a movie screening if you use the audience feedback to tweak your performance and perfect your package.

Finding Inspiration

Artists find inspiration from their own mediums as well as other art forms. While it is important to listen to the music of other artists that falls within your genre, you should not limit yourself to only the genres that you like. Listen to all kinds of music—classical, rap, gospel, country, jazz, and any anything else you can find. Pay attention to the way different artists combine melody, harmony, rhythm, and lyrics to tell their story or someone else's through their point of view. What vocal registers and colors do they choose? Do they sing the song straight or do they add other elements like riffs and licks? How does that change the message of the music? Think about what you do and do not like about each song, what makes it appealing to an audience, and whether or not the song and/or performance sheds light on your own work.

Just as in visual art, song styles can present different life pictures. In the same way that both Renaissance portrait painters and the photographers in *Life* magazine depicted real people in real-life situations, songs such as Brandi Carlile's "The Story" give a snapshot of real life. Others painters, such as Thomas Kinkade, depict an idealized life of perfection, just like "Love Story" by Taylor Swift. Some artists, such as Salvador Dalí, depict surreal worlds and views of the world that mix the inner and outer realities of life (Kleiner & Mamiya, 2004). Similarly, concept albums, such as The Who's *Tommy* and Pink Floyd's *The Wall*, tell complex, surreal stories through music. As you explore, always keep an open mind and take what you can use. You never know what may lead to a breakthrough.

Conclusion

The only way that you will be able to know if audiences are receptive to your ideas is to seek out opportunities to perform in front of others and listen to their feedback on your performance. When you receive feedback, evaluate it with an open mind. Discard both positive and negative nonspecific feedback such as "I just don't like it," "They look ridiculous," "You were fabulous," or "You are amazing." Instead, seek out detailed feedback such as "The guitars solo too much," "The vocals are out of tune," or "You really command the stage with great energy." That kind of feedback allows you to evaluate the source, analyze the comments in relation to your performance, and make changes if you think the critique is useful.

As you begin to develop artistically, you must accept that some people will not like what you do. Do not take it personally. Different people have different tastes. While developing your artistic voice, try out different ideas and approaches based on the feedback you receive and see if those ideas and approaches make a difference in the reception of your performance. When Broadway producers develop a show, they present "preview" performances and make adjustments according to the feedback before showing it to the general public. Often the creative team will even rewrite songs or entire scenes during the preview process. By using performance opportunities to see what works and what needs help, you too can develop your work over time to create authentic and engaging performances that align with your artistic goals.

Bibliography

Beck. (2012). *Song reader*. San Francisco: McSweeney's.

Brestoff, R. (1996). *The great acting teachers and their methods*. Hanover: Smith & Kraus.

Kleiner, F., & Mamiya, C. (2004). *Gardner's art through the ages*. Belmont: Thomson Wadsworth.

Petit, L. (2004). The objective and the psychological gesture. Michael Chekhov Acting Studio, New York. Retrieved from http://www.michaelchekhovactingstudio .com/articles.htm#action.

TAKIN' CARE OF BUSINESS

Most of the important things in the world have been accomplished by people who have kept on trying when there seemed to be no hope at all.

—Dale Carnegie

Exploring the Possibilities

If you do your own research on rock history, you will find that in the early days of rock and roll there were many overnight successes. Performers such as Elvis Presley were discovered early in their career and supported by record labels that helped propel their success. Today, most artists develop their careers over the course of several years. Some become local successes, some gain regional notoriety, and a few gain national attention. In my view, they are all successful as long as they enjoy what they do. This chapter will help you understand the current marketplace, explore what it means to become successful, and help you formulate a plan for success.

The Marketplace

Internet file sharing had a negative impact on record sales, but the economics of the music industry are far from dismal. Worldwide music industry revenue in 2010 totaled $64.6 billion with recordings contributing $35.1 billion toward that total (Disc Makers, 2013). If you have ever worked in retail, you have probably heard that sales have an effect on payroll. In essence, when sales increase, there is greater opportunity for workers to get a piece of the pie through increased work hours. The music industry is no different. Consumer demand brings in revenue and creates opportunities for new artists. With $64.4 billion in the marketplace spent on music, there are clearly enough sales to support tens of thousands of performers. This is not to say that you will become wealthy beyond your wildest dreams. In fact, that is probably a long shot. But you can make an honest and decent living as a musician. I personally think that, instead of focusing on "making it big," you are better off focusing on earning a living through music, and then any successes beyond your expectations will be a bonus.

Fame Isn't Everything

Many young people hold a major misconception of what it means to be a successful musician, by believing they are only successful if they are famous. Some of the most famous musicians of all time were not nearly as popular in their own lifetime as they are today. Take Johann Sebastian Bach for example. Today Bach is a household name, even among those who are largely unfamiliar with classical music. Yet Bach was hardly a household name during his own lifetime. Bach's entire career was confined to employment at five Lutheran churches, and his compositions were primarily written for the services and demands of his employers. Bach died in 1750, and it was not until his *St Matthew Passion* was performed again in 1829 that his music came to the attention of an international audience (Grout & Palisca, 1996).

When Bach was alive, he was not composing to be famous. He was composing because it was part of his job and it was something that he loved. He was working full-time as a musician and earning a living. He was successful. If he had changed his compositional style to cater to his perceptions of public tastes in order to achieve fame, it is quite possible that he would have never created the type of music that eventually earned him international recognition. The same is true for rock singers. There is nothing wrong with wanting and achieving fame, but don't confuse it with success. If Bach had quit composing because he was not famous in his first five years of composing, he would never have become a household name. We as a society need to redefine what it means to be a successful musician and acknowledge that earning a living by working with music every day of your life, whether for one person or one million, is indeed success.

Hybrid Careers

I cannot begin to tell you how many times I have heard parents say that they do not want their children to be starving musicians. Those parents believe that if their child is not among the very few who become famous, that child will not even be able to afford food. If their child sits back and waits for opportunities to appear out of thin air, the parents' fear may be well founded. However, if that young musician takes the career-building initiative, a healthy living wage is possible.

I believe the future for musicians is a "hybrid career": combining multiple revenue-producing musical activities to piece together a livable wage. As a musician, one of the best opportunities you have for producing income that supplements your performing is teaching. Teaching offers many great benefits for performers, from artistic exploration of genres outside of their own to networking with other musicians. As you introduce technical concepts to students, you will inevitably make discoveries that will inform your own approach to singing. Best of all, you are earning money by being involved with something you love.

Some artists add other music-related, revenue-producing activities besides teaching. Some with audio recording experience record demos for up-and-coming artists, audition tapes for high school students pursuing university degrees in music, or professional recordings of local concerts at high schools, churches, and community ensembles. Others repair instruments or tune pianos. If you are an entrepreneur with a strong interest in sales and networking, start a small booking agency for other local performers. Restaurants, brides-to-be, and corporate party planners often need help finding entertainment for their events. If you can provide a one-stop shop for those clients, you could easily build a sizable secondary source of income. Let's take a look at how a combination of pursuits can produce a significant salary.

- Suppose you teach private lessons (guitar, piano, voice, etc.) for twenty hours a week. If you charge $40 an hour, you will earn $800 per week, $3,200 per month. If you teach eleven months a year, your yearly income will total $35,200.

- Let's assume you play one gig a week, forty weeks of the year, and two gigs a week during the twelve weeks of summer. If you earned $100 per gig, you would net $6,400.

- Finally, let's assume you record auditions and local concerts on the side. If you do twenty audition recordings at $100 each, you will bring in an additional $2,000. If you also record ten local concerts and sell twenty CDs at each concert for $15 apiece, you will bring in an additional $3,000.

While some of these line items may not seem significant by themselves, when you add them together they total $44,600. That is $8,928 more than the national average salary for first-year public school teachers (2011–2012: Average starting teacher salaries by state, accessed 2013). It is a very livable wage.

The Parallel Career

Parallel careers differ slightly from the hybrid career. Whereas a hybrid career involves multiple jobs within the music industry, the parallel career includes a single job outside of the industry, paired with performing. Parallel careers often involve another aspect of the arts, but that is not always the case; some parallel careers are surprising. Randall Rader, Chief Justice of the United States Court of Appeals for the Federal Circuit, is also a musician who plays with other rockers at various conferences and meetings related to his law career (Sichelman, 2012). Dana Williams, former mayor of Park City, Utah, fronted a rock band while in office (Smart, 2013). Finally, six gynecologic-oncology surgeons from around the United States get together several times a year to perform in their group, N.E.D. (No Evidence of Disease) as a way to raise awareness of gynecological cancer (Mount Sinai Hospital, 2012). The possibilities are endless; just be sure that you really enjoy any parallel career you choose. If you are miserable at work, that misery will likely spill over into your music and have a negative impact on your artistry.

Prepare for Your Second Career

Even if you have a successful career as a rock star, there is a good chance you will reach the day when you will tire of life on the road. Many artists reach that point and pursue other careers. These could also be considered parallel careers since many artists return to the road from time to time to perform. Bryan Adams, the singer behind "(Everything I Do) I Do It for You" and "Summer of '69" began pursuing his interests in photography in 2001. He is now working as a professional photographer with exhibitions around the world, from Oklahoma City to Berlin, Toronto, London, Rome, and Moscow (Bryan Adams). Financial adviser Bert Padell encourages his rock star clients to look into the restaurant business as they retire. Alice Cooper owns restaurants in Phoenix and Cleveland (Strauss, 2006). Rock star Jon Bon Jovi took a unique take on the food industry and opened a restaurant where customers are asked to pay only what they can. (Parry, 2011). Grace Slick of Jefferson Airplane retired from rock in 1989 and began pursuing painting in the mid-1990s. Her work has been shown in over one hundred exhibitions throughout the United States and Europe (Grace Slick biography). I personally think it is always beneficial to consider long-term goals when planning for the future. Even if thinking long-term does not appeal to you, I believe it is encouraging to know that even superstars walk away from the business, and that does not make them any less successful. So if there is another career that interests you, why not start developing yourself along the way for the transition?

Nontraditional Careers

"Nontraditional" is a poor title for these careers, but it does accurately explain the concept. Instead of pursuing a life on the road, playing bars and festivals and pursuing rock stardom, some musicians find steady employment in venues that offer rock-influenced music in other formats. Cruise ships, theme parks, casinos, music theater productions, and vacation resorts all provide opportunities for rock musicians to perform, and the pay is quite good. Cruise ships pay as much as $1,000 a week and often provide free room and board. Performers in Broadway shows, many of which are composed by rock musicians, earn $1,807 per week (Minimum salaries—production agreement [Broadway & National tours], 2013). Many churches have abandoned traditional music for contemporary praise and worship. These churches often hire professional musicians on full-time contracts to lead and oversee the musical aspects of their services. There are numerous opportunities out there for people with musical talents; just do a little research.

Getting Signed

Many people believe that success will come if they can get signed to a record label. Yet getting signed does not necessarily mean that you will be successful. Record labels are for-profit businesses whose mission is to earn a profit, not pursue high artistic standards. If your work is making them money or they think that it will eventually earn them money, they will do everything they can to support you. If you stop making them money or they lose faith in your product, they may quickly drop their support for you and direct their resources toward another client. That could be after your second record, after your first, or before your first record is ever released.

If you do release an album, you may be surprised to find out that the payoff is not always as big as you would think. Take as an example the band 30 Seconds to Mars, whose album *30 Seconds to Mars* sold two million copies and achieved platinum status. Because of the way their contract was worded and the costs associated with recording and promoting the album, the band received no monetary compensation whatsoever for that album (Masnick, 2008). Labels must invest in the artist before the record is even available for purchase, through costs in recording the songs, mastering them, pressing CDs, and developing a marketing campaign. All of that money has to be recouped through revenue generated by album sales. If the initial investment was large and the album achieves only modest financial success, there is a chance the product sales will recover only the investment costs of the company, and there will be no profit for the artists. In fact, if the record company gave the artist an advance before the album was produced, the artists could even find themselves owing the label money.

In the recent past, record labels earned money mainly from record-sales commissions. But when the Internet reduced physical record sales due to widespread piracy, the labels took on a new strategy. The new approach is called the "360 deal." Instead of collecting commissions on record sales alone, the labels now collect a percentage of all revenue-producing activities including touring, commercials, movie licensing, television appearances, and more. The labels say this additional income allows them to promote artists in multiple areas (live performance, TV/film, Internet, etc.). If the record company is successful in its promotion, the artist may earn more than if they had only label support for their album. Then again, if the label does a poor job of promotion, the artist might still have to pay for it and give up even more of their earnings to the label.

How Artists Get Signed

The A&R (artists and repertoire) department of the record label scouts and signs new talent. A&R representatives stay on top of current trends and look for artists who fit a specific sound that the company believes will be marketable. Once the A&R representative finds an interesting artist, they take them to the A&R executive to see if the label will sign the artist to a record deal. While it sounds exciting, signing a record deal does not mean that the artist's career is about to take off. After an artist signs a deal, the label will often take time to develop him or her. That can mean that the label wants to take some time for the artist to mature. It could mean that the label likes the artist's sound but does not think the market is ready for the artist. In some cases, a development deal can actually be a tactic to keep the artist off of the market and not competing with other artists that the label has already signed.

Take the artist Lorde as an example of the artist-development process. An A&R representative from Universal took interest in Lorde after seeing a video of her performing at a talent show in New Zealand when she was only twelve years old. By the time she was thirteen, Universal Records signed her for a solo-artist development deal. It took three years of working on her writing with other artists before the label felt she was ready to release her debut single "Royals" (Rollins, 2013). Lorde was young enough to still live at home with her parents while she waited for things to progress. However, if she were in her twenties, moving back home to live with her mom and dad could be more of a challenge.

A New Business Model for a New Century—the Indie Artist

The Internet created a major shift in the business model for musicians that has many advantages for aspiring artists. Until the Internet age, an artist had to rely on major record labels to gain widespread access to the marketplace. Back in the 1990s, most musicians would book time in a recording studio to record a demo or an album. Today's musicians, because of readily available audio technology, can build home studios, record their own material, and purposely avoid major record labels for both artistic and monetary reasons. Radio Head left its label, EMI, in 2007 after fifteen years of collaboration and set out on their own (Thorton, 2011). Ani DiFranco has turned down every record deal she has ever been offered, instead preferring to release her work herself (Ani biography). In today's marketplace, there is a better chance than ever before to reach an audience without corporate support.

Resources to Get You Started

Online Distribution

As mentioned above, going independent is more popular than ever. Visit the following websites for more information about how to release your own album, in physical format as well as online through websites such as iTunes and Amazon.

- The Orchard—http://www.theorchard.com

- Tune Core—http://www.tunecore.com

- CD Baby—http://www.cdbaby.com

- Reverbnation—http://www.reverbnation.com

Books about the Industry

The following books cover everything from marketing to touring to making good business decisions. Studying these texts will give you more than enough information to get you started:

This Business of Music: The Definitive Guide to the Business and Legal Issues of the Music Industry by M. William Krasilovsky, Sidney Shemel, John M. Gross, and Jonathan Feinstein;

This Business of Music: The Definitive Guide to the Music Industry by M. William Krasilovsky, Sidney Shemel, and John M. Gross;

This Business of Music Marketing and Promotion by Tad Lathrop;

This Business of Concert Promotion and Touring: A Practical Guide to Creating, Selling, Organizing, and Staging Concerts by Ray D. Waddell, Rich Barnet, and Jake Berry;

All You Need to Know About the Music Business by Donald S. Passman

The Future of Music: Manifesto for the Digital Music Revolution by Susan Gedutis Lindsay

Teaching

Here are two great books to start with if you like the idea of a hybrid teaching/performing career.

The Music Teaching Artist's Bible: Becoming a Virtuoso Educator by Eric Booth

Make a Fortune Teaching Private Music Lessons: How to Quit Your Job and Become a Professional Musician in 30 Days or Less by Lloyd Steiner

Self-Development

Interpersonal relationships are incredibly valuable in this business. Begin with Dale Carnegie's book (*How to Win Friends and Influence People*) and then seek out other self-help titles of interest to you. Taking the time to sit down and think about how you interact with others can pay great dividends throughout your career.

Getting Yourself Out There and Formulating a Plan

Letting the World Know That You Exist

You may be the greatest singer in the world, but if no one knows that you exist, it doesn't matter how good you are. Thanks to the Internet, you can easily promote yourself globally with little to no investment. After you have defined your brand (see appendix E), you should begin building up your web presence. YouTube is probably the easiest and best place to start. The great thing about YouTube is that you can post both video content and audio files with still images. There are of course legal issues surrounding YouTube and the use of other people's work, including cover songs. I will leave it up to you to do your own research and make your own decisions as you proceed. What I can say is that many people use YouTube to find talent, in addition to watching videos for entertainment purposes. Posting cover versions of new hit songs can help you gain a following. Writing songs related to current events or a special cause is another way to gain attention. Once you have content online, start a Twitter account and share your work with your followers. You should then begin building your own website.

Your Website

There are six important components for a website: bio, photos, media, performance calendar, links, and contact info. Your website is your platform for your story to be heard. The bio is your chance to tell your story. Think about your brand and the life story you want to communicate, and work up a narrative that communicates that message to your audience. Photos give visitors a glimpse into your performance style, your personality, and your brand. The media section is where you will post videos and audio clips of your work. It is tempting to throw up as many clips as possible, but I strongly encourage you to resist the temptation and share only your best work. First impressions are important. You do not want the first impression to be, "She can almost do that song." You want the impression to be, "Wow, I've never heard anything like that!" Think of yourself as the curator of your brand. Take your time and build content slowly and deliberately. Building a career is a marathon, not a sprint. Next, keep a running list of all of your performances. Keep your past gigs listed to show your track record and post each new gig as soon as you confirm it. The links page can be a great networking tool. As you connect with other like-minded artists, ask them to trade links with you. That way fans who visit their site can find you, and visitors to your site can find them. Most importantly, create a contact page so you can easily be reached. You are better off using a website contact form than directly listing your contact information online. If you post your actual e-mail address, you will spend more time sorting through spam than responding to serious inquiries.

Here are a few companies worth researching as you begin to develop your website:

- Wix.com

- Weebly.com

- Dynamod.com

- Wordpress.com

Putting Together a Press Kit

In addition to developing an online presence, you should work on putting together a package of physical materials that you can distribute. A press kit is a package of materials that you will use to sell yourself to venues when trying to book gigs. You will also share it with the press when you are attempting to have your work covered in a specific publication.

Your first goal should be to find a photographer to help you capture a few shots that highlight your brand. If "industrial" is part of what you sell, take photos in an industrial part of town. If "love and peace" is part of what you sell, have a few shots taken with flowers and peace signs or the like. When you begin shopping around for a photographer, tell them the purpose and intent of the photos and let them know that you want to own the copyright. This is common practice among those who do these types of photo shoots for a living. The photographer will usually give you two to three hundred shots from your session to look over. You will then need to pick your favorite shots (usually one to five) that will then be touched up so that they look perfect. When trying to pick which shots to use, get feedback from people other than your significant other or family members. Since you are not simply looking for a good picture, be sure to tell anyone whose opinion you are seeking what you are trying to sell (your brand) and ask them which shots they think best communicate that message.

Once you have selected a photo, design and print business cards. There are numerous online vendors that provide design interfaces and who print high-quality products. You can often get a better deal if you order more than one product at a time. If that is the case, design a matching postcard with blank space on the back and eleven-by-seventeen-inch posters with blank space at the bottom. You will use the blank space on the postcards and posters to write in information about your upcoming gigs, for promotional purposes. When developing these materials, be sure that the look and message is consistent across all of your promotional materials.

After you have developed these basic printed materials, assemble them into a press kit. A press kit includes photos, publicity shots, reviews, references, your bio, and a business card, carefully organized in a high-quality folder. If you have a demo, you should also include a CD and/or video in your kit. Take your time putting together your press kit. Once it is out there in people's hands, you cannot take it back. Be sure that whatever you put in this folder fits your brand. The fonts, photos, and designs that you use must all reinforce your message and be consistent across all materials, including your website.

Writing a Business Plan

As a performer, you are the CEO of "You, Inc." Most businesses create a business plan at some time during their existence. A business plan can help you focus your thoughts, clarify your goals, and gain a better understanding of the market you are trying to enter. The outline below will help you create a business plan specific to your needs. For additional help, I recommend you contact your local Small Business Administration office and ask about SCORE (Service Corps of Retired Executives) mentoring.

Career Summary

While this is the first section in any business plan, you are going to write it last. This section will summarize the plan in one to two paragraphs. It is a summary of the entire plan that you should commit to memory so that you can clearly and quickly communicate your goals to others.

Market Summary

This section is meant to help you understand the marketplace for yourself in order to gain a better understanding of where you fit in and how you can break into the marketplace. To get started, answer the following questions.

Industry Description and Outlook

1. Which segment of the industry (indie rock, folk rock, punk rock, etc.) do you want to break into?

2. What percentage of the local music scene is comprised of your segment? What percentage of the regional music scene is comprised of your segment? What percentage of the national market is comprised of your segment?

3. Make a list of all of the venues that fit your segment in your local and regional market.

4. How far in advance do the venues book acts?

5. What is the growth rate of your segment?

6. Is the segment you're targeting an emerging, established, or declining segment?

Using this information, write a short summary for yourself about the opportunities in your area. After you have summarized the situation, address any issues that you see. Maybe there are so many venues that you really need to focus in on a small area. Perhaps there are so few venues that you are going to have to travel weekly in order to perform. Whatever the case may be, think about the issues at hand and how you will address them.

Identifying Your Target Market

Your target market is the primary demographic where you intend to sell your talent. For example, middle-aged dads, with one to three children, who are blue-collar workers. Trying to focus on too many demographics can often be a mistake because it turns you into a generic commodity instead of a unique brand. Think in terms of age, gender, occupation (including high school or college student), and socioeconomic background. Next you need to gather information about the following:

1. Size of the target demographic in your local area, the region, and nationally. U.S. Census data can be very helpful in determining these numbers.

2. Distinguishing characteristics of the demographic you are targeting. Find information on your potential customers' income bracket, average education, buying habits, and entertainment decisions.

3. How easily will you be able to gain market share? Explain your answer.

4. Make a list of resources for finding information related to your demographic (magazines, local papers, websites, forums, etc.).

5. What marketing tools will you use to reach your target demographic? These might include mailings, postcards, YouTube broadcasts, Facebook, website, etc.

Competitive Analysis

The competitive analysis section helps you identify other performers in your market who could be your competition. Assess their strengths and weaknesses and relate them to your own work. To begin, select four to five competitors and fill in the sections on the chart in table 8.1. It can also be useful to create a list of other competitors to keep an eye on. After you have completed the chart, create a short narrative of what you have found.

Table 8.1. Competitive analysis chart.

	Competitor A	Competitor B	Competitor C	Competitor D
Name				
Age				
Appearance				
How did they develop their career?				
Career highlights				
Demographics of their fan base				
How do they promote themselves?				

Competitive Advantages and Weaknesses

A competitive advantage is an advantage that your competition holds over you. These are usually traits or skills that they possess which may make it difficult for you to compete with them. The strengths of your competitors may take many forms. For example, they may be easy to work with or have a recognizable look or name, a good track record and reputation, solid financial resources, and/or strong technical skills. Write a summary of your competitors' advantages. If you think you will eventually be able to compete, write about your plan for competing in the areas where you believe you can. If you cannot compete, do you think it will hinder you? Is there anything you can do to eventually compete in that area (i.e., take voice lessons, lose weight, gain muscle, learn to play guitar, etc.)?

Weaknesses are the flip side of advantages. Are your competitors unable to satisfy industry demands? Do they have a poor branding and marketing strategy? Is their track record or reputation not up to par with what is expected or desired? Do they have limited financial resources? These are areas where you can easily compete and gain a competitive advantage. If you find weak areas in your competition, note the specifics of why they are having problems. This way, you can avoid the same mistakes they have made.

Barriers

What are your barriers to the marketplace? Barriers might include startup costs (publicity shots, websites, equipment, etc.), time constraints (day job, education, spouse, etc.), lack of contacts, financial restraints (debt, lack of income, etc.), and/or relationships (boyfriend, girlfriend, fiancé, spouse, friends, sick parents or relatives, etc.). How do you plan to cope with or overcome your barriers?

Optional: City Analysis

If you are considering more than one potential city to develop your career, do a competitive analysis of those cities with a chart and narrative (see table 8.2), just as you did above with your competitors. Ask questions such as, What is the cost of living? How many venues are there? What day job opportunities exist? What is the economic situation of the city? What contacts do you have in the city? How many other performers/bands are currently in the city? Write a summary of your analysis and identify areas that need further research and your game plan for clarifying the benefits and risks of your options.

Table 8.2. City analysis chart.

	Option A	Option B	Option C
Cost of living			
Cost of rent			
Cost of health insurance			
Cost of public transportation			
Number of venues			
Number of other performers in the city			
Contacts in the city			
Other employment opportunities			
The city's economic situation			
Nearest airport			

Brand Description

This is where you outline your brand. Reread Jonathan Flom's introduction to branding and write your brand description as if it were a one-minute introduction to someone you just met. You are never going to actually give this speech, but having the narrative down on paper will help solidify your brand and give you talking points for the future.

Marketing Strategy

Your marketing strategy should include four sections:

1. Market penetration strategy. How are you going to break into the marketplace?

2. Growth strategy. Once you begin landing gigs, how are you going to network, get the word out that you are working, and continue to book new gigs at new venues while also booking repeat gigs?

3. Branding strategy. How will you continue to reevaluate your brand and make it relevant to the industry? How will you stay current with market trends?

4. Communication strategy. How are you going to get the word out to the industry about what you are doing? How will you maintain your contacts?

First answer the questions in the sections above and then create a three-, six-, nine-, and twelve-month plan of how you will implement your strategy.

Financials

1. How are you going to fund your career? Do you have investors/ donors who are willing to help you?

2. How much do you anticipate earning from your music (monthly) and what expenses do you anticipate?

3. What is the difference between how much you will earn and how much you need to survive? How will you bridge that gap (day job, savings, etc.)?

4. How long will it take you to save up the equivalent of three months' salary? Six months' salary? Do you have other savings goals you need to work toward?

5. Identify changes in your spending habits that will enable you to meet your budget. If you need to give up certain items that you enjoy, can you offer them to yourself as a reward down the road for reaching certain performance, career, or financial goals?

Goal Setting

Now that you have compiled the above information, set goals for the next five years. Begin with each of the first twelve months, and then come up with a few general goals for the first, second, third, fourth, and fifth year. Finally, write a short description of your ideal situation in the next ten, twenty, and thirty years. The long-term goals can be brief, but at least think about them. Difficult choices will be a regular part of your life as a professional musician. Long-term goals can help you make sure the decisions you make align with the kind of life you would like to live. Next, write a brief bullet point under each goal outlining any steps you need to take in order to make the goal a reality. Refer back to this document often, and refine it as things change. People who set goals are more likely to succeed than those who do not. It takes time, but it is well worth it.

Goals Reached or Missed

In this section, keep a running log beginning with the date you finish your plan. You will make a note of every goal that you reach or don't reach. If you did not reach a goal, consider why, and write about it with a new strategy and deadline for achieving it. If you decide to drop that goal from your list instead of revising the date, explain why. This step is about holding yourself accountable. This is your running record of how your business is progressing, and it is for your information only.

"If It Was Easy, Everyone Would Do It"

When I got discouraged about the progress of my music career, my father used to tell me, "If it was easy, everyone would do it." Television makes the road to stardom look easy and it can easily cloud our judgment of what is realistic. For a long time, I did not quite understand what my dad meant; I felt as though I was working harder than anyone else already. What more could I do? I was fortunate that my father taught me the value of hard work early in life, and he made sure that I knew the only way to succeed was by giving everything I did 110 percent. But, I must be honest and say that I had no idea what hard work really was until I began pursuing a career as a professional musician. There is a thirteen-year period of my life when, at times, I held as many as six part-time jobs in order to get where I wanted to go. I literally worked from the time I woke up, around 7 a.m., until the time I went to bed, usually midnight or 1 a.m. I cannot tell you the names of any popular television shows during that period because there was no time to do anything but work. There were times when I felt as though there was no way that my life was ever going to get better, but things always improved. This chapter only skims the surface of what you need to know in order to succeed in the entertainment world. Is it difficult? Yes. In fact, it is beyond difficult. Pursuing a career is very likely going to be the hardest thing you will ever do in your life. However, you will never forget the journey, you will make amazing friends, create wonderful memories, and come out on the other side a stronger and smarter person with life skills that will serve you well in all other facets of your life. So go back to the beginning of this chapter, read it again, and then get to work. You can do this!

Bibliography

2011–2012: Average starting teacher salaries by state. Retrieved from http://www.nea .org/home/2011-2012-average-starting-teacher-salary.html [retrieved December 29, 2013].

Ani biography. Retrieved from http://www.righteousbabe.com/pages/ani-biography [retrieved December 26, 2013].

Bryan Adams. Retrieved from http://www.bryanadamsphotography.com/exhibitions [retrieved December 15, 2013].

Disc Makers. (2013). *Earning music as an Indie*. Retrieved from http://www.disc makers.com.

Grace Slick biography, http://www.areaarts.com/grace-slick/ [retrieved December 17, 2013].

Grout, D. J. A., & Palisca, C. V. A. (1996). *A history of western music*. New York: W.W. Norton & Company.

Masnick, M. (2008, August 21). EMI/Virgin records sues platinum selling band for $30 million . . . despite not paying them a dime in royalties. *Tech Dirt*. Retrieved from http://www.techdirt.com/articles/20080820/0204472040.shtml.

Minimum salaries—production agreement (Broadway & National tours), http:// www.actorsequity.org/agreements/agreement_info.asp?inc=001 [retrieved December 29, 2013].

Mount Sinai Hospital. (September 19, 2012). Rock band consisting of six gyneco- logic oncology surgeons to perform series of sold-out concerts as part of Septem- ber's gynecologic cancer awareness month [Press release]. Retrieved from http:// www.mountsinai.org/about-us/newsroom/press-releases/rock-band-consisting -of-six-gynecologic-oncology-surgeons-to-perform-series-of-sold-out-concerts -as-part-of-septembers-gynecologic-cancer-awareness-month.

Parry, W. (October 19, 2011). Rock star Bon Jovi's charity restaurant opens near New Jersey train station. *Lubbock Avalanche-Journal*. Retrieved from http:// lubbockonline.com/filed-online/2011-10-19/rock-star-jon-bon-jovis-charity -restaurant-opens-near-new-jersey-train.

Rollins, S. (September 23, 2013). Who is Lorde? 9 facts about alt-pop's newest sensation. *The Week*. Retrieved from http://theweek.com/article/index/250050/who-is-lorde -9-facts-about-alt-pops-newest-sensation [retrieved December 30, 2013].

Sichelman, T. (January 9, 2012). Chief Judge Rader & band DeNovo to "rock" San Diego's House of Blues. *Patentlyo*. Retrieved from http://www.patentlyo .com/patent/2012/01/chief-judge-rader-band-denovo-to-rock-san-diegos-house -of-blues.html.

Smart, C. (December 27, 2013). Park City's rock 'n roll mayor bows out. *The Salt Lake Tribune*. Retrieved from http://www.sltrib.com/sltrib/politics/57307318-90/ class-community-hall-mayor.html.csp.

Strauss, R. (April 11, 2006). Rock stars must plan for the day the music dies. *New York Times*. Retrieved from http://www.nytimes.com/2006/04/11/business/retirement/11rockers.html?pagewanted=print&_r=0.

Talbot, M. (2013). Antonio Vivaldi. In *Grove Music Online*. Retrieved from http://www.oxfordmusiconline.com/subscriber/article/grove/music/40120pg2.

Thorton, T. (July 22, 2011). The 10 greatest unsigned bands in history. *Sabotage Times*. Retrieved from http://sabotagetimes.com/music/the-10-greatest-unsigned-bands-in-history/.

CHAPTER NINE

WE DON'T NEED NO EDUCATION! OR DO WE?

I spent three days a week for ten years educating myself in the public library, and it's better than college. People should educate themselves—you can get a complete education for no money.

—Ray Bradbury

I f this were a textbook on how to become a biologist, this chapter would not be necessary. I could just tell you to go to a university and study biology. For the rock singer, the answer is not that simple. Unfortunately there are limited opportunities in higher education to learn the skills necessary for success as a professional rock singer. In order to be successful, you will need to take control of your own education and create your own opportunities. In some ways you may be better off. Whereas a university program must establish a standardized curriculum of learning for its students so that they all graduate with the same skill set, as an independent learner you can determine what you need to know and what you do not. Use this chapter as a guide to form your own educational plan. Then follow through with your plan and start teaching yourself.

Formal Training

I recently had a student tell me that she never knew you could take voice lessons and actually improve. Unfortunately, this is a statement that I hear way too often. I've also heard students and their parents justify not taking lessons by claiming that most professional singers never had formal voice training. That is a myth that I am happy to burst. A few simple Internet searches will reveal that the "King of Pop" himself, Michael Jackson, studied voice with Los Angeles voice teacher Seth Riggs. Miley Cyrus, Hayley Williams, Keith Urban, Taylor Swift, Luther Vandross, Natalie Cole, and Stevie Wonder have all taken voice lessons too (Products by Brett Manning, 2013; Lecturing & Teaching Experience, 2007). There are countless others who also study privately with teachers who do not list the names of their clientele in their marketing. The reality is that everyone needs a little help from time to time. This chapter will explore voice lessons and other educational opportunities to assist you on your journey to become a better rock singer and performer.

Private Lessons

While I'm thrilled that you are reading this book, I must be honest and say that reading this book alone is not enough to make you a terrific rock singer. In addition to working on the exercises in this book, a singer really needs to work with a voice expert one-on-one. In reality, when we are singing, we can never hear ourselves in the same way that others hear us. We have two types of hearing: sensorial-neural (vibrations that are received through our ear canal) and conductive (vibrations that are received through the bones in our head that surround the ear drum) (McCoy, 2004). When we sing, we hear ourselves with both types of hearing, but when our audience listens to us sing, they only hear us from the outside in (sensorial-neural). The only way you can truly hear what others hear is by listening to a recording, which itself may not be a perfectly accurate representation (see chapter 6). However, the best time to make vocal corrections is when you are in the moment, not after the fact, which is why I personally think the best results occur when you work one-on-one with a voice teacher who has experience teaching rock singers.

Finding a Teacher

Finding a voice teacher who is both willing to teach rock singers and capable of helping them achieve their goals can sometimes be difficult. There is no formal certification procedure for voice teachers. Other professionals, such as personal trainers, are required to take a certification test, which leads to a credential that lets clients know that the trainer is proficient in specific areas. For instance, a trainer may be certified in personal training and yoga but not group fitness classes. This specificity helps clients identify the trainer best suited to their needs. However, voice teachers do not have a nationally recognized certification system. Since teacher credentials are not certified by a national organization, you must do your own homework to determine teachers' qualifications and whether or not they fit your needs.

The most common qualification for teaching voice is a music degree from a university music program. There are a wide variety of degrees you may encounter when researching voice teachers: bachelor of arts (a general studies degree), a bachelor of science in music education (the standard degree for K–12 music teachers), a bachelor of music in voice performance (the most common degree for classical singers), and a bachelor of fine arts or bachelor of music in music theater (the most common degrees for music theater performers). You may also encounter teachers with advanced degrees such as the master of music (MM) or a doctor of musical arts (DMA) in either voice performance or voice pedagogy. There are also teachers who hold no degree at all and simply learned by doing. These teachers can be just as effective as those with a college degree. In fact, two of the finest teachers I have ever worked with fall into this category.

There are also several certificates that indicate a teacher has completed a specific program of study related to singing voice training. Instructors who have trademarked their teaching methods issue these certificates. Examples include Estill Voice Training, Speech Level Singing, the Morganix Method, Lisa Popeil's Voiceworks, and Somatic Voicework, and the Jeannette LoVetri method. All of these courses are specifically designed for training CCM (contemporary commercial music) singing.

There is no perfect combination of credentials for a voice teacher, which is why it is essential that you do your homework. Technical needs can vary drastically from singer to singer. Some performers need a teacher who specializes in the basics of posture, breath, and basic vocal function. Another student may be recovering from a vocal injury and will require a teacher experienced in working with damaged voices, called a "singing voice specialist." Advanced students may need detailed work on style and finesse and could benefit from an experienced professional performer with many years of performance experience. These professionals sometimes refer to themselves as vocal coaches. While some coaches are comfortable working on vocal technique, most prefer to focus on interpretation.

The Internet and word-of-mouth referrals are often your best resources when trying to find a teacher. Most voice teachers have some sort of web presence where you can find details about their background, the types of students they teach, and what their teaching philosophy is. Do not judge their teaching abilities by the quality of their websites. They are voice teachers, not web designers. Also, ask other musicians in the area if they have recommendations. If the same name keeps coming up in discussions, you may want to investigate that teacher on your own. After you've come up with a short list, contact the teachers and ask if you can observe a lesson or have a trial lesson. You should expect to pay for this initial session; these are professionals and their time is limited. Voice teacher rates vary widely depending on experience and location. In some areas you may find nationally known teachers who charge $50 an hour, while in other locations a teacher of that same caliber may charge $200 an hour. If you decide that you would like to work with a teacher on a regular basis, you will probably be asked to pay for a month in advance. It is very common for teachers to have cancelation policies that require you to give a twenty-four-hour notice before canceling a lesson to avoid having to pay for the missed lesson. Voice teachers deserve the same respect as physical therapists, counselors, or other professionals. If you miss a doctor's appointment without providing notice, you will be billed for it. Treating your teacher with the same respect will ensure that you get the most out of your lessons.

Classical/Bel Canto Methods

When seeking a voice teacher, you will likely come across instructors who say that they teach classical voice or bel canto. Unfortunately there are no standard techniques for either. What one teacher calls "bel canto" may be completely different from another teacher who also claims to teach a bel canto technique. When researching this category of teacher you will need to read their websites thoroughly and talk to current and former students to see if what they teach aligns with your needs. Read appendix A by Dr. Kathryn Green for more information about the similarities and differences between classical and bel canto techniques.

Contemporary Voice Methods

As mentioned above, there are several trademarked singing voice techniques that have been developed over the last few decades. There are many benefits of training with a teacher of a trademarked technique. Graduates of a specific certification program will usually teach a standardized terminology with uniform beliefs about how the voice works. For instance, if you go to any two Somatic Voicework teachers, you will be learning the same basic concepts about registration, volume, vowels, and pitch range. If you work with an Estill teacher, you will learn the same basic figures that all Estill students learn. Learning a codified technique can be helpful if you move around a lot and do not want to keep starting over each time with a new teacher. To help you gain a better understanding of the various options that are available, I suggest you do your own research using the web links below.

- Somatic Voicework (SVW)—online at SomaticVoicework.com.

- Speech Level Singing—online at SpeechLevelSinging.com.

- Singing Success—online at SingingSuccess.com.

- Estill Voice Training—online at EstillVoice.com.

- Lisa Popeil's Voiceworks—online at Popeil.com

What You Should Expect

You have probably heard the adage that one of the keys to small-business success is location, location, location. However, when it comes to voice teachers, that is not always the case. Many of the country's finest voice teachers work with students in their homes or apartments in order to reduce costs for themselves and their students. Renting a studio space or teaching out of a music store can be rather expensive and significantly cut into the teacher's income. There are of course fine teachers who do teach in a music store for the convenience of not having students in their own homes. Some open their own private studio space and hire other instructors to teach at their location. This is one business where location does not really matter. Just be sure that you feel comfortable wherever the lessons are being held.

When setting up a trial lesson with a teacher, ask them if they would like you to bring anything. If you play guitar or another instrument, you may want to ask if you can play and sing for them. Arrive early for your lesson and bring a bottle of water with you. Lessons usually begin either with the teacher asking you to sing for them or with the teacher playing the piano to lead you through a series of vocal exercises. There is no reason to be nervous when singing for the teacher. Voice teachers are in business to help you reach your goals and make singing easier; they are not there to judge you.

At some point, every student will work on vocal exercises. These exercises may seem awkward or sound strange, but they are designed to strengthen the voice and to help you get comfortable with new techniques for producing various tone qualities. Even if the exercise feels or sounds strange, give it your best effort. Some of my biggest breakthroughs arose from exercises that I thought were weird or ridiculous. You can only evaluate whether a teacher's approach will work for you or not by giving their methods 100 percent of your effort and attention. You may not notice immediate results, but if you like the teacher's approach, you should try one or two months of lessons with them and see what happens. If you are not seeing results in two to three months and you feel that you have been giving the teacher's advice your best efforts, then you should probably look around and see if you can find a teacher whose teaching style more closely aligns with your learning style.

Individual Learning Styles

It is important to realize that not every teacher or training method will work the same way for every student. If a close friend tells you that their teacher is the best they have ever worked with, yet that teacher does not connect with you, it is not necessarily because they are a bad teacher. It is possible that there are differences in teaching and learning styles between you and the teacher. For instance, kinesthetic learners tend to respond best by focusing on physical sensations. Aural learners learn better by hearing things than by feeling them. Visual learners respond best by visualizing what they are attempting to do, for example, singing through a dolphin nose. Because of these differences, different teachers may work better for different students. Even though most teachers make an effort to convey information in a way that will make sense regardless of learning style, sometimes a student and a teacher just don't click.

Taking Charge of Your Education

I've mentioned several times so far that you must talk with your teacher. What do I mean? Many times students will just agree with whatever they are told; they will not ask questions when something does not make sense, and they will not tell their teacher when they do not like what they are hearing. Conversely, there are students who will question everything, doubt every new idea that is presented to them, and spend the whole lesson talking instead of singing. Neither situation is ideal for either the teacher or the student.

Part of what makes teaching singing difficult for the teacher is that the teacher can neither feel what you are feeling nor see what is happening in your throat. Yes, they can see the lips and jaw, but they cannot see the whole tongue, the movement of the soft palate, or the vibration of the vocal folds. Voice teachers listen and can usually identify which movements within the vocal mechanism produce which sounds, but a teacher's best insight often comes from the student's feedback. When I ask a student, "How was that?" or, "What was that like?" their response can give me useful information. I may learn that a tone that sounds great actually hurts the student's throat. From specific feedback, I can also help a student begin to differentiate between sensations that are simply awkward and uncomfortable (which is acceptable) and painful (which is not acceptable). When I know what my student is experiencing, I can proceed according to the student's individual needs. However, if the student says something vague like, "It was okay," I am left with very little information with which to help the student.

How to Be a Great Student

To help your teacher give the best instruction, be sure to find time every day to practice making the new techniques comfortable, and make notes of any questions or concerns you may have while practicing. Write down questions that you have about specific pitches in songs that are not working or vocal exercises that are troubling you. If the teacher asks you to try something in a lesson, give it 100 percent of your effort. If the teacher corrects you several times in a row, feel free to say, "I'm sorry, I don't think I understand what you are asking me to do." If the teacher tells you something that is especially helpful, tell them, "That explanation really helps." Your verbal feedback is essential to seeing results. You also have to trust your teacher. If they tell you something sounds good, believe them. It is in their best interest to be truthful. If you go out into the world singing with an awful tonal quality and then say, "I study with John Doe," others may avoid that teacher. No teacher wants that to happen; it's bad for business.

You must also understand that what constitutes a good sound can be very subjective. If you notice that all of a teacher's students have a certain tonal quality that you really do not like and you notice yourself taking on aspects of that tonal quality, then that teacher may not be the right match for you. Rufus Wainright and Bruce Springsteen sing differently. They are both successful, and neither approach is necessarily better or worse than the other. Preferred vocal tone is a matter of personal taste and it is a teacher's responsibility to help you get where you want to go, whether or not it is a sound they love. If the two of you have fundamental disagreements, it is completely acceptable to seek out a new instructor.

Know When to Walk Away, Know When to Run

It is normal for the relationship between a teacher and a student to encounter difficulties. In our day-to-day lives, we all meet people whom we can connect with and others we cannot. The same is true for voice teachers. A truly professional teacher will understand this and should freely admit when a relationship is not working. If you encounter a teacher who will not acknowledge that his or her teaching style does not work for everyone, you should be cautious. If you are practicing and doing everything you are asked, then you have the right to expect that the teacher will try different approaches. If they are not willing to adapt their approach to fit your needs, it is probably time to move on and find a different teacher.

Abuse Is Not Okay

Unfortunately it is not uncommon for singers to tell stories of abusive teachers they have encountered. The abuse is usually verbal or emotional, but it can also be physical or sexual. Regardless of the type, abuse is unacceptable. Here are a few examples of comments that should be considered abusive:

- "What's wrong with you? I told you what to do, why can't you get it?"

- "You are clearly not listening to me or using my technique."

- "Your voice sounds like nails on a chalkboard; it is really hard for me to sit here and listen to you sing."

- "Of course you cannot sing it like me; I am a professional, you barely know what you are doing."

- "Well your voice is just ugly and there is no way you can sing that song."

- "You should wear tighter clothes so I can see your breathing."

- "Not everyone is meant to sing."

Believe me, there are teachers out there who make comments such as these to their students. I studied with one teacher who was noticeably drunk during my lessons. Another frequently told me that I sounded terrible and would dismiss me early from my lessons but would offer no useful advice as how to make things better. Even when I knew I was not singing as poorly as I was being led to believe, it was still hard not to let those comments affect me. I left both of those teachers and never regretted it for a second. Every human being deserves respect. Do not settle for anything less.

The Gray Areas

The relationship between singer and teacher is unique. The two of you must work closely together and talk about your body and your emotions. It is often helpful for the teacher to put their hands on your neck, shoulders, rib cage, stomach, or back to help draw your attention to those areas. Your teacher may even ask you to touch those areas on their body so that you can feel what an experienced singer does. This has been a teaching technique used by voice teachers for centuries. If the teacher asks to touch you, or for you to touch them, they are not trying to be inappropriate. However, when they ask, and they should ask first, you do have the right to say no. If they do touch you, it should feel medical in nature, like a physical therapist trying to inspect an injury. Caressing, tickling, poking, and hitting are not okay. Unfortunately, there are some teachers out there who take advantage of their position and prey on younger victims. If you feel as though a teacher is trying to take advantage of you, walk out of the studio immediately and talk to someone about the situation.

Because of the acting/interpretation component of singing, you may eventually discuss relationships and emotions in your lessons or coachings. Asking a student to talk specifically about the meaning of the text will often include connecting the text to the student's personal experiences. It is common for these types of discussions to include questions that explore connections to your family, life experiences, and relationships (platonic and romantic). If the conversation makes you uncomfortable, feel free to say, "I think I know what you are asking; let me try that again," or "I'm sorry, I just don't feel like talking about that right now." If you are not ready to have those conversations, you may not be ready to sing that song and that is okay. Songs are conversations between the artist and the audience about the human experience. Getting comfortable about telling your story in a safe environment is the first step to being comfortable telling it to a room full of strangers. At some point you have to go there or else your performances will seem flat and disconnected. World-class artists are always connected to every word they sing, which is why they appeal to their audiences and they are able to sell their records.

If It Hurts, It Is Probably Wrong

When you are learning to sing, your teacher will likely try many new techniques that may feel or sound strange to you. An experienced instructor knows the difference between sensations that occur when strengthening the voice and sensations that indicate something may not be functioning correctly. You must communicate with your teacher to protect your vocal health. Sometimes a great sound will not feel good for the first few weeks. As long as the sound is not making you hoarse, it is worth exploring. However, if you start losing your voice as you practice, tell your teacher. If the teacher does not know what to do to relieve the pain or voice loss, you may need to find someone else to work with. In general, if a new technique makes you feel a little tired or uncomfortable, it is probably okay. If it causes pain (beyond simple discomfort) and causes you to lose your voice, it is probably wrong.

Online Learning

The Internet has brought the entire world of knowledge into the home. It has completely revolutionized the way we learn, which has both positive and negative consequences. There are no regulatory agencies that control what can be published on the Internet. There are many articles concerning the singing voice on blogs and websites that have no grounding in voice science or commonly accepted vocal techniques. In fact, some of these resources offer advice that could be harmful. For instance, if you look up "how to sing death metal" online, you will find several videos of people sitting in their bedroom offering advice. Some of these "experts" demonstrate sounds that might sound quite good, but some of the techniques they advocate could easily lead to vocal damage. When engaged in self-learning, it is very important to remember that if it hurts, it is probably wrong. Just as with many other goods and services, let the buyer beware. Take what you learn from online resources, compare it to what you know to be true and what you experience for yourself, and decide what is worth keeping and what is worth ignoring.

YouTube

YouTube is an incredible resource for singers, with many great instructional videos available from some of the leading voice experts in the world. People like Jeannette LoVetri, Ingo Titze, Brett Manning, Lisa Popeil, Melissa Cross, and many others have produced YouTube videos. Videos of live performances can be educational as well. Comparing the sound a singer makes performing live without microphones to the recording can be eye-opening. You can also use YouTube to learn how to play instruments, write songs, use audio equipment, and record yourself at home. If you want to know about it, you can probably find a video on YouTube to help you learn.

Blogs

Many voice teachers maintain blogs as a way to market their voice studio and/or products. These blogs can be great resources for finding answers to specific questions, learning about different techniques, and investigating teachers or methods that interest you. Remember though, just because it is in print does not mean it is true. Do your research. If the person has a great reputation, you can probably trust what they have to say. If it seems that no one knows who the blogger is and they have listed questionable credentials, be careful. Here are a few blogs to get you started:

- Lisa Popeil—http://www.lisapopeil.com/blog.asp
- Claudia Friedlander—http://www.claudiafriedlander.com/
- Brett Manning Studios—http://www.brettmanningstudios.com/blog
- Voice Lessons to Go—http://voicelessonstogo.com/blog/
- D. Brian Lee—http://vocalability.com/blog/
- Jeannette LoVetri—http://somaticvoicework.com/

MOOCs

MOOC stands for "massive open online course." MOOCs are the major anchors in the movement to transfer the postsecondary educational experience out of the traditional university and into the user's home. Most MOOCs are offered free online with a paid option to take a test and earn a certificate of completion. There are several organizations offering a collection of courses on one centralized website (listed below). MOOCs are great resources for learning about music history, music theory, accounting, marketing, and nearly every other academic subject you can think of. While MOOC certificates are no substitute for the credentials offered by a traditional university, they do offer an educational benefit at a fraction of the cost for those not interested in obtaining a formal degree.

- Coursera—https://www.coursera.org/

- Udacity—https://www.udacity.com/

- edX—https://www.edx.org/

University Courses

Several universities offer courses and degrees online. One attractive option for performers is Berklee Online, a division of the Berklee College of Music in Boston, Massachusetts (http://online.berklee.edu/courses). Berklee offers courses including music production, songwriting, voice, music business, arranging, and improvisation. These courses are a great option for many students because they provide an opportunity to receive a world-class education from any location and do not require full tuition.

Reading

While I am thrilled to have your attention in this book, I must admit that it is not the definitive source for all things rock 'n' roll. Then again, no single book fits that description. Each chapter of this book provides a bibliography with references for books, magazines, and journal articles that you can consult for further reading. I'd also like to recommend a few of my favorite books on singing and music history:

- *Rockin' in Time: A Social History of Rock and Roll* by David P. Szatmary;

- *Rock of Ages: The Rolling Stone History of Rock and Roll* by Ed Ward, Geoffrey Stokes, and Ken Tucker;

- *Rolling Stone Encyclopedia of Rock & Roll* edited by Rolling Stone;

- *Ultimate Vocal Voyage* by Daniel Zangger Borch;

- *The Contemporary Singer: Elements of Vocal Technique* by Anne Peckham; and

- *Sing! The Vocal Power Method* by Elisabeth Howard.

Conferences

Conferences offer great opportunities to learn and interact with leading experts in the voice community and music industry. I've listed a few of the most popular conferences that are well worth your time and effort to attend:

- National Association of Music Merchants—http://www.namm .org

- Voice Foundation Annual Symposium: Care of the Professional Voice—http://www.voicefoundation.org

- South by Southwest (SXSW)—http://www.sxsw.com

- West Coast Songwriters—http://www.westcoastsongwriters .org/conference

- I Create Music ASCAP Expo—http://www.ascap.com/events awards/events/expo

- Songwriters MCs Music Conference—http://scmcmusic.com/

- Songwriting & Music Business—http://songwritingandmusic business.com/

Majoring in Rock 'n' Roll

I wish I could provide you a long list of well-known schools that offer degrees in rock 'n' roll, but unfortunately I cannot. There are only a few universities that offer degrees in commercial voice: University of Denver, Towson University, Columbia College in Chicago, The New School for Jazz and Contemporary Music, Berklee College of Music, and Belmont

University. The next best thing for many aspiring rockers is a degree in music production. As a music production major you will learn your way around a recording studio, while also learning about the business side of things. Some programs also provide ensemble experience and private instruction in voice or another instrument. Many of these programs are offered by universities in larger metropolitan areas where there are plenty of opportunities for gigging and applying your skills.

There are also several alternative paths worth considering. A bachelor of arts degree in business, marketing, or communications at a university in a community with an active live music scene can be a great option. During the day you will learn how to run your band like a business, and at night you can gig around town and build a fan base while networking with other musicians.

If you also have an interest in acting and dance, you could choose to study music theater. Jason Mraz (Jason Mraz, 2012) and Nicole Scherzinger (Nicole Sherzinger biography, 2013) were both music theater majors at one point in their careers. As a music theater major you will learn how to put on a production, act, run lights and sound, design sets, dance, and sing. While your schedule will be extremely busy, you will be spending every day developing your performance skills. Other creative people who are also interested in songwriting and performing music other than show tunes will surround you. That type of environment can be extremely inspirational and motivating.

You also have the option of pursuing a music education degree and becoming a music teacher. Just be aware that most music-education voice curriculums in universities have repertoire requirements that fall primarily within the classical genre. This can be frustrating if you have no interest in singing in Italian, French, and German. Voice performance is also an option, but you must understand that it is a degree that is designed to prepare you for a career as a classical singer. Most voice-performance programs will not allow you to sing anything but classical music. If you love that repertoire, you will probably really enjoy the degree program, but if classical music is not one of your passions, you may be very unhappy.

Conclusion

While there are unfortunately very few traditional educational paths for rock singers, there are more options than ever for educating yourself. By working with a professional voice teacher, taking online courses, and reading on your own, you can teach yourself many of the skills that are necessary for success in this business. As long as you keep an open mind and never stop learning, you cannot help but improve.

Bibliography

Jason Mraz. (2012). Retrieved from http://www.mtv.com/artists/jason-mraz/ [retrieved December 1, 2013].

Lecturing & Teaching Experience. (2007). Retrieved from http://www.sethriggs.com/resume.html [retrieved November 1, 2013].

McCoy, S. J. (2004). *Your voice, an inside view: Multimedia voice science and pedagogy.* Princeton: Inside View Press.

Nicole Scherzinger biography. (2013). Retrieved from http://www.biography.com/people/nicole-scherzinger-20980747 [retrieved December 1, 2013].

Products by Brett Manning. (2013). Retrieved from http://justforsingers.com/products-by-brett-manning [retrieved November 1, 2013].

APPENDIX A
Classical Training and Bel Canto
Kathryn Green

W hat is bel canto and why do people consider it the gold standard for voice training? While some people use the term to mean classical singing, it actually refers to a specific art of singing that flourished in Italy from the early eighteenth century through the first decades of the nineteenth century. Simply translated as "beautiful singing," "bel canto" most accurately refers to a style of singing that emerged at a moment in history when the prevalent musical forms had already shifted from choral polyphony to opera, heralding the rise and reign of the operatic solo singer.

Author James Stark suggests that bel canto is a method of singing that embodies the qualities of chiaroscuro, appoggio, register equalization, and a pleasing vibrato (1999). This appendix will introduce some of the similarities and differences among various bel canto/classical approaches to help you gain a better understanding of why teachers of these methods often disagree about the fundamentals of vocal technique.

Resonance

Simply stated, chiaroscuro is a resonance strategy. It is safe to say that it is one of the hallmarks of a trained classical sound. The idea of producing a tone that has both roundness and brightness can be traced back as early as 1774 in Gimbattista Mancini's treatise on singing (Foreman, 1969). It is probably the most recognizable quality we hear in classically trained singers. This identifiable timbre of the voice contains a high-frequency ring that, without the use of a microphone, can be heard over a full orchestra, while simultaneously producing warm low frequencies.

By raising the soft palate, lowering the larynx, and expanding the pharyngeal walls, one achieves this desired warmth in the sound. The resulting quality creates a cultivated western European sound that is distinctly different from an untrained voice or a voice produced by any other means. Classical voice teachers commonly instruct students to "open the throat" to produce this quality of voice production. The desired position of the larynx in the throat can vary from teacher to teacher, depending upon cultural and aesthetic ideals. Some teach that the larynx should descend, as if in a yawn, whereas others advocate that this approach results in an overly darkened or swallowed sound.

Those who ascribe to the low laryngeal position often use an easily recognizable "tucked-in-chin" posture quite opposite to the elevated chin posture often seen among those trained in the French manner of singing (Miller, 1997). Joan Wall states, "A relaxed neck and a slightly tilted (upward) head position helps avoid a jutting chin and unnecessary tension on the throat-neck area," suggesting an approach to posture that allows for a flexible laryngeal position and that differs from the "tucked-in-chin" stance of lowered laryngeal advocates (Blades-Zeller, 2003).

Breath Management and Posture

Appoggio refers to the management of breath and posture in its simplest translation. One still hears the eighteenth-century admonition in modern-day voice studios to sing before a candle but not allow the flame to flicker, as a means of "holding back" the breath, associated with this concept of appoggio. Richard Miller considers appoggio first and foremost a postural attitude, resulting in the high sternum position maintained in the "noble posture" of the Italian-schooled singer (1997). This manner of posture allows for upper-chest expansion of the rib cage and is considered the superior method of breathing in the bel canto tradition. However, there are classical methods found in Germany that place much greater emphasis on low-belly breathing, which has a direct impact on one's ability to maintain the Italian noble posture. It produces a low-diaphragmatic breath, rather than the high-chest intercostal breathing of the Italians, and has little to do with the upper chest expansion associated with the Italian school. Concepts of proper breathing from England involve back breathing, rounding the shoulders forward and feeling the expansion in the lower back upon inspiration. The posture required for this type of breath management is the antithesis of the high chest expansion advocated by those of the Italian school. Miller states,

> The Italian School stands in direct opposition to systems which advocate lowered sternum and collapsed thoracic cage, and equally so to those techniques which aim at fixing the costals or the diaphragm. Even more decisively, the Italian School considers the low-breathing techniques and outward abdominal pressures of the German School to be functional violations, contrary to natural processes. (1997, p. 41)

There are clearly very different methods of breathing and posture within established classical voice pedagogies, yet all them are considered approaches to good classical voice training, depending upon one's orientation.

Registration

The human voice has at least two registers, including a full, lower speech-like sound and a thinner or sweeter high-pitched sound. As early as 1592, Lodovico Zacconi refers to them as *Do di Petto* (chest voice) and *Do di Testa* (head voice) in his treatise, *Prattica di musica* (Stark, 1999). Successfully balancing these registers is perhaps the most challenging aspect of vocal training. Classical singers train to mix the two registers intentionally to hide the break and create a seamless tone quality from top to bottom. Often this training strategy requires female singers to sing in their head voice down to pitches that would naturally occur in a more speech-like production and requires male singers to strengthen their chest voice up to pitches that would naturally make the voice flip or break. Many classically oriented pedagogues consider training the male voice with falsetto as a way of promoting more ease in the top part of the mixed voice, but others do not adhere to this notion and consider the falsetto register less important in developing the legitimate male voice (Blades-Zeller, 2003). The same issue occurs with respect to the chest voice in training the female voice. It is not uncommon for a young female singer to be discouraged from using the chest voice in any vocal range. However, other classical methods advocate strengthening both the chest and head registers independently of each other in both male and female voices (Reid, 1978).

Vibrato

Use of a straight tone or beginning with a straight tone and moving to vibrato is not a strategy that is embraced by any classical tradition, except perhaps the English choral tradition. In classical singing, vibrato is expected to be even and consistent from the first moment of vocal onset. It should exhibit neither a wobble nor a tremor and is one of the chief attributes of a beautiful voice. As universal as this aesthetic desire is for an even vibrato, research shows variances in pedagogical approaches for achieving the desired consistency. Franco Corelli, Barbara Doscher, and Bert Coffin all attribute faulty vibrato to the improper flow of breath. Corelli, who successfully eliminated a fast vibrato (*caprino*) early in his career, states, "I believe this *caprino* is caused by breath that has not found its proper point of placement. When the breath was taught to go to the right place, the voice became steady" (Hines, 1982, p. 631). Doscher views a vibrato that is "out of whack" as a conflict between the airflow and the resonance track (Blades-Zeller, 2003, p. 61). Bert Coffin believes that an irregular vibrato is a sign that there is a fight going on between vocal fold vibration, vocal tract resonance, and the breath (Doscher, 1994, p. 204). Cornelius Reid, on the other hand, attributes issues with a faulty vibrato to improper muscular coordination at the vocal fold level. Reid states, "The first obligation of the teacher in such instances is to immediately proceed to the problem of registers and re-establish them in their divided form, with closest attention being given at all times to the purity of the vowel quality" (Reid, 1978, p. 141).

Conclusion

In today's culture, "bel canto" is a catch-all term used by a wide range of vocal pedagogues to imply the highest standard of vocal training. As a result, the term has become an ambiguous marketing tool aimed toward anyone seeking a voice teacher. A casual search on the Internet may reveal dozens of teachers who suggest that their vocal method is based upon bel canto principles, including some who teach CCM styles and genres. Whatever the claims, the reality is that no consensus exists among music historians or voice teachers as to the precise application or meaning of the term. As William Earl Brown stated, "No definite system of bel canto has descended to us, except by word of mouth from singer to singer" (Brown, 1957, p. iii).

This very brief survey of the elements of voice training reveals a variance in methods and aesthetic values among voice teachers and singers from earliest history up to the present day. If there is no universally accepted classical training, then it puts into question the notion that classical training is an appropriate foundation for all good singing. If it cannot be defined as a specifically prescribed set of parameters known and practiced by singing teachers and professional singers alike, then it becomes less clear what a classical foundation actually means. Some techniques from various classical traditions may be of use to the CCM singer while others may not. Each singer must determine, through research and self-assessment, what is best for their functional approach to training the instrument.

Bibiography

Blades-Zeller, E. (2003). *A spectrum of voices: Prominent American voice teachers discuss the teaching of singing*. Oxford: Scarecrow Press.

Brown, W. (1957). *Vocal wisdom: The maxims of Giovanni Battista Lamperti*. Malboro: Taplinger Publishing.

Doscher, B. (1994). *The functional unity of the singing voice*. London: Scarecrow Press.

Foreman, E. (1969). *A comparison of selected Italian vocal tutors of the period circa 1550–1800*. Ann Arbor, MI: University Microfilms.

Hines, J. (1982). *Great singers on great singing*. Garden City: Doubleday.

Miller, R. (1997). *National schools of singing: English, French, German, and Italian techniques of singing revisited*. London: Scarecrow Press.

Reid, C. (1978). *Bel canto: Principles and practices*. New York: Joseph Patelson Music House.

Stark, J. (1999). *Bel canto: A history of vocal pedagogy*. Toronto: University of Toronto Press.

Dr. Kathryn Green is professor of voice and voice pedagogy, director of the graduate voice pedagogy programs at Shenandoah University, and director of the CCM Voice Pedagogy Institute at Shenandoah Conservatory.

APPENDIX B
Vocal Exercise Patterns

The basic patterns illustrated in this appendix are great for working on a new technical concept. Use them to build stability, strength, and stamina. See figure B.1 for a three-note pattern, figure B.2 for a five-note pattern, figure B.3 for a five-note descending pattern, and figure B.4 for a 1-3-5-3-1 arpeggio. Once you are comfortable with a technical concept, try advancing to an octave. See figure B.5 for an octave arpeggio and figure B.6 for an octave scale.

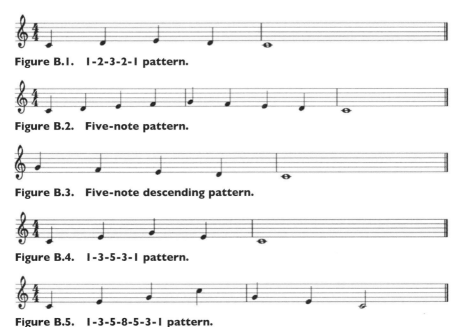

Figure B.1. 1-2-3-2-1 pattern.

Figure B.2. Five-note pattern.

Figure B.3. Five-note descending pattern.

Figure B.4. 1-3-5-3-1 pattern.

Figure B.5. 1-3-5-8-5-3-1 pattern.

When you are feeling secure with a technique, you will want to try working with up-tempo exercises that cultivate flexibility. Refer to figure B.7 for a nine-note scale, figure B.8 for nine-note turns, figure B.9 for an extended nine-note scale, and figure B.10 for an octave and a fifth arpeggio.

Figure B.6.   Octave pattern.

Figure B.7.   Nine-note pattern.

Figure B.8.   Extended nine-note pattern.

Figure B.9.   Nine-note into 1-3-5-8-5-3-1.

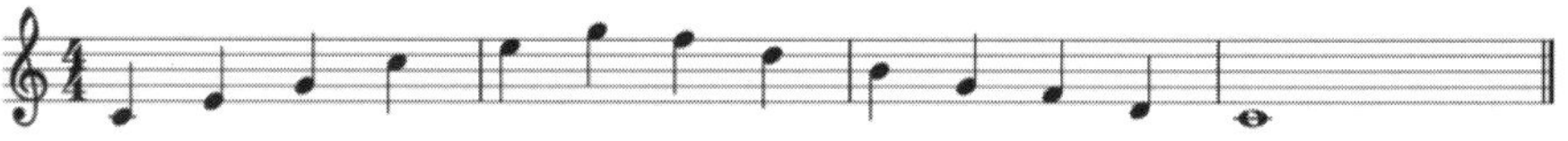

Figure B.10.   Octave and a fifth pattern.

APPENDIX C
Breathing for Singing
Christina Howell

E veryone can breathe. Yet breathing for singing has been set apart. Entire books have been written on it and specializations have been claimed. Some singers and teachers of singing treat breathing and breath management as the one remedy for every vocal issue at the expense of more direct technical solutions. In classical vocal circles, respected pedagogues name breath management the most important foundational technique. How then should the rock singer approach breathing for singing? Understanding the basics of respiration provides a good foundation for the rock singer who wishes to benefit from implementing breathing strategies to improve singing.

Respiration

In chapter 2, you read that respiration is the result of an increase and decrease in the volume of the chest cavity. When you inhale, muscles contract and increase the volume of your chest cavity, or thorax. When the diaphragm muscle contracts and flattens out, through connections within the thorax, it stretches the lungs downward. At the same time, muscles between the ribs contract and expand the rib cage, causing the lungs to stretch outward. Since the lungs are organs and not muscles, they cannot move on their own, so it is this expansion of the thorax that makes them get bigger or smaller. When volume increases, pressure decreases. Since air wants to move from an area of higher pressure to an area of lower pressure, the expansion of the lungs draws air into them resulting in inhalation.

Exhalation would be the opposite phenomenon, in which the volume of the thorax decreases, air pressure increases, and in order to equalize the pressure below and above the vocal folds, air leaves the chest cavity via the larynx. Reduction of the volume of the thorax can be the result of natural recoil of the muscles that caused inhalation. You experience this muscle recoil during a normal cycle of respiration. Additionally, activation of other muscles can cause a more forceful reduction of the volume of the thorax, such as when you cough or blow out a candle. Imagine an inflated pool float. You can simply open the valve and allow the air to leave the float, or you can apply pressure to the outside of the float and make the air leave more forcefully. Depending on the strength of the pressure on the outside of the float, the speed and pressure of the air coming out of the valve will vary. In exhalation, the abdominal muscles contract and increase pressure on organs within the abdominal cavity. Since these organs neither increase nor decrease in volume, the abdominal contraction simply displaces the abdominal viscera and puts upward pressure on the diaphragm. Adding the upward movement of the diaphragm to the inward movement of the ribs decreases thoracic volume and increases the air pressure within the lungs.

If the vocal folds are closed during this process, as in singing, the increase of air pressure within the lungs builds beneath the vocal folds. You can feel an extreme version of this increase if you take a really big breath and start the process of clearing your throat without actually following through on the action. Since the force of the air can be such that the relatively small muscles of the vocal folds cannot stay closed in resistance to it, singers develop means by which they can manage both the air pressure beneath the vocal folds and the rate at which air is released. Sometimes, this process happens without singers actively thinking about it. As long as the voice is responding appropriately for the needs of the singer, no further exploration of breath management should be necessary. However, if you are experiencing difficulties related to either too much or too little air pressure, exploring breathing strategies can be helpful.

In breathing for singing, singers need to supply the vocal folds with just enough air pressure to sustain phonation for the duration of the pitch. Just like Goldilocks, singers should strive for neither too much nor too little. Things get complicated when the vocal folds change thickness and length, as we learned they do in chapter 4 when we read about registration. Shorter and fatter vocal folds that are more strongly closed, such as in chest registration, can resist a greater amount of air pressure. Longer and thinner vocal folds, as found in head voice registration, need less air pressure to sustain phonation. Additionally, without intervention, breath pressure naturally tends to weaken the longer phonation lasts (see figure C.1). Therefore, controlling breath pressure becomes important to the singer who experiences issues related to the above.

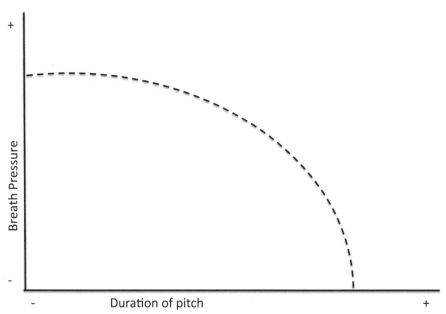

Figure C.1. Upon inhalation (left), breath pressure is at its maximum. Breath pressure (Y axis) will rapidly decrease with duration (X axis) unless the singer makes a deliberate choice to manage exhalation.

Increasing Breath Pressure

Some singers do not naturally provide sufficient air pressure to sustain phonation at the desired level and will want to increase breath pressure levels. For example, a singer just learning to use chest registration may not be accustomed to providing the kind of breath power the chest register needs. As you already learned, reduction in volume of the chest cavity causes an increase in breath pressure. If needed, singers can cause this volume reduction in a more forceful way by strongly engaging muscles of exhalation, such as the abdominal muscles, when approaching a problematic pitch area.

Decreasing Breath Pressure

More commonly, however, a singer will need to decrease breath pressure. Since a certain amount of air is always escaping during phonation, the chest cavity consistently becomes gradually smaller over the duration of the pitch. To reduce pressure beneath the vocal folds, the singer must reduce the force with which the volume of the chest cavity reduces. Just as more forceful volume reduction creates higher breath pressure, less forceful reduction reduces breath pressure. To reduce breath pressure beneath the vocal folds, avoid strong contraction of the abdominal muscle group, since that contraction reduces abdominal volume, displacing viscera upward into the diaphragm. Strong contraction of the abdominal group can result in breath pressure that is stronger than necessary. Additionally, singers should pay attention to rib cage movement. If the rib cage regularly collapses during phonation, that reduction in volume increases breath pressure. (See sustained "/s/" exercise in the "Practice Maintaining an Expanded Rib Cage" section of this appendix.)

Sustaining Subglottic Pressure

As a singer sustains any note, the natural recoil of the muscles of inhalation will cause a rapid reduction in breath pressure over the duration of the note. In order to counteract this natural tendency, a singer must maintain a steady amount of breath pressure beneath the vocal folds by both resisting the natural tendency of the rib cage to collapse and by gradually increasing the upward pressure on the bottom of the lungs via the abdominal muscles (see figure C.2). Often, singers naturally have enough upward pressure without conscious intervention to sustain phonation for a sufficient time if they are simultaneously resisting the urge to collapse the rib cage. However, if a phrase or note is particularly long, increased muscular activity in the abdominal muscles as the phrase continues can help you maintain sufficient breath pressure.

Vocal folds respond to breath pressure changes. Since the vocal folds change shape along with variations in pitch and registration, the required amount of breath pressure may also change accordingly. In order to maintain the desired vocal fold configuration and degree of vocal fold closure, you must consistently control breath pressure beneath the vocal folds throughout the phrase. Controlling this pressure during phonation allows you to control

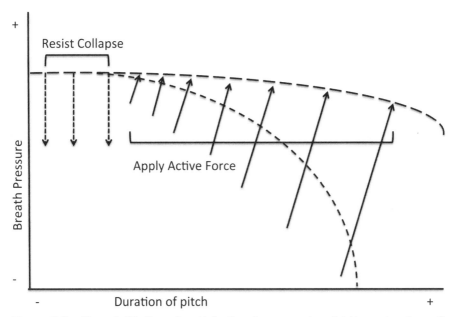

Figure C.2. **Upon initiation of a pitch, the singer must resist the natural recoil action of the rib cage in order to prevent breath pressure from rapidly falling (left). As breath pressure naturally decreases, the singer must use inward contraction of the abdominal muscles to gently press the abdominal contents into the diaphragm, thus increasing breath pressure (applying active force). These two actions allow the singer to manage the decline of breath pressure when sustaining a pitch (as displayed by the upper dashed line).**

the degree to which your vocal folds close and facilitates the balancing of registers, especially in transition areas between registers.

As discussed above, reduction in breath pressure results from a less forceful reduction of volume in the thorax. Since the diaphragm muscle is passive on exhalation, and we know that abdominal contraction displaces the abdominal viscera upward and reduces thoracic volume (increasing breath pressure), controlling the speed and pressure of exhalation becomes the responsibility of the only muscle group that can apply muscular antagonism, the muscles that control the ribs. Ideally, a singer will not only resist the urge to strongly contract the abdominal muscles to avoid reducing the thoracic volume from below but will also maintain an expanded rib cage while sustaining any tone. These two activities together can make the pressure and speed of exhalation consistent.

Practice Maintaining an Expanded Rib Cage

- Take a relaxed, deep breath and release it on a strong and harsh /s/. How many seconds did it take to get to the end of your breath? Was it the same strength all the way through?

- Take a relaxed, deep breath and release it on a gentle /s/. How many seconds did it take to get to the end of your breath? Was it the same strength all the way through?

- Place your hands on your head with elbows out to the sides of your body. Take a relaxed, deep breath and release it on a strong and harsh /s/. How many seconds did it take to get to the end of your breath? Was it the same strength all the way through?

- Place your hands on your head with elbows out to the sides of your body. Take a relaxed, deep breath and release it on a gentle /s/. How many seconds did it take to get to the end of your breath? Was it the same strength all the way through?

During the /s/ exercise, each sustained /s/ probably got longer and more consistent than the last one. The first example had you strongly contracting your abdominal muscles and allowing the rib cage to collapse inward. It was probably very difficult to maintain any kind of strength after the first second or two, and the /s/ was probably rather short. The second exercise encouraged less forceful abdominal activity, which probably allowed you to not only maintain the same strength throughout the exercise but also to sustain the duration of the /s/ probably longer than the first. The lifting of your arms in the third exercise encouraged a consistently open rib cage but still asked for strong abdominal contraction. You were probably able to maintain a more consistent strength in your /s/, and its duration was a little longer than in the previous two exercises. Finally, the last exercise encouraged a consistently open rib cage as well as less abdominal activity and was probably not only the easiest to maintain a consistent strength but also lasted the longest.

Even though the sustained /s/ is simply an air exercise, and singing will include more elements, remember that the vocal folds react to variations in breath pressure, so an increase or decrease will affect the sound of your voice. To support the thicker vocal fold closure of chest voice, a singer will require a greater amount of breath pressure than that required for the thinner closure of head voice. Imagine a singer who regularly sings in a loud, chest-dominant registration but regularly has problems with notes beyond a certain range. The breath strategy the singer is currently using, which works so well with chest-dominant low tones, may be overwhelming the vocal folds when he or she tries to get them to work in a higher and thinner configuration.

As you saw in the /s/ exercise, resisting the engagement of abdominal muscles while simultaneously maintaining an open posture in the ribs will reduce breath pressure, making those upper tones easier to manage.

Practice Maintaining an Expanded Rib Cage While Singing

- Try the same exercise as above while sustaining a vocal tone. Is one strategy more successful with lower tones? Higher tones? Does your registration (chest or head) make a difference?

- Try the same exercise as above and move between having your arms at your sides and above your head while you ascend or descend in pitch. Does raising your rib cage make a difference when you ascend? When you descend?

Controlling the inward and outward motion of the ribs gives the singer access to the most dependable method for controlling breath speed and pressure, muscular antagonism (see chapter 2 for further discussion of muscular antagonism). Since there are muscles that work in opposition to each other in this group, a singer can maintain an outward expansion of the ribs, while at the same time either allowing a gradual chest cavity volume reduction or even speeding up the volume reduction, depending on vocal needs.

Breathing Strategies

In his book *Your Voice: An Inside View*, Dr. Scott McCoy outlines four basic strategies of breathing for singing. In all four methods, the thorax expands to allow air into the lungs and contracts to expel air from the lungs. The four methods differ in how the expansion and contraction are accomplished. Clavicular breathing allows inhalation via upward expansion of the thorax through pronounced lifting of the shoulders and upper rib cage as one might see after a sprinter has finished a race. Dropping that upward expansion accomplishes exhalation. This method allows for a large amount of air to enter the body but has little to no ability to control its release. Thoracic breathing allows air to enter and exit the body primarily via an expansion and contraction of the rib cage. Because opposing muscles control this movement, there is ample opportunity to control exhalation. Abdominal breathing allows for the expansion of the thorax only via the relaxation of the abdominal muscles and, therefore, the downward movement of the lungs. This method allows a significant increase, over thoracic breathing alone, in the amount of air entering the body but because of the lack of muscular antagonism, offers little to no ability to control exhalation. A combination of thoracic and abdominal breathing provides the advantages of both methods, an increase in the amount of air and an ability to control its release. Thoracic-abdominal breathing is the method associated with most classical singers.

In 2009, Jennifer Cowgill investigated somatyping as a means to determine breathing strategy. Her research indicates that body type seems to dictate the natural breathing tendency of singers. Mesomorphs, people who have an athletic build, showed activity high in the rib cage with little abdominal movement during inhalation. Endomorphs, or those who are overweight, showed movement lower into the abdominal region, while ectomorphs, lean body types, tended to breathe high and wide in the chest. Furthermore, she found that there were no statistically significant variations in the respiratory function of these singers, even though their respiratory movements were different (Cowgill, 2009). These results imply that since singers with different body types naturally breathe differently, their breath management strategy should suit their physicality. If the objective of breath management is to maintain a consistent breath pressure that is just enough for the type of phonation needed by the singer, then the singer should breathe in whatever manner feels natural and accomplishes that objective.

Experiment with this concept on your own. Try each of the four breathing methods previously described and take note of what you experience as your lungs expand in new directions.

- Clavicular breathing: Do you get more air when you inhale? Can you control the sound on the release?

- Thoracic breathing (exclusively using the outward motion of the ribs): If you are used to singing classically, you may feel as if you are inhaling much less air. Does this make your rock singing easier or harder? Try exhaling 80 percent of your breath and singing on only the last 20 percent of air. Can you get the rock sound more easily?

- Abdominal breathing: Does this give you more air than you are used to? Does it make the rock sound easier or harder?

- Thoracic-abdominal breathing: This method may give you more air than you are used to. Can you control the release? Does this make a rock 'n' roll chest-dominant sound easier or harder?

- Is there another combination of the above that makes the rock sound easier?

What about the Rock 'n' Roll Singer?

Rock singers have specific vocal needs that vary with the singer and the style. In the twenty-first century, virtually all rock singing benefits from electronic amplification and requires a singer to produce tones only loud enough to reach a microphone two to three inches away. Rock melodies do not demand the singing of long, continuous phrases. In rock singing, laryngeal function can often benefit from a slightly elevated laryngeal position. Breath-management strategies developed for classical singers make assumptions that require maximized breath volume, maximized ability to create high acoustic vocal amplitude, a comfortably low larynx, and sustained, continuous breath pressure over long phrases. These assumptions do not meet the needs of the rock singer. Breathing strategies that take the rock singer's needs into account include inhalation only sufficient for the needs of shorter phrases, ability to control exhalation in specific circumstances without a need for continuous maintenance, and no need for a laryngeal drop.

Therefore, breath-management strategies that do not include abdominal movement during inhalation are appropriate. After all, the low breath associated with abdominal breathing encourages a low laryngeal position. Inhalation that primarily includes movement in the upper chest is especially appropriate for the athletically built or extremely lean rock singer. Rock singers should engage the abdominal muscle group in order to give sufficient power to the primarily chest-dominant vocal mechanism, while at the same time being careful to avoid creating too much breath pressure. Rock singers should develop the ability to control exhalation, especially during notes of high intensity in a high-pitch range. Breathing should serve the vocal outcome and you should choose the method that allows you to achieve your desired sound. Singing, such as that found in rock and roll, allows for many variables. Remembering that the goal of breath management is to match breath pressure with vocal need and remembering that the vocal needs of the rock artist differ from other genres allows for experimentation with breath function to find the method that works best.

Bibliography

Cowgill, J. (2009). Breathing for singers: A comparative analysis of body types and breathing tendencies. *Journal of Singing, 66*(2), 141–47.

McCoy, S. (2004) *Your voice: An inside view.* Princeton: Inside View Press.

Miller, R. (2000). *Training soprano voices.* New York: Oxford University Press.

Dr. Christina Howell is associate professor of voice at Clayton State University in Morrow, Georgia.

APPENDIX D
Phonetic Symbols

These symbols are used to notate vowels and consonants throughout the text. Examples are provided for each symbol.

Symbol	Examples
/a/	mama, nana
/ɑ/	father, ponder
/i/	see, me
/I/	it, sit
/ɛ/	Fred, Ed
/o/	so, go
/ɔ/	sought, ought
/u/	sue, shoe
/ʊ/	put, foot
/ng/	sung, flung
/m/	hum, murmur

APPENDIX E
Branding Yourself
Jonathan Flom

Chances are you've heard the word "brand" and you may be vaguely familiar with the notion of branding. But have you ever really stepped back and stopped to think about the power of the brand? It occurred to me while watching television that Verizon commercials emphasize the color red, while their main competitor AT&T uses orange and blue. When I see a phone commercial, I know instantly which company is pitching their product because my brain has been trained to recognize the company's colors and fonts. Similarly, when I was preparing Thanksgiving dinner, I knew it was the time of year for Lexus to advertise their "December to Remember" campaign because I heard the song that accompanies their holiday commercials every year. I didn't need to hear the voiceover or see the luxury cars on the screen; my brain just jumped right from the song to the product.

Whether it's a product we love and use, one that we opt not to purchase, or one that we aspire to afford some day, the fact is that good marketing uses the power of branding to provide a shorthand to product recognition in our brains. This approach relies on strong imagery, memorable phrases, and consistency. Over time, the combined effect of these three factors leads to instant product identification. We know what we're getting when we drive down the street and see the McDonalds "golden arches" or the Target "bullseye." A great deal of information is conveyed to us just from seeing those signs because they have become a part of our culture. That is the power of branding.

Performing artists are now beginning to discover how branding can work for them. After all, as a singer you're your own business ("You, Inc.") with a product to sell, whether your intended buyer is a record label, an agent or manager, or a paying audience. Like the big businesses and services that find success through consistency of memorable images and phrases, performing artists can also etch themselves into the consumer consciousness by learning how to use the same approach.

The first step in the process is to accurately identify the product you're selling. And you must be specific. To use Matt's example in chapter 8, Lady Gaga is a singer. But so is Dolly Parton, right? Are their products the same? Both are strong women who tell stories through song. Both are blonde (sometimes) and both have had mainstream pop music success. However, if you know these two artists, you know that they could not be more different. There is nothing generic about either one of them. Both have had immensely successful careers by developing a persona, being true to themselves, and baring their souls for their fans through music and live performance. But Gaga's brand has shock value. She uses an approach that could almost be called performance art, capturing the audience by dressing wildly and using grand stage theatrics. On the other hand, Dolly Parton has always been the girl next door who for some reason never seems to age. When you listen to Lady Gaga, you imagine her performing in an extravagant costume and dancing on the stage with an army of back-up performers, surrounded by pyrotechnic effects and grand lighting design. When you hear Dolly Parton, you see yourself sitting with a friend and gossiping over coffee in the comfort of your living room.

Each artist knows who she is, and neither tries to be something she is not. Dolly does not try to adapt and appeal to Gaga's audience, nor vice versa. Some people like Lady Gaga, some like Dolly Parton, some like both, and I'm sure some prefer neither. But both are doing just fine, even considering that a good number of people don't care for their music. The concept of branding means being true to yourself or your product and accepting the fact that some people won't want to buy what you're selling.

As an acting teacher, I struggle to understand why so many young actors feel they need to be everything to everybody. They work with different headshots and audition packages just to be sure they demonstrate how "right" they are for different parts in different shows. Rather than attempting to embed their personal and specific style, approach, and abilities into the minds of casting directors, they try to adapt themselves and transform into whatever the current role being cast demands. With actors like this who try to demonstrate versatility at every turn, I have observed that the good ones get called back a lot but have a very low callback-to-hire ratio. My theory is that they make a good enough impression with their talent and their range to get past the first audition, but once they get to the second or third round the director finds someone who is equally talented but better suited for the role. In short, the actor who is best for the role will generally land it.

I suspect that the same issue arises for singers and bands that try to emulate whatever is "hot" at the moment instead of trusting that what they have to offer is unique and special. Instead of asking them to constantly be what someone else wants, I encourage my students to create their own brands and stick with them. I tell them that they should be as specific and consistent as possible with their brands. I warn them that they might decrease their frequency of callbacks when they narrow their range in auditions, but when they *are* called back they will be more likely to book the role because they are right for the roles for which they're considered. Furthermore, when casting directors see actors audition several times, they get to know the product that the actors are selling and begin to think of them for other roles suited to them even before they come in and audition.

In my book *Act Like It's Your Business: Branding and Marketing Strategies for Actors*, I walk readers through the long and detailed process of creating a personal brand and then marketing it through materials such as headshots, resumes, and websites. Although I train students to perform for stage and film and this approach was written for actors, I believe singers and recording artists can apply the same techniques to create their own brands as well. To get you started, here are a few tips:

- Start collecting adjectives. Think of five to ten adjectives you would use to describe yourself (your essence, not your physical description). Then ask various people you know to offer you five adjectives to describe you. Are you serious or carefree, thoughtful or impulsive, suave or nerdy, or focused and determined or whimsical? These are just a few examples of what I mean by descriptions of your essence. Compare what you said with what others observed and determine the three or four words that really capture you the best.

- Consider role models. Are there performers with whom you feel some sort of connection? It could be a physical likeness or the spirit or nature of the artist. You can even qualify the comparison, such as "I'm a young so-and-so" or "I'm like the female version of so-and-so" or "I have the wit of so-and-so and the sensitivity of so-and-so." Could you compare yourself in this way to any other artists?

- Put it all together into something tangible. For example, if the adjectives you amassed led you to describe yourself as vivacious, energetic, and optimistic and your role models are performers like Pink and Gwen Stefani, then you probably gravitate toward their style of performance. Your brand might be "Vivacious with Optimistic Energy" or some variation on that, and your music should reflect that description.

- Once you select a brand, it should guide all your decisions, from what clothes to wear to what photos to choose to what kind of repertoire will suit you best. For every decision you must make, ask yourself, "Is this consistent with my brand?" It will take courage and patience, but I really believe that if you disregard and avoid all choices not consistent with your brand once you decide on what it will be, it will pay off in the long run.

As I said, this idea of branding is a fairly new phenomenon among the artistic community, at least on a conscious, intentional level. But it's hard to deny the power of a recognizable logo and catch phrase being seen repeatedly and associated with a product that's dependable and reliable. I encourage you to do some serious self-exploration and come up with your own personal "golden arches" and then give it a try. The good news is that if you try and fail or if you grow and change, you can always rebrand. Companies do it all the time. But before they flood the marketplace with a lot of mixed information, successful businesses spend a good amount of time pitching themselves in one undeviating way.

Jonathan Flom is the musical theater program coordinator at Shenandoah Conservatory and author of Get the Callback *and* Act Like It's Your Business.

GLOSSARY

The vocal terminology definitions in this glossary are courtesy of Karen Hall, *So You Want to Sing Music Theater*.

A&R: An acronym for "artists and repertoire," a title for those in the music business who scout new talent for record deals.

air: A subjective quality of recorded vocals that makes them appear more intimate. To add air, engineers will boost the frequencies between 12 and 14 kHz by 3 to 5 dB.

amplitude: A measurement of air pressurization used to define how loud a sound is.

attenuate: To reduce.

audio engineer: A trained professional who operates the soundboard and related audio equipment in live performance and/or the recording studio.

audio spectrum: The collective frequencies that comprise a complex sound. Also known as "sound spectrum."

baby boomers: The generation born between 1946 and 1964, after the conclusion of World War II.

back phrasing: When a singer intentionally sings off tempo by singing before or after the written beat.

bandwidth: The distance between two frequencies. The bandwidth between 400 Hz and 600 Hz would be 200 Hz.

BBC: The British Broadcasting Company, a government-controlled media company in England.

chest mix: Singing that is not pure chest register production. The chest register dominates, but a small amount of head register is also present. It differs from classical singing in that the amount of chest voice used at any pitch level is more significant than in classical production.

chest register: Also sometimes called "chest resonance," it is singing produced primarily by the thyroarytenoid muscles of the larynx. It is also described as a sound employing heavy registration with excessive resonance in the lower formants. Some music theater voice teachers include chest voice in their definition of the belt voice, while others do not. The use of these muscles in music theater singing is still being debated. Chest register is used with more regularity and at higher pitches in music theater singing than in classical singing.

chiaroscuro: A term derived from art. When applied to singing, it refers to a balance of high and low resonance in the voice.

chord: A combination of two or more notes played simultaneously.

contemporary commercial music (CCM): A generic descriptor developed to describe all types of nonclassical singing. CCM styles are cabaret, country, experimental, folk, gospel, jazz, music theater, pop, rock, and rhythm and blues. This term was developed to call CCM styles by what they are rather than what they are not—nonclassical.

cover song: A performance of a song originally performed by another artist.

cricoid cartilage: A solid ring of cartilage located below and behind the thyroid cartilage.

cricothyroid muscle: A set of paired intrinsic laryngeal muscles that are used primarily to control and assist the folds to vibrate by stretching them. The sound produced by the cricothyroid is commonly referred to as "head" register. In the classical female voice, the use of head register dominates each pitch, while in the music theater female voice most singing is thyroarytenoid dominant. The cricothyroid muscle also controls pitch and consequently is used in all vocal production.

decibel (dB): A logarithmic unit used to measure sound pressure to quantify volume levels.

Digital Audio Workstation (DAW): An electronic system used for recording and editing music.

distortion: A quality of sound that is created by electronically altering the amplitude of harmonics and partials in a complex sound. The resulting quality is often described as harsh, fuzzy, or gritty.

embelish: To add additional notes or rhythmic figures to a melody.

epiglottis: The cartilage that covers over the larynx during swallowing.

falsetto: High, light register, applied primarily to men's voices singing in the soprano or alto range.

formant: A resonance of the vocal tract. Formants are sound potential rather than actual sound or a result of vibrating vocal folds. Each sung vowel shapes the vocal tract differently. The different vowel shapes determine the resonance/formant. The vocal tract produces several formants: labeled as F1, F2, etc. from the lowest to the highest.

forward placement: A term used to describe a sensation of the voice vibrating in the frontal bones of the face.

fundamental: Lowest partial of a spectrum, the frequency of which normally corresponds to the pitch perceived.

gig: Music business jargon for a job as a performer.

glottis: The space between the vocal folds.

harmonic: A frequency that is an integer multiple of a given fundamental. Harmonics of a fundamental are equally spaced in frequency.

head mix: Female music theater singing that is not pure head register production. The head register dominates, but a small amount of chest register is also present. It differs from classical singing in that the amount of chest voice used at any pitch level is more significant than in classical production.

head-mounted microphone: A wireless microphone that wraps around the head to position the diaphragm near the mouth for performers who frequently move around the stage. Most often found in music theater and pop performances.

head register: A term used to describe singing produced primarily by the cricothyroid muscles of the throat. It derived its name from the vibrations felt in the head area while producing higher pitches. These vibrations are sympathetic and not produced in the head region. Although classical singing is dominated by the use of head voice, the use of chest voice is dominant in contemporary music theater repertoire.

inharmonic: In music, inharmonicity is the degree to which the frequencies of overtones (also known as partials) depart from whole multiples of the fundamental frequency (harmonic series).

intended vocal distortion: Distorted vocal qualities that are intentionally created to achieve a special effect.

Kilohertz: A kHz, or kilohertz, is a measurement of frequency equal to 1,000 Hertz. Kilohertz is unit of measurement for alternating current, audio signals, and a measurement of wireless signals.

larynx: The cartilaginous box-shaped part of the respiratory tract located in the neck that includes the vocal folds. It is sometimes referred to as the "voice box." It is about the size of a walnut and attaches at the top to the hyoid bone. The larynx is capable of movement up and down, and this movement is the subject of a great deal of scientific investigation in belt singing. The scientific data generally shows that in belting, the larynx assumes a high position, whereas in classical singing, it is in a lower position.

legit: The term used in music theater to describe male and female classical singing. It is a slang term shortened from the word "legitimate." This term came into use to delineate between vaudeville and legitimate theater when legitimate theater first began. There are two types of legit singing: traditional and contemporary. The traditional legit sound has the qualities of classical singing, and the contemporary legit sound, while head-voice dominant, is more speech oriented. The speech component in contemporary legit singing results in a vocal sound that employs less classical resonance and has a brighter quality as opposed to the darker quality found in the traditional legit sound.

minstrel show: An American entertainment consisting of comic skits, variety acts, dancing, and music, performed by white people in blackface or, especially after the Civil War, black people in blackface. Minstrel shows lampooned black people and began with brief burlesques and comic *entr'actes* in the early 1830s and emerged as a full-fledged form in the next decade.

mix register: Used in music theater to describe a female singing sound that is a blend of head and chest register. The sound can be head-register dominant with some chest or chest dominant with some head register. This mix blend can occur at any pitch level. Mix register is sometimes referred to as "blended" or "coordinated" register.

overtones: Partial above the fundamental in a spectrum of sound.

partial: A partial is a higher tone produced at the same time as the lowest tone that helps to determine the overall quality of the sound. Overtones that are not whole-number multiples of the fundamental are called partials. In musical sounds, including singing, harmonic overtones strongly dominate. Partials, if present, lead to roughness and make correct intonation difficult to achieve. In singing, they are generally only found in damaged and dysfunctional voices.

phantom power: A forty-eight volt (48 V) power supply that is transmitted from a soundboard through a microphone cable. Phantom power is required when using condenser microphones.

power chords: Two note chords played on guitar consisting of only the root and fifth. The resulting sound is powerful and tonally ambiguous due to the absence of the third.

presence: A subjective quality of recorded vocals that makes them appear more powerful. To add presence, engineers will boost the frequencies between 4 and 7 kHz by 3 to 5 dB.

recording engineer: A trained professional who operates the soundboard and related audio equipment in the recording studio.

register: A unified group of tones that have the same texture or quality. In classical singing, the use of the head register predominates whereas in music theater singing, especially for women, the use of chest register is favored.

register balance: Describes the amount of chest and head register function in a sung tone. In music theater singing, this balance varies depending on the size of the voice and type of repertoire being sung.

resonance: The peak occurring at certain frequencies in the vibration of sound.

riff: A brief, relaxed phrase repeated over changing melodies. It may serve as a refrain or melodic figure, often played by the rhythm section instruments or solo instruments that form the basis or accompaniment of a musical composition

singer's formant: A high-spectrum peak occurring between about 2.3 and 3.5 kHz in voiced sounds in Western opera and concert singing. It is associated with the "ring" in a voice and with the voice's ability to project over the sound of a choir or orchestra.

source: A theory that assumes the time-varying glottal airflow to be the primary sound source.

space: The most basic definition of space is that every note written on the page can serve as a point of departure. Space has several characteristics: The pitch can be changed either up or down while respecting the harmony; the note can become more than one note (ornaments, repeated notes, etc.); the note can be started earlier or later than written; and the duration of notes can be changed.

stomp box: A solid metal or plastic box constructed to function on the stage floor that encloses an effects processor and allows the user to control it with their feet.

subglottal pressure: Air pressure in the airway immediately below the level of the closed vocal folds.

360 deal: A contract with a record label that requires the musician to pay a percentage of all earnings (live, TV/Film, internet, etc.) to the record label.

thyroarytenoid muscle: A paired intrinsic laryngeal muscle that comprises the bulk of the vocal fold. It is also called the vocalis muscle. The medial belly constitutes the body of the vocal fold. It is the primary muscle used in the production of the lower pitches in a singing voice. It is also commonly referred to as the chest voice muscle. Music theater singing is often characterized by predominant use of the thyroarytenoid or chest voice muscle. Music theater singing often uses this muscle at higher pitches than classical singing.

thyroid cartilage: The largest laryngeal cartilage. It is open posteriorly and is made up of two plates (thyroid laminae) jointed anteriorly at the midline. In males, there is a prominence superiorly known as the "Adam's apple" visible from the outside as a protrusion in the middle of the throat.

timbre: The unique qualities of an instrument or voice created by differences in the amplitude of the harmonic overtone series that distinguish one instrument from another.

tube (vacuum tube): An electronic device that controls electrical current through a vacuum in a glass bulb. Tubes are found in the earliest electric recording and amplification devices and are still valued today for their unique tone qualities.

vaudeville: A theatrical genre of variety entertainment popular in the United States and from the early 1880s until the early 1930s. Each performance was made up of a series of separate, unrelated acts grouped together on a common bill.

vibrato: The periodic modulation of the frequency of phonation.

vocal folds: The scientific term for a paired system of ligaments in the larynx that oscillate to produce sound. The vocal folds are sometimes referred to as vocal cords. The vocal folds consist of two wedge-shaped, multilayered bundles of muscles with ligamental edges covered by a mucous membrane. The vocal folds are a complex tensing and relaxing system; they can shorten, contract laterally, vary both length and thickness during vibration, and even part of them can tense while the rest is relaxed.

INDEX

ABOUT THE AUTHOR

Matthew Edwards is an assistant professor of voice and voice pedagogy and a music theater styles specialist (pop, rock, country, R&B) at Shenandoah University. His current and former students have performed on Broadway, off-Broadway, in national and international tours, at theme parks, on national TV (including *American Idol*), and on major motion picture soundtracks and have appeared on the Billboard music charts. As a performer, he has extensive experience in opera, theater, and music theater with companies including New Jersey Opera, Tri-Cities Opera, Ashlawn Opera, Acadiana Symphony Orchestra, Dayton Pops, Cincinnatti Opera, Lyric Opera Cleveland, Atlantic Coast Opera Festival, Theatre Lab, KNOW Theatre, and many others. He has received awards from the Metropolitan Opera National Council Auditions, the Dayton Opera Competition, and the National Association of Teachers of Singing. He was a NATS intern under Jeannette LoVetri and Dr. Scott McCoy and is a certified Somatic Voicework teacher. He has authored articles for *American Music Teacher*, NYSTA *VoicePrints*, *Southern Theatre*, *Journal of Voice*, and *Journal of Singing* and book chapters for *The Vocal Athelete* by Dr. Wendy LeBorgne and Marci Rosenburg and *A Dictionary for the Modern Singer* by Dr. Matthew Hoch. Edwards regularly presents at conferences and universities throughout the United States and is a faculty member at the CCM Voice Pedagogy Institute, where he teaches Somatic Voicework, the Jeannette LoVetri method. More online at EdwardsVoice.com.